1895

BREEDING
A LITTER

This book is devoted to enhancing dogs' lives with their owners. Three generations of Alaskan Malamutes with their owner.

BREEDING A LITTER

The Complete Book of Prenatal and Postnatal Care

Beth J. Finder Harris

HOWELL BOOK HOUSE

New York

Maxwell Macmillan Canada
Toronto

Maxwell Macmillan International
New York   Oxford   Singapore   Sydney

Copyright © 1993 by Beth J. Finder Harris

All rights reserved. No part of this book may be reproduced or transmitted in any form or by any means, electronic or mechanical, including photocopying, recording, or by any information storage and retrieval system, without permission in writing from the Publisher.

Howell Book House
Macmillan Publishing Company
866 Third Avenue
New York, NY 10022

Maxwell Macmillan Canada, Inc.
1200 Eglinton Avenue East
Suite 200
Don Mills, Ontario M3C 3N1

Macmillan Publishing Company is part of the Maxwell Communication Group of Companies.

Library of Congress Cataloging-in-Publication Data

Harris, Beth J.
    Breeding a litter: the complete book of prenatal and postnatal care/Beth J. Finder Harris.
        p.   cm.
    ISBN 0-87605-414-9
    1. Dogs—Breeding.   2. Puppies.   I. Title.
SF427.2.H37   1993
636.089'082—dc20   92–23789
                                                                CIP

Macmillan books are available at special discounts for bulk purchases for sales promotions, premiums, fund-raising, or educational use. For details, contact:

Special Sales Director
Macmillan Publishing Company
866 Third Avenue
New York, NY 10022

10 9 8 7 6 5 4 3 2 1

Printed in the United States of America

In loving memory of
Leonard V. Finder
and Fritz Bieth,
who believed all things are possible

Contents

Acknowledgments

Many PEOPLE have helped to make this book possible. These people deserve a special acknowledgment for their contributions to making this book a reality: Maxwell Riddle, for his strength of convictions and unwaivering faith in my abilities; Irv Levine and Anne G. Finder Levine, for their continuous support; Danielle Philippa, who has always shared my love of all infant creatures; Nancy Scanlon, D.V.M., for originally encouraging me, and the late Elsworth Howell who, many years ago, suggested I write on this subject.

A very special thank you to Eugene Borman, D.V.M., of Old Towne Animal Hospital, who graciously devoted a great deal of time, effort and energy helping with all technical aspects of this work; Jan Walker for her delightful artistic contributions. Jane, Debi, Monte, Dorothy, Joe, Margaret, Dan and Ray, thank you all. Acknowledgment is also given to all those who contributed photographs, sharing the unqualified love and pride they feel for their pets.

Introduction

THIS MANUSCRIPT is dedicated to those who desire to engage in a breeding program of better-bred dogs. Not elitist in aspect, this book is devoted to enhancing dogs' lives with their owners through a candidly spoken medical and psychological direction of rearing puppies in the best of all possible environments.

Usually there is nothing that can replace positive, practical firsthand experience; however, when working with the lives of well-loved pets, the acquisition of some basic knowledge proves essential to maximize success.

Here is a straight-forward commonsense guide to sound practices in breeding a bitch and rearing of her offspring. The body of this work focuses upon helping you optimize your efforts, rearing superior and emotionally stable, physically sound puppies.

Whenever contemplating a breeding there are several specific areas of focus that first need to be addressed. If you desire to breed because you see dollar signs from your dog's litter, you will be disappointed. Established breeders of good repute are first devoted to their breed in general, and then specifically to their own dogs. They choose to breed for a variety of reasons established upon sound reasoning and practical, successful experiences. They have, above all else, an ultimate, long-range goal in mind other than the mere production of puppies.

Conscientious breeders find vast rewards bringing new life into the world with each well-planned and prepared-for litter of successive generations. They have the added bonus of making new friends through their puppy buyers. These people do not breed dogs with the expectations of fabulous monetary returns. Invariably, rearing a litter proves a losing proposition when financial rewards are considered. Why then do people continue to dedicate themselves to breeding dogs? Because short- and long-term satisfaction are obtained when a breeder's program is proven.

The success of breeding is proven through dog shows that were founded to prove a program's superiority. Today, while still fulfilling this function, dog shows have also become a family endeavor: a sport where participants of all ages and abilities may compete, from the youngest and most novice, to the professionally experienced. The sport encompasses a wide variety of interests and levels. There is literally something for everyone: from Obedience and Field Trials, Tracking and Hunting Tests, to the conformation ring.

BREEDING
A LITTER

Dog shows are, by definition, the place where the quality of a breeding program is proven.

Joyce Weichsel

1

Breeding Responsibly

BY DEFINITION, a breeder is anyone who successfully undertakes the breeding of two dogs. It does not matter if this person has plans covering years of time, encompassing multiple breedings, or is one who plans to breed but a single litter.

A BREEDER'S OBLIGATIONS

Many people who breed dogs recognize their obligations. They are perfectly willing to accept the responsibilities assumed when bringing new life into the world. These people offer their brood matron superior prenatal and postnatal care. They carefully research the pedigrees of the dogs they have brought to a breeding. Conscientiously, they ensure the sire and dam are X-rayed (hips and elbows), along with being checked for other problems that may afflict their breed.

These breeders carefully select the homes in which the puppies are placed. Once a sale has been made, they provide detailed instructions for feeding and follow-up veterinary care. These dedicated people maintain a follow-up program, staying in touch with their puppy buyers. They ensure that puppies and grown dogs have optimum emotional as well as physical care. These responsible breeders are also prepared to take back or help to relocate at any age a dog of their breeding should the owners be incapable of keeping the animal.

There is nothing wrong with breeding and being a breeder per se. *Education* is, however, the key word for every person who contemplates this activity. It does not matter if this is for a single litter or for an entire breeding program encompassing years of forethought. People who sell puppies must be aware of those prospective buyers who, during the interview process, disclose that they do not want to show, they only want to breed dogs. Dog shows are, by their very definition, the place where the quality of a breeding program is proven.

All prospective puppy owners require adequate education. They need to be clearly informed that it is far easier to place a puppy from champion parents, or parents that are working successfully on their titles, than it is to sell a puppy from untitled parents. A breeder should keep the entire breed's welfare in mind when making puppy placements. *When confronted by the type of purchaser who insists upon breeding alone, it is best not to make the sale.*

Most breeders carefully place their puppies in responsible homes with responsible people. Sales of pet-quality puppies *without* restrictions on breeding them is a real crime perpetrated on the overpopulated canine world. Some people "reason" that since Nature provided their pet with the means of reproduction, they should take advantage of this regardless of the animal's quality. Dogs do not have the same libido as people. It is not necessary that every dog be bred, nor is it imperative for each champion to reproduce.

Each day of the week, in any newspaper, one can find numerous advertisements for puppy sales from "planned" breedings. Often these sellers panic because the buyers they anticipated do not materialize. Some of these breeders are people who feel they are "entitled to recoup" the expenses of their initial purchase and subsequent upkeep of their pet. As a result, they feel entitled to breed just once.

These people do not realize the costs involved in properly rearing a litter: stud fees (and transportation costs to get to the stud dog); veterinary fees (radiographs, brucellosis tests and artificial insemination if required); proper nutritional support for the dam and puppies and advertising expenses. These people are only able to see dollar signs before their eyes with the arrival of each new puppy into the world.

Ask Questions—Give Information

When people call for a puppy, the first question to be asked by the breeder is, "Pet or show quality?" Many newcomers to the realm of the better-bred dog are under the misconception that show dogs are not pets. They have no idea that the family dog that loves to eat ice cream cones and table scraps (on occasion) can also be a fine show dog. People need to know that champions are, after all, still dogs—and family members first. A show career encompasses but a brief span of time in the lives show dogs share with their families. These people also need to know that show dogs may be eligible for a breeding program *only* if they are able to reproduce either their own quality (what every breeder strives for), or better quality (closer to the breed's Standard) in each successive generation.

It is important to make it perfectly clear to a prospective client that the price of a puppy is never predicated on the animal's sex. You, as the breeder, should fully explain the differences between the show prospects and pet-only puppies in the litter. Even more important, and it must be made clear, that any puppy sold not to be shown is not to be bred. Be a strong advocate of neutering these puppies by spaying (ovarian hysterectomy) or castration. Take the time to explain fully and in a positive manner that withdrawal from a breeding program does not affect a dog's personality. Nor does neutering cause a dog (male or female) to become fat and sluggish with the proper nutritional requirements and exercise levels.

One benefit derived from neutering is that castrated males will almost never chase after neighborhood females in season; nor will a spayed female attract destructive neighborhood males. Another benefit is that many neutered animals live longer and healthier lives than their unneutered counterparts, thereby giving their owners additional years in the pleasure of their company. Finally, some states offer a price reduction in their licensing programs to owners of neutered animals.

Offer your puppy purchasers additional information about the types of neutering available. Vasectomies and tubal ligations can be performed at a very early age. These males and females retain their respective physical characteristics but are incapable of reproduction. It is generally suggested that males be castrated after reaching a physical maturity in order to develop traditional physical characteristics. Early spaying (before the first season) prevents a bitch from fully developing her female hormones and traditional physical characteristics. Very often and as a result, these females develop male characteristics, but not male character traits.

Prospective clients are often willing to neuter a pet puppy in return for a price reduction, or the possible difference in price between a show prospect and pet-only puppy. These people can be proud of their puppy selection and the breeding behind it. They have the added bonus of feeling good about the fact that their new family addition has come from a dedicated breeder, a person who so evidently cares strongly about the breed's welfare in general.

It is important to educate *all* prospective owners. This educational program should also include those who purchase show-prospect puppies. These people will be exhibiting and eventually possibly breeding. If this information is correctly extended to them, they will in turn be able to carry on your tradition of offering sound information to their own puppy owners. The breeder who educates all owners is a breeder of fine repute.

By all means, let your prospective purchasers know that of course "papers" are available for pet-quality puppies. Inform them that these dogs may compete in Obedience and Field Trials. It is highly important to be candid with buyers from the beginning, making it perfectly clear why each animal being individually registered is not necessarily a breeding program candidate.

As prospective clients view the puppies, teach them the physical differences between a show prospect and a pet-quality puppy in order that they may make an informed decision. The differences may be any number of physical variables that do not closely meet your breed Standard's requirements, that designate a

3

specific puppy as pet quality. Stress the fact that lack of any of these physical qualities does not diminish a puppy's potential as a marvelous pet.

It is important to disclose that while your pedigree offers generations of champions behind your litter, there has never been a dog that is perfect. Some dogs may approach perfection, being closer to their breed's Standard than others. Take the time to explain your breed Standard fully. Let your clients know why it was written, the history and purpose of your breed and why any deviations from the Standard are unacceptable for a breeding program.

Most people are reasonable and will accept such explanations. They will show evidence of acting conscientiously upon your advice as a dedicated breeder. There are many people who desire a well-bred dog in their home as a pet, but who cannot afford the price of a show prospect. These people can nevertheless offer a superior home, a supportive and loving environment to the pet-quality puppy.

During prospective owners' interviews, introduce the subject of obedience training. Every dog, from the finest purebred to the "all-Americanbred," at the very least deserves some basic obedience work. Most people will exhibit an interest in training when given a brief background about the basic rules and regulations of obedience, and how competition is judged, be it the Canine Good Citizen Test or Obedience Trial. Offer information about the challenge and excitement of training and competition. Encourage your clients by letting them know that bonding and communication with their dog is immeasurably enhanced by such training. Additionally, beyond opening communications, this training will last the lifetime of the dog. While anyone can breed a "pretty" dog, it is in competition where dog-and-owner bonding are all that matter.

The American Kennel Club's rules and regulations state that the offspring of purebred, registered parents are entitled to registration papers. *Unlimited* registration for offspring applies *only* to those dogs the *breeder designates*. Any offspring issuing from pet-quality dogs (should this occur), are not eligible for registration if so designated on the individual's Registration Application form.

Some people are undecided about a name for their puppy at the time of purchase. Too often these people fail to submit their dog's individual Registration Application in a timely manner. The breeder, upon signing the application, must make it perfectly clear to these clients that the dog is not registered until the application has been received within the AKC offices. It must also be made known to the new owners that should the *application* form become misplaced or lost, a duplicate application would be extremely hard to obtain. In some cases, the AKC has refused to issue a duplicate, and the dog remains unregistered. Let these people know that once their dog is individually registered, duplicate certificates of ownership, if needed, may be obtained for a nominal sum.

When interviewing prospective homes for puppy placement, stress not only the positive aspects of your breed, but also the "no-no's" according to your breed Standard. Be honest about your breed's personality. Describe not only the best in the breed, but also any minor or major negative breed quirks. Present a positive and sincere attitude when offering information about all the opportunities available with your breed, including local affiliations and national clubs and trials.

If these basic guidelines of being a responsible breeder are followed in making placements of puppies into responsible homes, if you offer an educational program in addition to your careful breeding program, then you are indeed a "breeder" and truly worthy of this title.

Each breed is unique, carrying individual physical and character traits that set it apart from all others.

Artist: Jan Walker

2

Designer Genes

$\mathbf{Y}$OU ALONE are ultimately responsible for making the decision to breed your bitch. Exercising your option to breed, however, should also be influenced by your veterinarian. Veterinarians have an obligation to all dog owners to strongly suggest *not* breeding (and clearly, why) if a matron- or stud-elect should have any deleterious condition, abnormalities or disorders that could detrimentally influence the breeding or offspring.

MEDICAL CHECKLIST

Some of the conditions that require the withdrawal of a dog from a breeding program are cataracts, cleft palate, hernias, hip dysplasia, an ununited anconeal process, hydrocephalus, stenotic nares, chondrodysplasia, deafness and monorchidism (of the sire). Additionally, certain dogs may have other conditions innate solely to their breed. Acquired diseases such as vaginitis, canine brucellosis, metritis, prostatitis and other inflammations can also produce a deleterious effect upon conception or the offspring.

OFA

The Orthopedic Foundation for Animals, Inc. (OFA), has established a universal set of criteria for soundness in hips and elbows. Most veterinarians use a mild and safe, brief-acting anesthetic to relax dogs prior to their being radiographed. This allows the animal to be positioned correctly, in accordance with the guidelines established by the OFA. Some dogs are, however, so naturally relaxed and trusting even when being positioned, that a few veterinarians are willing to radiograph without the use of anesthetic. It is important to radiograph the bitch well in advance of her estrus, before her eggs ripen at the onset of mature ovulation.

After the animal has been radiographed, the X-rays are sent to OFA headquarters in Missouri. There, the radiographs are "read" by selected board-certified veterinary radiologists who specialize in this field. Approval of the X rays by the OFA is made in the form of a certificate that is coded with the dog's name, breed and individual number. This certified approval is indicative of your dog's physical soundness in accordance with the OFA standards. A physically sound dog should be a requirement for any breeding program.

CERF

All breeding program candidates should also be checked by a board-certified veterinary ophthalmologist for any genetic or traumatically induced defects and diseases of the eye. Standards established by the Canine Eye Registration Foundation (CERF) should be met before a breeding is made.

Sperm Viability

Always have the stud's sperm quality checked prior to a breeding. Even though he may not be in peak physical condition, the stud may be able to provide suitable sperm to effect fertilization. Dogs that have been on certain medications immediately prior to a breeding may produce insufficient numbers of sperm, sperm of a low motility or deformed sperm. Dogs over six years of age and those not used on a regular basis may also produce sperm low in motility. This usually results in smaller-sized litters or breeding failures. Only veterinarians and certain clinicians are medically trained and equipped to determine sperm quality for breeding.

The male's libido is, generally speaking, of a somewhat more delicate nature than that of the female. In order to maintain his libido, the male should ideally be kept apart from the bitch during her estral cycle until the optimum time for breeding has arrived.

All Bases Covered

The physical and emotional well-being of the matron-elect has a profound effect upon the future of her offspring. Ideally, you should have her conditioned to be free of superfluous fat without being overly lean, firm and vigorous well prior to and through the confinement during her estral cycle.

In addition to the earlier criteria, other conditions should also be met shortly prior to the onset of your bitch's estrus. Have a recent (fresh) fecal sample checked by veterinary technicians for signs of parasitic infestation. Do not wait to initiate appropriate treatment if, after a microscopic examination, such treatment is indicated.

Unless your female is already being treated with preventative heartworm medication, have a blood sample taken as well. Should microfilaria prove to be present when the laboratory report is returned, your dog will require serious extensive therapy to recover. If such is the case, dreams of breeding this particular female during this cycle (and possibly for the future) must be abandoned.

Check the inoculation record of your bitch. If she is due for regular vaccinations (DHLPP, corona and rabies), bring all inoculations up-to-date prior to the onset of her cycle. Quite a few breeders follow a preventative program of additional booster inoculations even when not directly medically required.

It is possible to have your bitch inoculated and wormed subsequent to a breeding. It is *best*, however, to do so *beforehand*. While there are newer and safer drugs being marketed each year, it is nevertheless taking a calculated risk to the fetuses to booster, inoculate or worm a bitch during her pregnancy.

Never assume that your female does not have any parasitic infestation just because you see nothing in a gross examination of her stool. Only by microscopic examination in almost all cases can any parasitic infestation be determined. Unless you have the proper training and equipment (including a variably powered microscope), you are not qualified to make these determinations.

Never initiate the inoculation or worming of a female that has already been bred. Even when considering it in the best sense, worming is, to a degree, toxic. Inoculations are drugs. Putting either toxic substances or drugs into your matron during her pregnancy can be risky to the fetuses. Only your veterinarian is able to determine the best program for your matron, including the time and type of precautionary measures.

Your veterinarian should be willing to set aside time to explain in terms you understand the initiation of any program (medical or supportive therapy) intended for your dog, and should candidly describe why this program is in order for your matron-elect. Should you question or feel uncomfortable with the program as outlined, do not be afraid to consult another practitioner. However, be tolerant of the veterinarian who, possibly having had an emergency, was short of time. Never hesitate to make an appointment to talk.

While almost all veterinarians are genuinely concerned about the welfare of their clients, two- and four-legged alike, few achieve a "Marcus Welby" status in the dog world with an exemplary manner. If the veterinarian you use is repeatedly brusque and does not appear to be kindly dispositioned toward your female, if she repeatedly and uncharacteristically retreats from the vet, seriously consider seeking another medical facility.

ASSESSING QUALITY

All dog owners have some conception about the ideal dog, type and personality. Everyone's first dog is their "best" dog. Although subsequent dogs may prove to be better, smarter or more handsome, the first for most people remains the best in their minds. The ability to realize *objectivity* when assessing the merits (or lack thereof) of a brood matron-elect is *critical* to desired puppy quality. As a newcomer to the field, learning to be objective about your own dog can be a hard task. Indeed, objectivity has proven to be an elusive quality even for many who are well established in their chosen breed.

Learning to acquire objectivity for a breeding program, having what is termed an "eye" for a dog's merits, may be achieved through contact with established breeders and professional handlers of good reputation. Even some breed experts find it difficult to assess the merits of their own dogs.

Each breed is unique, carrying individual physical and character traits that set it apart from all others. Each has its own peculiar problems beyond sharing those common to many breeds. If you do not already know those problems that beset your breed, as well as the strengths and weaknesses your matron-elect may carry to her offspring, these qualities need to be explored before breeding. While no dog is perfect, some dogs more closely approach a breed's ideal Standard than do others. These dogs may prove themselves to be worthy of breeding through the quality of their offspring. Hopefully, your dog is one of them.

SELECTING A STUD DOG

Do not be afraid to approach well-known experts for help. Most of these people maintain a sound perspective, desiring only the best for their breed's reputation. Your female's breeder may also offer assistance when selecting a potential sire.

When considering a stud, be aware that genetically inherited structural, breathing and skin problems may be found among certain breeds and dogs. Only consider those stud dogs that closest meet their breed's Standard. Breeding dogs is not like mixing coffee and milk; one does not end up with café au lait. Lack of merit in one animal is never compensated by the other. For example, if your female has too profuse a coat, do not breed to a male that is essentially hairless. You will end up producing a variety of puppies, some too profuse in coat, and others lacking length and density of coat representative of the breed. Always, no matter what criteria you use as a measurement, breed to the ideal dog according to your breed's Standard and one which complements your bitch.

Timing is essential when contemplating a breeding. Solidify your plans well in advance of your bitch's estral cycle. Contact stud owners no less than several months prior to your planned breeding. It can take a considerable amount of time to contact owners of dogs that may prove suitable for your female. Some people even plan their program several years in advance of a breeding.

SETTING TYPE

Request and compare copies of the stud dogs' pedigrees. When selection has been narrowed to a few candidates, compare these pedigrees to that of your female. The best breedings are generally those where the pedigrees exhibit several

LET'S SEE SOME PEDIGREE

Request and compare copies of potential stud dogs' pedigrees.   *Artist: Jan Walker*

outstanding ancestors common to both the stud and brood bitch-elect. This is how breed "type" is set.

The formula for establishing and maintaining type is a simple premise. As an example, the sire's sire should be the same dog as the dam's grandsire. This can be reversed to effect a line breeding on the dam's sire as well. Known as "close line breeding," such a formula makes it possible to set type within a breed.

Type can be either good or bad. Line and inbreeding can increase the possibility of producing superdog. It must be recognized, however, that at the same time it can also, through augmentation by percentages, produce animals possessed of undesirable characteristics.

When few or no ancestors are common to the sire and dam, the breeding is known as an *outcross*. Some outcrosses are excellent, others are not. When outcrossing, all genetic variables increase considerably. Some puppies may resemble the sire, the dam, a combination of the parents or a remote ancestor.

Bloodlines and origins are important to any successful breeding.

Since outcrossing is an educated guessing game, you will be unable to know in advance what your puppies will look like or how they will behave.

Line breeding is generally the safest course for newcomers to practice. Both the sire and the dam of the litter share multiple common ancestors. Line breeding is safe. You work with known qualities previously united through the ancestors. By line breeding you will be able to know in advance, to some degree, what your puppies will look like and how they will behave.

Inbreeding is perhaps the most misunderstood of all breeding formulas, particularly among newcomers. *Inbreeding should be done by only the most experienced breeders*, those who have a strong grasp of genetics and who have known the direct ancestors for at least the first few generations. *Type*, that elusive quality, *is firmly set by inbreeding*. Good or poor quality, the characteristic traits are intensified. While there is the opportunity of producing superior puppies, there is the risk of bringing very poor specimens into the world. Increasing genetic traits and characteristics by intensely multiplied factors, the best and worst of the ancestors must be carefully evaluated before an inbreeding is attempted.

Newcomers should inbreed or outcross only under the advice of a successfully experienced breeder, one who knows the antecedent dogs well and the risks involved. *This format of breeding does increase additional risks of birth defects.* Evisceration (puppies born with intestines external to the body), cleft palates and hydrocephalus are but a few of the birth anomalies that can occur in any breeding, but are intensified risks with inbreeding when done by those lacking adequate genetic information.

If the dogs being considered have already sired one or more litters, inquire about their offspring's quality. If it is geographically feasible, visit offspring from various litters. Note not only the excellence (or lack of merit) of their conformation, but be cognizant as well of the dogs' personalities and temperaments in their individual environments. If you are unable to personally see the ''get'' of the studs you are considering, request and obtain photographs of them in various growth stages. Obtain photographs of the sire's parents and the dams of the litters whenever possible.

When reading the pedigree, make note if the stud's line is consistent for quality through repeated generations of titled forebears. Inquire about any known recessives (possible drawbacks in the dog's background) and what strengths he may bring to your litter. Make your selection of a stud dog not simply through geographical accessibility, but rather because this particular animal is the wisest choice (through his genetic makeup) for your female. Be positive that he has much to offer your breed.

If the dog you select is being actively campaigned in field, hunting, obedience or conformation competition, he may not always be available for a physical union. You may find that you will have to plan your breeding program around the dog's availability if you insist on a physical union. Alternative methods to a natural breeding are available and viable. Covered in another chapter, these include cooled and frozen semen breedings.

If you are perhaps someone who does not actively exhibit or belong to a local or national breed club, the assistance of an established stud owner will prove invaluable. The dog's owners will express a continued interest in your proposed litter. Prior to a breeding contract they should readily express a willingness to help you by answering questions and assisting with puppy placements in good homes. Through their active participation they will have proven to be the type of stud dog owner who does not terminate the business relationship once the breeding itself has been achieved.

While you may have already established a solid support system for yourself through the sire's owner and your bitch's breeder, the following chapters offer you additional guidelines for physically and emotionally maximizing your litter. Here you will find sound basics from conception through whelping, providing a safe and supportive environment. As a breeder, your obligations are carefully defined, as is the puppies' presentation to prospective owners and your selection of their future homes. The investment of time, effort, money and devotion that a litter brings is rarely if ever compensated, except by the emotional largesse through which a healthy litter rewards the breeder.

DESIGNER GENES

Radiographs of the dam's hips and elbows should be made several months prior to the breeding. The veterinarian should give her at this time a complete physical in reference to her future breeding. An unvaccinated bitch, or one with an extremely low immunity, may respond well to inoculation at this time; a substantial increase in colostral immunity is also provided to her puppies. The

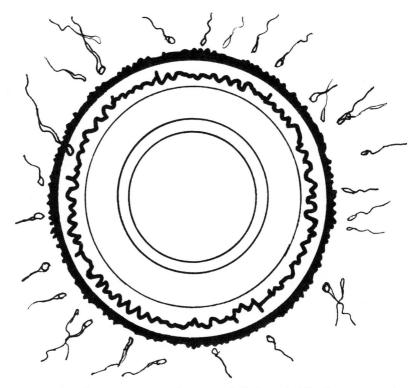

The conception of a puppy occurs when a zygote is formed at the time a spermatozoa penetrates an egg's wall. *Artist: Jan Walker*

dam should be in a peak physical condition, neither under- nor overweight at the time of a breeding.

A wide variety of factors can impact sperm. As a result, the stud dog should also be radiographed at least six weeks prior to the time of breeding. Normal, healthy sperm, resembling a pollywog in its early stages, is composed of a head and a tail. A sperm's structure is delicate, easily altered by chemicals, heat and recent illnesses. Factors affecting the viability of sperm may result in spermatozoa appearing with two heads, two tails, missing heads or tails or deformed heads and tails.

Deformed sperm are incapable of penetrating an egg's wall to form a zygote. Immature males and those recently physically ill may not have healthy sperm production, or may have a low sperm count. Ideally, therefore, only males in peak physical condition should be bred. They may be bred on alternate days over an extended time period to successfully produce viable sperm on each occasion.

The sex of each puppy is determined by the sire's sperm. The dam determines the number of puppies that can be conceived by the amount of eggs she releases during ovulation. Studies have reported healthy sperm remaining viable within a "friendly" (normal and not infected) uterus for as long as six days. Breedings should optimally occur every other day during the bitch's full estrous period, in order to allow the stud sound opportunity to recuperate and rebuild a strong viable sperm "bank."

The conception of a puppy occurs when a zygote is formed at the time a spermatozoa penetrates an egg's wall. Fertilization of the eggs occurs in the oviduct. It is at this moment of conception that a puppy's genetic makeup is set for life. From this moment onward, a breeder may only support the litter by offering the optimum environment, first for the dam and later for the puppies themselves.

Once fertilized, the zygote descends into the uterine horn's lumen. There, it "floats" unattached while being nourished by "uterine milk" for approximately 18 to 20 days before actually becoming implanted in the uterine wall. The formation and attachment of canine placenta is not unlike the processes found in other carnivores.

Individual breed characteristics are transmitted through genes which are located within chromosomes. During conception, the reproductive germ cells of the sire and the dam unite, replicating the parents in type (when both the sire and dam are of known, purebred ancestry and of the same breed). Each contributes 39 chromosomes to every puppy conceived to make up the 78 chromosomes contained in all reproductive cells. The result is that each puppy born in a litter receives half its chromosomes from the dam and the other half from the sire.

Genes are contained within the 78 chromosomes (39 pairs) found in each dog. Individual characteristic traits are contained within the genes. These traits include the sex, size and shape, eye color, tailset, coat quality and color of each puppy. Included, also, are the essential character or personality traits of each individual. The predisposition toward certain forms of behaviors are found genetically within the seven Groups of dogs: Sporting, Hounds, Working, Terriers, Toys, Non-Sporting and Herding. Representatives of these Groups individually exhibit a variety of behaviors, such as guarding, herding, scent-hunting, sight-hinting, retrieving and pulling, as clarified examples.

Not all genes are created "equal." Some genes are recessive while others are dominant. Complex factors determine whether either the dominant or recessive genes of any breeding are beneficial or detrimental to the desired combined result sought in the offspring (puppies). Many researchers spend their lives studying the effects of genetics, the hereditary factors involved when offspring of parents are created.

The genetic history of a puppy is not strictly found in the immediate ancestry of sire and dam. It is also based on earlier antecedents such as the grandparents, great grandparents and even earlier generations. Thus personal knowledge of the individual dogs making up a pedigree is critically important when considering a breeding, and that is why the help of a successfully experienced breeder within a given bloodline and breed is so invaluable.

Unless you have already obtained a background in the study of genetics in general, it may take you as a breeder years of practical hands-on experience to successfully determine which breedings will be best and why. The study of genetics, the successful breeding of dogs and optimizing puppies are not suggested for an impatient individual who desires success yesterday without having acquired a sound basis of knowledge in the breed and individual dogs' backgrounds.

The discipline of breeding, the successes and heartbreaks, is founded in learning the practical aspects of linebreeding, inbreeding and outcrossing of the various bloodlines available. Each breed and each bloodline carries with it certain traits, characteristics that are desirable and undesirable. Certain genetic pools may even constitute what are known as "lethal" genes. It takes years of concentrated study and effort, trial and error, to achieve a successful breeding program in any breed and type of dog.

Any person who breeds dogs should obtain at the very least a fundamental grasp not only of the study of genetics, but the focus of the breed Standard involved; and importantly, *why* the Standard is devised as written *and* the background several generations behind each pair of dogs being united. Even with the most scientific approach, breeding dogs involves a cerrtain amount of luck. Not unlike a spin of the roulette wheel, there is a "numbers game" of percentages in breeding dogs. It helps, therefore, to stack the percentages toward the successful side of each endeavor. Simplified, this equates to breeding the best female you have been able to obtain to the male best physically and genetically complementing your bitch.

Two wrongs do not make a right. Before selecting a stud dog, you must first look as objectively as possible at your bitch. If she is not close to your breed Standard's ideal in more than your opinion alone, *she should not be bred*. Nor should you select a sire based on a compromise of attributes between the two animals.

16

Outcrossing is like a mix-and-match game. Think, for example, of building a kaleidoscope. Genes are all the tiny different colors and shapes placed at the far end. Each color and shape represents different possible genetic combinations. To get all the pretty shapes reflected in the various forms (genetic combinations), the end of the kaleidoscope must be rotated. Each rotation produces an excitingly new aspect of the color/shape combinations. Each rotation (breeding) produces exciting new genetic combinations reflected as individual animals. No rotations produce identical pictures. No breedings (including repeat) produce identical dogs.

Temperaments

Your puppies' temperaments are affected not only by their genetic predisposition toward certain character traits, but by their environment as well. The greatest factor influencing your puppies' behavior is initially through their dam, her relationship with you and generalized perception of her environment. Her perception and acceptance of outside stimuli such as, for example, strangers who come to view the litter can set an indelible example for her offspring. Therefore, no bitch should be bred who has an unsound temperament. If the temperament is the overt product of abuse, and the female exhibits exceptional redeemable qualities given an optimum supportive environment, breeding is a possibility. The attitude of the dam will always be reflected at least to some degree in every puppy.

The neonatal period, between birth and the first eight to ten weeks of puppies' lives, is the most critical time. It is at this time that they acquire much of their dam's temperament as the result of their intense focus and relationship with their mother. If your dam is nervous or neurotic, she will communicate these aspects to the offspring. If, however, your matron-elect is confident of her role and position within your household, and she is openly and outwardly friendly, these character traits will be acquired by her progeny.

Puppies and older dogs can and do learn through mimicking those closest to them, their dam and siblings. Inherited predisposition toward certain behaviors is believed by many geneticists to be but about 10 percent inherited and 90 percent acquired. The predisposition of the inherited 10 percent of character traits does, however, remain with the puppies as they mature and go through life.

The environment in which a litter is reared, therefore, is of paramount importance to having well socialized and confident puppies. As a result, it behooves anyone who engages in a breeding program, whether for a single litter or a long-term endeavor encompassing multiple years and litters, to breed *only* those dogs that most closely meet the breed Standard's physical criteria, as well as those animals exhibiting the ideal temperament.

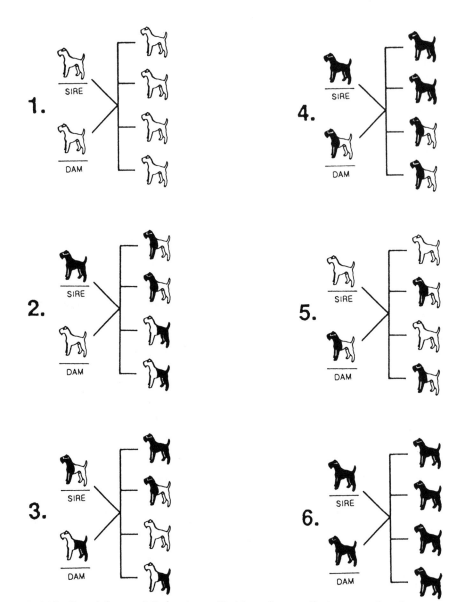

Individual breed characteristics are transmitted through genes. During conception, the reproductive germ cells of the parents unite, replicating them in type. The result is that each puppy born receives half its chromosomes from the dam and the other half from its sire.

Simple Mendalian Chart

MALE MEDICAL ASPECTS RELATED TO BREEDING

A major focus of this book is to give every breeder-owner enough useful information to rear puppies to the fullest potential. Equally important is the ability to develop a heightened awareness and a strong sensitivity to the dogs' physical and emotional well-being. Through such an advanced awareness, the earliest signs of many problems may be detected. Thus may be avoided undue physical and emotional stress and expenses for all, two- and four-legged alike.

The majority of male-female relationships are successful without extraordinary measures or help. Abnormalities discussed here are beyond the normal experience though not considered rarities. Essentially, males generally appear to be more free of breeding problems than females. They are somewhat more simple physiologically because they do not carry puppies.

The normal intact male produces spermatozoa stimulated by the hormone FSH, one of the two basic and essential hormones that a female's ovary also requires to produce viable eggs. When examined, the normal males' testes appear smooth, one like the other without variation. Upon gentle palpation during an examination, both testicles should be of closely similar if not the same in size. The palpated weight and density of the two should feel equal.

Some males may have one testicle that is small, not having developed normally. The passageway for sperm may be absent, or it may be so narrow that semen cannot be ejaculated. During the time when a male is stimulated by the presence of a receptive female in estrus, the testes may actually become somewhat enlarged and slightly firmer to palpation. During this period of stimulation it is not unusual for the prostate gland to enlarge, becoming sore or even painful. This condition may be first noticed by the owner when it has caused the male to walk in a manner different from usual. The male may also exhibit other signs of discomfort such as, for example, repeatedly licking the scrotum.

The average male is capable of breeding physically before emotional maturation occurs. Attempted use, however, of a dog that is too young may prove ineffectual because of infertility resulting from his age. Some young males appear to be physically mature, but may prove too emotionally immature to consummate a breeding.

If the penis has been previously injured, a dog may be incapable of effecting a natural breeding. It is also possible in some cases after an injury to the penis that the male will be unwilling to attempt mounting a female. Occasionally it has been found that the penis has developed incorrectly; one developmental abnormality is a curved penis bone. In this case, while the dog is fertile, it is unable to sufficiently direct the penis to allow a natural breeding. These males may still be used by breeding through artificial insemination.

The most common male problem found by veterinarians is that of testes that do not descend into the scrotal sac. In some cases the testes have been known to descend and not remain in the scrotal sac, being drawn back up through the inguinal ring into the abdominal cavity. Countless times veterinarians have also encountered males whose testes lie directly in front of the correct location.

Depending upon complex factors, including the genetic ancestry of the male, undescended or improperly located testicles remain a problem common to many dogs.

Contrary to a popular myth, injected hormones such as testosterone or LH-FSH will *not* cause testicles to descend "normally" into the scrotal sac. It is possible in some cases that testes are retained because the inguinal ring closes too early, before the male matures enough to allow their descent. Some slow or failed cases of testicle descent can be medically treated. Not a complex surgery, the testes are placed by the veterinarian into the corresponding scrotal sacs and the inguinal ring is surgically closed. However, it must be noted that after such surgery a dog may not be shown.

A dog with but one testicle located in the scrotum is still a fertile animal. The retained testicle is somewhat more prone to develop a cancerous tumor than one normally descended. The retained teste will also produce more male hormones (e.g., testosterone) than is normally found. This increased hormonal level can make the male a bit too strong in behavioral attitudes.

When breeders bypass some of the safeguards established by nature and breed animals not able to reproduce naturally, the risk of breeding problems is greatly increased in the litter and future generations. As a result, any dog that fails to have testes normally located in the scrotum should never be considered for a breeding program.

FEMALE MEDICAL ASPECTS RELATED TO BREEDING

The majority of normal females begin their estral cycles between six and ten months of age. Some few females, however, do not begin cycling until two-and-a-half years old. The giant breeds being somewhat slower in their physical maturation are also the slowest to develop hormonally. Only on a rare occasion does a small breed not cycle by fourteen or sixteen months of age.

The normal pre-estrus may be noted by a swelling around the vulva as early as six weeks before the estrus begins. The area just above the vulva may also exhibit early signs of pre-estrus by becoming enlarged and soft to the touch. Swelling is individualistic; some females swell profusely through their season, while in others the swelling is negligible to the point of being inconspicuous. The area of swelling is initially moderately firm to the touch, and as full estrus approaches the swollen area becomes softer.

If males are present, they may exhibit a slight behavioral change during this early estrus period, sniffing and licking the area where the female has recently urinated. Many repeatedly "chomp" their jaws together quickly, developing a foamy salivary excess immediately after sniffing or licking such a site. They may also exhibit increased signs of interest in the female's vulva and, if she does not sit or snap, sniff and lick this area as well.

The next noticeable sign of pre-estrus is the bleeding. Each female is different, although family lines are often predisposed toward similarities in their cycles. Nor is it always indicative of a female's fertility. Some females may never bleed or swell, and notice of their cycle may be made only by a companion dog's behavioral response to their change in scent caused by pheromones.

The duration of an average estral cycle is three weeks. The length of time varies from one female to another, even within close family relationships such as full sisters or mothers and daughters. Never assume by a female's family history that her cycle will be like that of her dam or granddams. A few females attain a full estrus by three to five days, and are out of season by the week's end. At the other end of the spectrum, many do not achieve full ovulation before 17 days. Full estrus normally occurs, however, by 10 to 14 days, and completion of this stage occurs within a week of ovulation. Determination of full estrus is usually best made by an experienced stud.

A veterinarian can confirm estrus through one of several various testing methods, any of which can be used to determine the optimum time for breeding. One accurate method is making a slide from a vaginal smear. The veterinarian uses a sterile swab to obtain a sample from inside the vagina. This sample is placed on a slide and examined after being dyed with a product known as methyl blue. Once treated, the slide is examined under a microscope for specific changes in the epithelial cells' structure. During the estrous cycle these cells undergo a progression of changes, normally indicative of the various and progressive estral stages.

In simple terms, the following closely describes changes made by the epithelial cells during a normal estrous cycle. The normal structure of a cell may be said to resemble a fresh egg that has been removed from its shell. The first and most obvious changes seen under a microscope are those of the cell walls, which become irregular in shape. As the days of the cycle continue, the cell walls and the nuclei seem to almost disappear. The albumen, the clear area surrounding the cell's nucleus, appears grainy in texture, as if grains of fine sand have been deposited upon the surface of the disintegrating cell. The cells' condition is "cornified." When most of the epithelial cells have progressed to this point of cornification, the female is in full estrus: she is ovulating and ready to conceive.

A substantial percentage of females do not cycle according to the rules. They may produce the pheromones (scent) that stimulate the male prior to or even after her ovulation. Waiting for a female to "flag" for the male and present her rear quarters for a breeding may not always be a good test either. Experienced studs are rarely fooled by even the most duplicitous female.

Some females have prolonged terms between their cycles. The normal time between cycles is six to seven months. Yet some females may cycle every three to four months, and others once a year. Some are very slow even to begin cycling. At the present time there is no reliable method to artificially cause a female to cycle. A few females respond positively to hormone treatments. After initiation, the treatment is suddenly withdrawn. This causes a small percentage of these females to begin cycling. Pregnant mares' serum, which is not readily available in this country at this writing, has proven effective in producing a complete fertile cycle for those cases of females that have had prolonged anestrous cycles.

Any hormone treatment must be approached conservatively. Hormones used to initiate cycles, treat unwanted pregnancies, control ovarian cysts or even stop cycles for the owner's convenience can result in breeding changes. Rarely do such treatments result in severe problems, but such hormone treatments can and do affect fertility in some cases.

Some maiden females may never stand and present themselves to the male. They will need help throughout the breeding process. Some bitches take an active dislike to the chosen stud and refuse to stand. For a natural breeding to be effected in these cases, the dogs will require manual assistance.

It has been well documented that any emotional stress of the bitch can also produce a lower conception rate. Such stress may be caused by shipping a female to the stud for breeding and then shipping her back to her owner *directly* afterward. The zygotes (fertilized eggs) do not attach to the uterine horn wall for approximately two weeks. Undue stress of the matron can cause a spontaneous abortion. Higher pregnancy ratios could be effected by leaving the female with the male for a longer period, until such time as the fertilized eggs have had the opportunity for uterine attachment.

The vaginal structure can also influence a breeding. If the vagina is defective in structure, it may prove physically impossible to obtain a natural breeding. A relatively simple examination of the female prior to breeding could help prevent or treat any problems that might be present.

Serum progesterone tests may also be utilized to determine the optimum time for a breeding. This test is costly for those females who have prolonged cycles. The serum progesterone test is a relatively quick examination for egg releases, by checking for the presence of increased levels of progesterone, the egg-releasing hormone. The difficulty of this test is, however, that it can prove costly. The serum progesterone tests are conducted by the veterinarian every other day.

One of the most common problems in effecting a breeding is low thyroid productions. In certain breeds and some genetic lines, nearly 50 percent of the animals are low thyroid producers. The problems of hypothyroidism are subtle and can be determined only by the veterinarian submitting a blood sample for laboratory testing.

There are also those females incapable of cycling as the result of inadequate food quality. This can mean that they are receiving insufficient nutritional value; additional support feedings, a change of diet, and adding supplements may bring the female to a more robustly fertile condition.

Weather and living conditions can also play an important role in a bitch's cycling. Snaps of heat or cold and prolonged darkness can cause delays in a female's cycle. Prolonged low-light conditions, such as those found in northern climes, cause a number of females to suppress their cycles during this period. It should also be noted that when females are housed together, one female can stimulate the others into either a true or a false estral cycle.

Many of the problems encountered can be hereditary. If such is the case, it would be wise to seriously consider a change of direction in particular genetic lines.

22

3

Orchestrating
the Breeding

NATURAL BREEDINGS do not always occur. Orchestrating
a breeding takes time, effort and a considerable amount of planning. Timing is
critical to breeding a litter. *More breeding failures occur through poor timing
than from any other factor.* Slides made by your veterinarian from vaginal smears
normally indicate the optimum time for breeding, but even when you think
everything has been satisfactorily coordinated, your female may not stand for
the male, and he may not be interested in your bitch.

If normal, your female's vulva will enlarge and soften as she nears ovulation. She will playfully "flag" the male, signaling her readiness to conceive
during this peak estrogen level. The dogs will usually at this time engage in a
period of foreplay. He will attempt mounting within minutes, and if she is ready,
she will stand. If she has a tail, she will whip it aside, presenting her rear
quarters to the male. This is an overt invitation for him to mount. Some females,
particularly those never before bred, allow a male to initaite a mounting, but will
then slip out from under him.

Under certain conditions it is necessary to provide extra assistance in order
to consummate a breeding. The "if" scenarios include but are not limited to: if
the male is considerably larger and heavier than the female; if she is reluctant to
stand, although slides or a serum progesterone test say she is ovulating; if the
male lacks interest, or if you have a type of dog that routinely has problems in
obtaining a natural breeding. Manually assisting a breeding is a common and
sound practice. Assisting insures that neither dog becomes injured.

Small dogs are best bred on a large table covered with a nonslip surface. Rubber-backed area rugs or bath mats are perfect. Use of a table saves the handlers' backs. The dogs may prove reluctant to "perform" on a table if they are not used to routine handling and grooming at an elevated level. Some males are reluctant to mount the female if she is overly handled, making him feel crowded and "threatened" by too many people.

Larger dogs and giant breeds are bred on the ground, on a nonslip surface where they can obtain good purchase. A stair riser is excellent for the male to stand on when mounting a larger female. A female much smaller than the male can be positioned toward the rear portion of a grooming or card table that has folded legs. Nor are all females able to physically withstand a male's advances. She may require assistance to stand under the force of his thrusts and weight. Handling a mating is often real physical exertion for the breeders as well.

There are females who, although they may be sweet pets, actively resist being bred. It may be wise to muzzle females with either tape, gauze, an old stocking or a velcro muzzle before a breeding is attempted. Muzzling prevents a bitch from nipping or biting either the handler or the dog's face as he mounts and penetrates. A growling female or one that overtly displays fear can leave a male reluctant to mount. Having someone hold the female's head by each cheek may sufficiently bolster the male's confidence to attempt the breeding.

Your female may respond confidently to a steadying hand on her stifle if she sags under the male. She can also be supported (depending upon her size and breed) by a dish, bath or beach towel slung under her belly. Stretched between two people immediately in front of her rear quarters or just behind her forelegs, the towel prevents her from sagging. She may require a second steadying hand at her head. It may take three or even four people working together to get a breeding when handling very large and heavy dogs. One person holds the female's head, two stretch a towel slung under her and the fourth physically assists the male to mount, aim or remain penetrated until a tie can occur.

When mounting, a male normally grabs and holds the female by her rear quarters, his forelegs wrapped around her "waist." Balancing on his hind legs, the male pulls the female into him. Although he is not usually too high, he may appear so, as his head and shoulders ride up along her neck. An unassertive stud may feel inhibited and reluctant to mount when those assisting are too close to the female. Use of a towel allows those helping to support the female from an uninhibiting distance. Nor should her head be held so closely that the male is inhibited from mounting fully, laying his forequarters up by her shoulders.

Not every female holds her tail far enough to one side when flagging. The person supporting her stifle, or holding one side of the towel, may be required to also hold onto her tail. At the same time, this assistant may have to assist the male's aim, tipping her vulva. Those dogs not routinely comfortable with having various portions of their anatomy handled may prove recalcitrant to such intimate maneuvers during this sensitive time. Some males require help in directing their penis in order to successfully breed naturally. Nor is it uncommon for certain males to have a downward curving penis bone. As the result of this curving, these dogs often have problems when breeding and must be manually aimed.

The penis substantially engorges once the male achieves penetration. The glans, which appear like a large knob, is located near the base of the penis. After penetration and during a tie, the glans swells beyond the dimensions of other penile tissue. This large and rigidly swollen "knob" keeps the coupling pair connected. The female's vaginal wall muscles automatically contract in response to the penile tissue engorgement. Thus "locked" together, the condition is known as a "tie." While a tie is not absolutely critical for conception, it is nature's way of helping to insure impregnation.

The stud releases his ejaculate in three distinct portions. The amount of between 2 to 15 milliliters varies according to the dog and breed type. The first fraction of the ejaculate, from the urethral glands, consists of a watery fluid devoid of sperm. The ejaculate's second portion, from the testicles, contains the spermatozoa. The third fraction, also without sperm, is the largest portion of the ejaculate.

On the average, most ties last from 10 to 45 minutes. *A briefer tie is not indicative of an incomplete ejaculation or one of insufficient quality or quantity.* Nor does a longer tie insure a greater conception rate. It is the female who determines the number of ova ripened to accept fertilization. The offspring's sex is determined by the sperm. Only one viable sperm can penetrate an ovum, thus creating a puppy.

ASSISTING A BREEDING

Outside ties are relatively common with certain types of dogs. Large, heavy-bodied, short-legged breeds and some Toy breeds are known to often tie outside when breeding. Males who do not penetrate deep enough during their pelvic thrusting are prone to tie outside the female's body. Virgin males and breedings attempted too early in the female's cycle can also result in an outside tie.

An "outside tie" is readily visible in smooth-coated breeds. Rough- or long-coated breeds should be manually checked, however, for the presence of a rigid, swollen glans, indicating a tie outside. Small breeds are easily held together. One hand is gently pressed against the female's abdomen and upper thigh, the other presses firmly (but not forcefully) against the male's hindquarters. Handling large or giant breeds requires greater physical exertion. Here an outside tie can be prevented by the male's handler, who encircles the rear quarters of both dogs with both arms. By exerting slight pressure with the handler's chest against the male's rear, and locking hands together in front of the female's thighs, a handler is able to keep the dogs pressed firmly together.

A breeding is not necessarily lost should an exterior tie occur. The pair may be held together as described, ideally until the penile swelling begins to subside, or for approximately ten minutes (whichever occurs first). An obviously

The dogs should remain rump-to-rump until the tie is completed. Large breeds are manually assisted by a handler to encircles the pair's hindquarters with his arms.

Artist: Jan Walker

tired male can be allowed to dismount, but must be prevented from turning. Instead, he is held immediately adjacent by about 90 degrees to the female's side. The handler manually holds the penis in place for as long as possible while the male ejaculates. Ten minutes is usually sufficient time for keeping the dogs coupled in this manner.

When a male stops the pelvic thrusting and appears to be resting, he is ready to be turned. Many indicate an instinctive desire to turn. It is uncomfortable for the female when a male remains astride, appearing to ''rest'' on her. Some males instinctively rotate a rear leg over the female's hindquarters when turning. Others may not have the instinct or ability of turning independently. It is neither uncomfortable nor dangerous to the dogs, should the male be turned manually.

The dogs should remain rump-to-rump until the tie is completed. Although the dogs are turned, the male continues to ejaculate. Eventually penile swelling decreases. When this occurs, and the vaginal walls are no longer stimulated, they cease rhythmic contractions.

When managing large and giant breeds, having the ability to sit on a low chair or stool during a tie saves a handler's back. Once the dogs are turned, large breeds are manually assisted by a handler encircling the pair's hindquarters with his arms. At this time the handler may sit, obtaining better leverage.

Some breeding pairs require additional handlers, helping to keep the dogs

26

together and preventing injury to one or both. Dogs have been known to turn somersaults or otherwise attempt pulling away during the tie. Having additional handlers available to help keep the dogs from moving too freely prevents injuries.

Ties extending over a prolonged period of time can cause problems. Dogs, like their handlers, tire rapidly when closely confined to a single position. Occasionally some dogs have become irritable during an extensive period of enforced stillness. The dogs must, however, be kept closely restrained, as still and as quiet as possible until the tie has completed.

Should a tie prove to be prolonged, there is a step easily taken, keeping all involved in good spirits and health. While confined rump-to-rump, the dogs can be laid onto their sides. This position appears to help even the most excitable dogs remain calm and quiet.

Getting dogs of any size prone requires well-orchestrated timing. If the breed is medium or small, two people can easily manage the dogs onto their sides. If the breed is a large one, however, as many as three handlers may be required: one for each dogs' forequarters, and a third person ''hugging'' the pair's rears together. Through a well-coordinated effort even the largest dogs can be handled.

Agitated dogs are able to actually prolong a tie. However, it is very rare for dogs to require assistance to obtain a separation. If dogs are forced to separate before the penile tissue has had time to diminish sufficiently, the male can be irreparably damaged. A dog's penis is not all tissue and contains a bone as well. If a breeding is improperly handled, the bone can be broken and the tissue damaged. The female can also be injured by forcing an early separation of the tying pair. Attempts to stop a tie are, therefore, not normally wise. There are those few times, however, when hastening the process of termination, if at all possible, is a good idea. If the dogs are small enough, the male may be rotated, turned back to the original mounting position. Once both dogs are in the original stand/thrust position, a reinforcing pressure on the male's rear quarters can bring enough relief, allowing the swelling to diminish. Use of a cool towel, or even ice, held against the testicles can help to facilitate reduction of the swelling.

BREEDING ALTERNATIVES: ARTIFICIAL INSEMINATION

Psychological and genetic studies, and other scientific advances, have made this age a most exciting one for the better-bred dog. Among these advances is artificial insemination, a practice now more than ever common to small animal husbandry. Following years of research, trials and errors, discoveries have been made that allow sperm collections to remain viable through a prolonged time period. As a result, breeding to a ''superstud,'' inaccessible before through ''geographical undesirability,'' has now become feasible.

''Artificial insemination'' is the introduction of sperm into a female's genital tract by instruments. The procedure involves sperm collection and evaluation of volume, quality and motility. When the female is not present for a direct breeding, the semen is separated by portion, then placed in "straws" for storage and transport.

Use of artificial insemination prevents spread of diseases by eliminating direct contact of the animals. This method overcomes incompatibility by personality or size in the mating pair, and it overcomes geographical difficulties. Superdogs can build up semen banks for worldwide use or use for after the dog is no longer capable of producing viable sperm or no longer alive.

Artificial insemination can produce pregnancy failure. When performed properly, however, artificial insemination reportedly achieves a pregnancy rate near that of natural breeding. While *fresh extended or frozen semen* offers breeders a greater geographical selection of possible studs, use of these methods does have certain drawbacks. Not all veterinarians have the training and facilities to properly prepare either fresh-cooled or frozen semen for insemination. The processes of cooling or freezing semen can weaken and kill sperm. Because of possible reduction in viable sperm, adequate facilities and preparation become paramount. There is now an expanding network of veterinarians who have been successfully trained in these methods.

Types of Artificial Breeding

Fresh-cooled semen collected for immediate shipment (by express delivery) is diluted with special extenders designed for this method of insemination. These breedings have proven to be a viable alternative to natural breeding or direct fresh insemination where both the male and female are present. Previously frozen semen has also proven a viable alternative to natural breeding and fresh-cooled insemination. Fresh-cooled semen has geographical shipping limitations, but use of frozen semen allows a superstud to cross international boundaries.

One day, canine embryos may also be transplanted. This procedure is already utilized in the large animal field (such as cattle and swine) for livestock improvement in geographically deprived areas. It may also be possible for future canine embryos to be transplanted into a surrogate dam of the same or even a different breed: one known to successfully carry multiple full-term puppies. Nor is it impossible that in the future embryos taken from their dam will be "suspended" through freezing, flown around the world and surgically implanted within a surrogate mother. Thus one day an outstanding work, show or field trial bitch in one country may be bred to a superstud in another, to produce superior offspring without losing valuable time in her field.

The ramifications of such ideas are staggering. Currently there are great variations in breed type from one country and area to another. With a geographically limited gene pool, dogs in some areas may not be as close to their Standard as are others elsewhere. Through use of fresh-cooled or frozen extended semen, boundaries are disappearing. The future of breeding dogs looks forward to the prospect of genetic access to the world's best studs, rather than the best from a local area.

There are a number of reasons why and when use of artificial insemination may be the best or only recourse to obtain a litter. There are females who, although in full estrus, may not give off the correct pheromones (scent) stimulating the male, enticing him to breed at the right time. She could have a physical abnormality such as a vaginal stricture or underdeveloped (juvenile) vagina preventing a natural coitus.

He may be an inexperienced or overeager male and ejaculate prematurely. A curved penis causing "aiming" difficulties can prevent dogs from achieving a natural union. Physical abnormalities may prevent a tie, and in certain cases be the cause of a prolonged one. Or, for a variety of reasons including medical, the stud may not be desirous of breeding.

For some, use of frozen or cooled semen remains controversial. Insemination by these means is nevertheless growing as a viable alternative method. While not necessarily less costly for the breeding of small or medium-sized dogs, the cost may be less than shipping a bitch, especially those of large and giant breeds. Breeding artificially becomes economically practical and feasible when faced by certain complicating factors such as shipment of a nervous female, perhaps one never before away from home, or inclement weather, being either too hot or too cold for safe shipment. At various times of the year and depending upon weather conditions, the airlines justifiably place an embargo on live animal shipments. Until recently, therefore, distance and weather played an important role in a stud's accessibility.

Beyond the expense are the possible effects from the rigors of shipping. The emotional stress caused by shipping has been known to drive females abruptly out of season. Shipping a female for a physical union is also not a litter guarantee, and shipping the female home directly after a successful breeding may cause her to abort. Even moderate emotional stress from a flight can cause an early release of hormones. Release of hormones at this time prevents the fertilized eggs (zygotes) from becoming implanted in the uterine horn wall. The zygotes normally attach to the uterine wall via the placenta, approximately 18 to 20 days after conception. Objectively then, fresh-cooled or frozen extended semen is easier and less expensive to ship than some bitches and does provide a viable alternative to natural breeding.

The Mechanics of Artificial Breeding

Most artificial inseminations consist of semen freshly collected in a sanitized, artificial vagina. This procedure is best performed by vetinarians with both dogs present. You may decide that you want to acquire mastery of artificially inseminating your own dogs if you are engaged in a serious breeding program, and have a breed that is routinely inseminated artificially. Complete artificial insemination kits are marketed throughout the country by reputable firms. The best of these kits includes a videotape that details the complete process, the necessary materials and a step-by-step guidance manual.

If you are concerned about your ability to perform an artificial insemination, speak candidly with your veterinarian. This person knows you, your capabilities and your relationship with your dog. When appropriate, a vet may offer you firsthand artificial insemination instruction. Conversely, if you do not intend to use this method on a regular basis, your veterinarian may dissuade you from attempting this procedure.

A "teaser" scent is almost inevitably a requisite for stimulating semen collection. Few males are able to effect a collection when not stimulated either by a "teaser" female (one in full estrus), or by use of an artificial estral scent. Once emotionally "turned on" through scent (dogs' most powerful sense), the male is stimulated directly behind the bulbus glans by a hand on his sheath. As the penile tissue begins to engorge, the sheath is pushed back to reveal the bulbus portion. The artificial vagina used for collection is held just over or below the dog's penis until ejaculation is complete. If a manufactured vagina is not available, another clean receptacle may be used for collection.

Ejaculate is passed in three distinct phases, with a normal volume of (depending on the dog and breed) between 2 and 15 milliliters. The first portion from the urethral glands and prostate serves as a lubricant. Consisting of a watery, clear fluid, it is devoid of sperm. The second ejaculate portion from the testicles contains the sperm. The third portion is composed of prostatic secretions to help propel sperm into the uterus. When both the male and female are present, the entire ejaculate is immediately injected into the female without having been separated into the three portions.

If the sperm is to be preserved by cooling or freezing for later use, only the second, sperm-bearing portion is preserved (the first and third are discarded). When prepared for storage, the sperm-bearing portion of the ejaculate is diluted with extenders. Untreated semen remains viable for only a short time (some only 15 minutes). Properly handled chilled semen remains viable for approximately 24 hours. Semen correctly treated with extenders and prepared for frozen storage keeps indefinitely. Only a qualified veterinarian should perform fresh-chilled or frozen semen breedings.

When the insemination is direct, the entire ejaculate is drawn from the receptacle into a sterile syringe. Air is also drawn into the syringe at this time. The air pocket following the seminal injection offers an extra "push," getting sperm deeper into the female's vagina. Some practitioners use an additional (second) syringe of air to help propel the semen even further.

Before any collection is made, the female has had a pipette (a thin, flexible sterile plastic tube) measured to her body's proportions. The semen-filled syringe is attached to the pipette and *gently* inserted into her vagina. The pipette is directed up and forward, slowly and carefully, into her vaginal canal (sloping forward toward the cervix). To avoid perforating the wall and vagina, the pipette must *never* be forced. Should the pipette not slip in easily, it must be withdrawn either part or all of the way, and the insertion reinstituted.

Once the pipette is in position, the syringe's plunger is depressed *slowly*. When all the ejaculate has been expelled from the syringe, it is removed from the pipette. After being refilled with air, the syringe is reattached and the plunger again slowly depressed. The plunger must never be withdrawn while attached to

30

the pipette. Should this occur, the ejaculate would be withdrawn from the female. After the pipette has been removed from the female, some practitioners will insert one or two sterile-gloved fingers into her vagina, stimulating her vaginal wall contractions. The bitch is then helped to retain the ejaculate.

Elevating the female's rear quarters also helps to insure effectiveness of the insemination. She should be kept in this position for at least five to ten minutes. A seated owner or assistant can easily hold a small female positioned head downward. Larger-breed females may have their rear quarters elevated wheelbarrow-fashion. The object is to keep the ejaculate as high and forward in the female as possible. Some practitioners recommend walking her for approximately fifteen minutes directly after having been elevated. Because vaginal contractions appear to stimulate an impulse to urinate, she must *not* be allowed to do so for at least one hour, if not two hours, following insemination. Crating her during this time period will prevent her from urinating.

OTHER FACTORS AFFECTING CONCEPTION

Weather conditions can also have a deleterious impact on a successful breeding. Weather either too hot or too cold can affect prime sperm production. This environmental factor can also cause a female to become temporarily infertile.

Other factors affecting litter conception rate can be multiple and interactive: 1) the age of the dog and bitch (too young or too old), 2) The health of both animals, 3) medical therapy (including flea controls) close to breeding time, 4) the breeding environment, 5) the mental state of the sire and dam at the time of mating, 6) the mental state and physical well-being of the bitch subsequent to the breeding and throughout her term, 7) some dogs genetically predisposed to a low conception rate. The most common conception failures are caused by poor timing, lack of adequate physical care and poor emotional support of both the sire and dam.

Certain countries have embargoes on dogs entering their rabies quarantine area. The preparation and shipment of either frozen or cooled semen usually bypasses red-tape boundaries and has produced conceptions worldwide. Be advised, however, that presently certain kennel clubs must grant permission to register offspring from artificial insemination if the semen is flown from one country to another. Additionally, at the present time, the United States Department of Agriculture must issue a special import license before any semen can be imported from abroad.

ABNORMAL SEXUAL AND BREEDING BEHAVIORS

Rarely seen, true nymphomania is an exaggerated sexual response in the female. Most commonly this condition is associated with other forms of abnormal sexual behavior. Some females will exhibit a variety of estral signs, making them extremely attractive to males. While they may "flag," present their rear and signal a willingness to breed, they will almost never permit a male to mount. There can also be evidence in this condition of normal estral signs such as an enlarged vulva and blood-stained discharge. True nymphomania is believed to originate from a prolonged estral cycle, one during which an excessive amount of the female hormone estrogen is produced. The cause of this excessive estrogen production is believed to be cystic ovaries. A prolonged swollen appearance of the genitalia may be indicative of nymphomania. Another indication is prolonged periods of excessive sexual desire, usually without allowing a breeding. Should a breeding occur, it is usually without conception, as most females of this condition are sterile. Females suffering from the condition of true nymphomania may often be nervous, irritable or even occasionally vicious. They may, at times, mount and ride males whenever present. If no males are convenient, they may attempt to mount and ride various family members of any age and either sex. Toys have also been employed for the expression of masturbation.

Successful treatment of true nymphomania is rare. A few veterinarians have had moderate success through massaging or rupturing the ovarian cysts by laparotomy. Sometimes effective treatment has been achieved through hormone injections that help to establish a normal and regular cycle. The success of therapy is not by any measure consistent. Most veterinarians recommend spaying as the normal and only viable course of treatment.

Hyperestrinism is another condition where the animal suffers from an excessive production of the female hormone estrogen. This condition leaves the female totally devoid of sexual desire. Through her scent, however, she remains an attractive nuisance to males. Again, cystic ovaries are the most common source of this problem. The dysfunction of the pituitary or adrenal glands should never go unchecked by the veterinarian, as their impairment may also cause hyperestrinism.

Vaginitis, another relatively common condition, also exhibits signs similar to those of a female in estrus. Although attractive and stimulating to males, a female with this condition will not exhibit signs of sexual desire. Other factors that can attract and stimulate males and appear to be caused by an estral cycle are infections of the vulva, cervix, bladder and anal sacs. The elimination of a possible infection and determination of a true estrous cycle is best made by your veterinarian, someone trained and equipped to make knowledgeable and definitive diagnoses.

Males can also suffer from hyperestrinism. The condition in this sex is usually caused by a Sertoli cell tumor, which is located in a testicle. Additional signs of feminism may be exhibited if the male's heightened state of estrogen stimulation is caused by this tumor's presence. The following signs may occur together, or they can occur as single symptoms: bilateral and symmetrical loss of hair, nipple enlargement, loss of muscular development around the neck and shoulders, a feminine distribution of fatty deposits and an atrophy of penile tissue. Male hyperestrinism is treatable and the effects of femininity are often reversible, provided the dog is presented to a veterinarian in a timely manner.

Satyriasis is the male counterpart of nymphomania. Found only occasionally, it is an exaggerated form of sexual desire. True satyriasis as a disturbance in the dog's libido (located at the center of its cerebral cortex) is a very rare condition. Temporal lobe damage, which also can manifest itself in such behavior, is equally rare. Occasionally a disease of the penis, prepuce or urethra can stimulate behaviors replicating those found in true satyriasis. An enlarged prostate and secondary urethritis accompany the condition of satyriasis. Usually exhibition of satyriasism is found in a spoiled or bored dog that lacks sufficient mental stimulation and the challenge of physically rigorous exercise. Many such spoiled animals have established themselves as the alpha personality in a household. Frequent masturbation characterizes satyriasis, with mounting attempts often directed toward household members—adults, children and other pets alike, regardless of their sex.

True satyriasis is rarely found. As a result, males that characteristically exhibit such behavior patterns should be examined by their veterinarian to determine the origins of their behavior. A thorough physical examination will disclose if such behaviors stem from physiological or environmental and psychological factors. Veterinary treatment is usually effective and satisfactory through administration of specific medications. Engaging the dog in a regular program of rigorous exercise also helps to control acquired negative behavioral impulses.

BREEDING FAILURES—CAUSES AND SOLUTIONS

Infertility can be the result of a wide variety of sources. Congenital defects, infections, medications and tumors of the reproductive system of either sex may result in breeding failures. Among females, endocrine imbalances may be the most common causes. Egg implantation failure resulting from either physiological or psychological sources is a cause of infertility. Impotence, whether temporary or permanent, can also stem from a wide variety of causes. As an example, a male kept under close confinement may suffer a temporary sterility.

Psychological and environmental factors can, and do, strongly influence fertility. Some house pets may be reluctant to breed at all, while others will breed successfully when not in the presence of their owners. Rough handling or distractions during a supervised breeding can affect conception rate. Dietary insufficiency or obesity affect reproduction ability. Many cases of temporary infertility or impotence can be successfully brought into control through therapeutic veterinary intervention.

The veterinarian should thoroughly examine both the male and female before a breeding is initiated. Ideally, the sire- and matron-elect should be in a good state of health, lean and physically strong. They should have blood drawn for a brucellosis test no less than several days prior to the first mating. The reproductive organs of the male should be examined. The veterinarian should also make a slide from a semen sample to assess the quality, motility and quantity of the sperm.

A breeding should take place in an atmosphere conducive to a natural completion of the mating. The atmosphere should be free of distractions, allowing the dogs to concentrate fully on what they are supposed to be doing. A backyard where neighbors hang over the fence to watch, or even a next-door party is a strong distraction for any coupling pair. Children zooming through the yard and nearby dogs barking are also major disturbances to a successful breeding.

Age and timing are the strongest factors in the reproductive ability of both sexes. The passage of years can cause an older dog, male or female, to become infertile. The best conception rates occur when the correct breeding time is determined. A female's flagging enticement of the male is not enough. Daily examination of vaginal smears helps to accurately define the optimum time for a breeding. Good conception rates occur when females are bred twice within 48 hours, and during the first three days of true estrus. Some females' slides indicate a longer breeding period. Bred no more than three times on an every-other-day basis, over a 72-hour period, a strong conception rate is almost always assured.

4

Detecting Pregnancy

THERE IS no infallible method to confirm a pregnancy very early in term, before 21 days. There are those few exceptional individuals who, by having developed an exceedingly close rapport with their female, may be able to detect a pregnancy as early as 10 days. Through a heightened awareness, they are able to observe minute subtle changes in their bitch. Those people who are able to determine pregnancies by two weeks and matrons who so strongly show hormonal changes are the exceptions to the normal course of early pregnancy determination.

The earliest signs of a pregnancy are often behavioral. Through initial hormonal changes, a bitch may need additional physical attention. Or she may appear to be depressed and withdrawn from her owners and normal routine. In these cases, a strengthened emotional support helps such sensitive females to retain their pregnancies.

Other changes are physical in appearance. Often, it is how the bitch carries herself; she may appear to move differently once bred. Her appetite may also change radically, sometimes within hours of a successful breeding. Such behavioral changes may be exhibited by either a depressed or increased desire for food intake. The expressed behavior can also be that of a need for variation in the diet.

Some females become coprographic: that is, eating feces, either their own or, in rarer cases, that of other dogs. This form of aberrational behavior is often fostered by unclean living conditions, a dietary insufficiency, a mineral/vitamin deficiency or a combination of factors.

Bred Jan / Due Mar	Bred Feb / Due Apr	Bred Mar / Due May	Bred Apr / Due Jun	Bred May / Due Jul	Bred Jun / Due Aug	Bred Jul / Due Sep	Bred Aug / Due Oct	Bred Sep / Due Nov	Bred Oct / Due Dec	Bred Nov / Due Jan	Bred Dec / Due Feb
1 5	1 5	1 3	1 3	1 3	1 3	1 2	1 3	1 3	1 3	1 3	1 2
2 6	2 6	2 4	2 4	2 4	2 4	2 3	2 4	2 4	2 4	2 4	2 3
3 7	3 7	3 5	3 5	3 5	3 5	3 4	3 5	3 5	3 5	3 5	3 4
4 8	4 8	4 6	4 6	4 6	4 6	4 5	4 6	4 6	4 6	4 6	4 5
5 9	5 9	5 7	5 7	5 7	5 7	5 6	5 7	5 7	5 7	5 7	5 6
6 10	6 10	6 8	6 8	6 8	6 8	6 7	6 8	6 8	6 8	6 8	6 7
7 11	7 11	7 9	7 9	7 9	7 9	7 8	7 9	7 9	7 9	7 9	7 8
8 12	8 12	8 10	8 10	8 10	8 10	8 9	8 10	8 10	8 10	8 10	8 9
9 13	9 13	9 11	9 11	9 11	9 11	9 10	9 11	9 11	9 11	9 11	9 10
10 14	10 14	10 12	10 12	10 12	10 12	10 11	10 12	10 12	10 12	10 12	10 11
11 15	11 15	11 13	11 13	11 13	11 13	11 12	11 13	11 13	11 13	11 13	11 12
12 16	12 16	12 14	12 14	12 14	12 14	12 13	12 14	12 14	12 14	12 14	12 13
13 17	13 17	13 15	13 15	13 15	13 15	13 14	13 15	13 15	13 15	13 15	13 14
14 18	14 18	14 16	14 16	14 16	14 16	14 15	14 16	14 16	14 16	14 16	14 15
15 19	15 19	15 17	15 17	15 17	15 17	15 16	15 17	15 17	15 17	15 17	15 16
16 20	16 20	16 18	16 18	16 18	16 18	16 17	16 18	16 18	16 18	16 18	16 17
17 21	17 21	17 19	17 19	17 19	17 19	17 18	17 19	17 19	17 19	17 19	17 18
18 22	18 22	18 20	18 20	18 20	18 20	18 19	18 20	18 20	18 20	18 20	18 19
19 23	19 23	19 21	19 21	19 21	19 21	19 20	19 21	19 21	19 21	19 21	19 20
20 24	20 24	20 22	20 22	20 22	20 22	20 21	20 22	20 22	20 22	20 22	20 21
21 25	21 25	21 23	21 23	21 23	21 23	21 22	21 23	21 23	21 23	21 23	21 22
22 26	22 26	22 24	22 24	22 24	22 24	22 23	22 24	22 24	22 24	22 24	22 23
23 27	23 27	23 25	23 25	23 25	23 25	23 24	23 25	23 25	23 25	23 25	23 24
24 28	24 28	24 26	24 26	24 26	24 26	24 25	24 26	24 26	24 26	24 26	24 25
25 29	25 29	25 27	25 27	25 27	25 27	25 26	25 27	25 27	25 27	25 27	25 26
26 30	26 30	26 28	26 28	26 28	26 28	26 27	26 28	26 28	26 28	26 28	26 27
27 31		27 29	27 29	27 29	27 29	27 28	27 29	27 29	27 29	27 29	27 28
		28 30	28 30	28 30	28 30	28 29	28 30	28 30	28 30	28 30	
		29 31		29 31	29 31	29 30	29 31		29 31	29 31	

Continuation (bred day / due date): 28 29 30 31 → Apr 1 2 3 4 | 27 28 → May 1 2 | 30 31 → Jun 1 2 | 29 30 → Jul 1 2 | 30 31 → Aug 1 2 | 30 → Sep 1 | 30 → Oct 1 2 | 30 31 → Nov 1 2 | 29 30 → Dec 1 2 | 30 → Jan 1 2 | 30 → Feb 1 | 28 29 30 31 → Mar 1 2 3 4

Corresponding date calendar for breeding and whelping.

PREGNANCY TESTS

There are a variety of tests that can help in detecting a pregnancy. Many of these tests are only as good as the technician or veterinarian administering them. Palpation has long been accepted as de rigueur for detecting a pregnancy. The optimum period for an expert to perform the palpation is 21 days past conception. At this time the puppies feel, upon palpation, round and enlarged like eggs.

Fertilized eggs do not attach to the uterus's lumen (wall) until approximately 18 days past conception. Determining a pregnancy at this time is not always possible if the female tenses during palpation. Should the clinician performing the palpation not be an expert and roughly handle the female at this time, an abortion can be caused by separation of the newly attached placenta from the uterine horn's wall.

When utilized properly, ultrasound has proven to be a successful method of determining pregnancy. Working on the same principle as sonar, safe and noninvasive as a test, the process of ultrasound consists of bouncing radio (sound) waves off internal organs. Ultrasound detection produces moving imagery (sonargram) on a television monitor. The principle behind ultrasound is the determination of how a structure's density reacts to the sound waves. As ultrasound waves return to the screen, distinct images are then produced through a computerized re-creation of the form probed. Although perhaps known for the detection of pregnancies and type, ultrasound is primarily utilized to investigate a wide variety of medical conditions. The bombardment of these ultrasound (beyond the range of hearing) radio waves allows technicians to look inside organs such as the heart, liver, kidneys, bladder, uterus and others. Through use of this noninvasive and painless technique, specific problems can be investigated and identified without requiring exploratory surgery.

The ultrasound form of pregnancy detection is not, however, fail-safe. Such sonar imagery can be erroneous. If the test is improperly handled, or performed too early in a pregnancy, an owner may be told that the bitch is not

While there are a variety of tests which may successfully determine a pregnancy, the best test is time. *Greyhound: Patricia Gail Burnham*

Many bitches are inclined toward denning once they become pregnant. This Alaskan Malamute carefully covered the entrance to her den with brush, instinctively to hide it from possible predators.

pregnant. This can have a deleterious effect on puppies if the dam is not given adequate supportive therapy throughout her entire term. Poor testing, or an erroneous diagnosis, may also give an owner the information that the female is pregnant. Ultrasound is only as useful as the proficiency of the technician handling the test. Ultrasound is most effectively performed 30 days past conception, when puppies' structures have had opportunity to gain in density.

A blood test has also been developed, which, while fairly effective, may not be fail-safe either. Most accurate between 22 and 36 days past conception, blood is examined for a specific substance known to have a high correlation with pregnancy. This sophisticated test is performed at either a fully equipped veterinary laboratory or an outside laboratory, one that works in close association with veterinary hospitals.

A conservative approach is wise. Therefore, keep in mind that any female exhibiting a positive response to testing may not necessarily be pregnant. If a bitch is maintained with an adequate diet on the supposition that a breeding has been successful, utilization of early pregnancy tests is unnecessary. Time alone is, in reality, the ultimate "test" of a pregnancy. By all means go ahead and test if early knowledge of pregnancy is critical to your peace of mind.

FAILURE TO CONCEIVE

If the female is a working animal, hard physical labor may prevent the retention of zygotes before uterine horn attachment becomes possible. The zygote (early embryo) may also simply fail to attach to the uterine horn wall. In some cases of pregnancy failure, the eggs die shortly after fertilization occurs. Causative factors can be physical or emotional stress or result from a genetic defect. Certain medications, such as various flea agents, are known to cause a variety of birth defects.

Having conceived, it is also possible for a matron to "withdraw" her pregnancy through either a spontaneous abortion or absorption of the fetuses during a relatively early stage of development. Physically, the dam may lack a diet adequate to nurturing the production of a healthy litter. Or the female can appear to be pregnant one day (with visible and palpable physical swelling of the abdominal area), and not appear to be pregnant 24 hours later. It is also possible that the bitch is in a false pregnancy, has been misdiagnosed as being pregnant, thereby reabsorbing her litter!

Bacteria are always present to some degree in the orifices containing mucus. Many are ingested and transferred by licking, migrating through the intestines. Most bacteria are harmless, neither preventing nor interfering with a healthy pregnancy. Bacterial infections from the vagina are too often credited with traveling through the cervix to foster pregnancy failure. This is, however, an infrequent occurrence. Remember when culturing that some forms of microorganisms are normally present and cultured in the anterior portion of the vagina.

Brucellosis prevents pregnancy and causes sterility in both the dog and bitch. A bitch who has brucellosis will spontaneously abort, should fertilization occur. Testing for the presence of brucellosis in order to prevent further spreading of this contagion is critical to the sire and matron dam and success of the breeding.

Never hesitate to call your veterinarian for a consultation should your bitch exhibit any suspicious abnormal signs during any portion of her term. Your veterinarian is your best friend, your ally in helping you to construct and maintain all forms of supportive therapy throughout all phases of your bitch's pregnancy.

Many products are available that do not offer adequate consumer information, and too few can safely be utilized directly before breeding and during pregnancy. The best rule is, therefore, one of chemical abstinence and moderation in all other areas.

PSEUDOPREGNANCY (FALSE PREGNANCY)

Not all females are created equal. Some are naturally endowed with a far greater nurturing drive than others. Once this condition is generated, many of these bitches repeatedly suffer one false pregnancy after another, usually after each estral cycle. The onset of a false pregnancy is believed to be caused by a hormonal imbalance. Many females persistently having this condition ovulate longer than the normal three-to-five-week period.

A false pregnancy may exhibit the exact physical and behavioral symptoms as that of a true pregnancy. Not only is there often the behavioral change of the instinct to ''nest'' or ''den,'' but usually changes occur in the appetite. Changes in appetite may not only be an obvious desire for increased food intake, but also include ''morning sickness'' at any hour of the day or night. Other normal signs of a false (or true pregnancy) can be a depression of appetite lasting as long as several weeks. Later, in both conditions, there is exhibited a continuously ravenous appetite. Whenever depression of an appetite occurs and persists for more than 24 hours, it is time to consult with your veterinarian. Such depression may well be indicative of other more serious concerns than that of initial hormonal responses.

As in cases of true pregnancies, the pseudopregnant female can exhibit inability to ingest normal amounts of food during a regular feeding period. She may leave all or part of her meal, returning periodically to sniff and nibble. With this behavior, it is helpful to provide smaller feedings throughout the day. Once she has passed her pseudopregnancy, a normal feeding routine can be resumed.

Another change that can occur is the eating of stools. Although coprophagy (eating of stools) is normally considered to be an acquired vice, it can also be indicative of problems other than behavioral. Food assimilation problems, dietary insufficiency, and/or a diet that lacks adequate vitamin-mineral support may cause a female to exhibit this behavior. She may also exhibit this form of behavioral aberration if she is habitually contained in unclean quarters. Multiple daily cleanings of any living area may be required (as opposed to cleaning thoroughly once daily). Sound supportive changes in diet with a vitamin/mineral supplement help to control or eradicate this behavior. Admonishing the female in stern vocal tones at the moment she initiates this is a good reinforcing measure of your displeasure. Corporal punishment is unnecessary and ill-advised.

Physical changes also can and often do occur during a pseudopregnancy (false pregnancy). Whether bred, the affected female is able to complete many physical symptoms accompanying a normal pregnancy. She may exhibit signs of weight gain (even when on her normal diet) and a gradual enlargement of the mammary glands with obvious colostrum and milk production occurring between 50 and 70 days from her estrus. She may also swell and relax her pelvic structure and vulval area. Some females produce cervical mucus. In unusual although not entirely rare occasions, the pseudomatron may actually engage in labor, through all its stages! Many of these ''mothers'' gather toys or other objects to nurse and nurture.

Clinical signs of whelping in pseudopregnancy cases usually occur beyond the calculated whelping date. Although not bred intentionally, cases of ''known'' false pregnancies should nevertheless be examined by your veterinarian, who may suggest employing palpation, radiographs or a blood test to entirely rule out a true pregnancy.

40

Spaying (ovariohysterectomy) is recommended for those females who are not to be included in a breeding program. Persistent episodes of false pregnancies can be indicative of health problems including, but not exclusive to, the condition of ovarian cysts. Not to be treated offhandedly, these continued pseudopregnancies also appear to promote malignant changes in the mammary glands, particularly in older females. In extreme cases of false pregnancies, mastitis may occur in those bitches producing a heavy milk flow. Treatment is best effected by a coordinated effort between you and your veterinarian. While the application of massage and hot and cold packs are helpful to relieve this painful condition, they are not always desirable. At times these measures actually promote stimulation of the mammaries, resulting in an increased flow of milk.

It has been said by many experts in the field (veterinarians and long-term breeders) that females consistently producing symptoms of repeated false pregnancies must have ovarian cysts. While often true, this axiom is not always accurate. When spayed later in their lives, a few of these females proved to have no ovarian cysts. What they had in common was a very strong instinctive drive for motherhood. When given the opportunity, matrons of this nature will usually readily adopt newborns, including other animals.

Some bitches' eating habits undergo radical changes during a pregnancy. This Alaskan Malamute is picking (and eating) fruit. *Wotan Alaskan Malamutes*

5

Diet

A FAT ANIMAL is an unhealthy breeding candidate. Overweight dams often have difficulties whelping and may require a cesarean section. Problems encountered with superfluous fatty masses during this time can be life-threatening to the dam and her puppies. A strict regimen of care for the matron must be followed before breeding, during her gestation (pregnancy) and after whelping. The regimen includes a balanced diet, rigorous but not strenuous exercise and maintenance of a sound mental attitude. Animals possessed of a sound physical condition also normally maintain emotional stability.

The variables of sound nutrition during any dog's life's stages are myriad and complex. There is no "right" formula to follow that can promise peak condition with vibrantly healthy puppies. The nutritional requirements of dogs beyond mere basics vary from breed to breed, and from one individual to another. The individualistic requirements are determined by the dog's metabolism, complex assimilation factors, immediate environment, mental attitude and weather.

Some commercial foods require an inordinately high intake volume to maintain a dog in an adequate-only condition. "Adequate" is never good enough. An optimum diet is required to maintain a dog in a peak physical condition and sound emotional state. Animals that are merely sustained are incapable of maximizing their physical potential or retaining a superior mental attitude.

The optimum is for dogs to ingest only moderate amounts during any feeding. Ideally, multiple meals offered daily at twelve-hour intervals are best for an adult dog's digestive system. Loading a stomach with but a single meal in a 24-hour period taxes digestive abilities. Taxing of digestive capabilities may also prevent full digestion—absorption of the meal. Digestion includes all chemical and physical changes that allow food to be absorbed and send increased blood flow through the stomach's capillary system. This stimulates increased gastric secretions that are abetted by the enzymes found in the oral mucosa to break down food particles for processing.

Large ingested volumes of any food type slow gastric emptying time. These food masses may ferment in the stomach, and gas is created. Distention from gas causes the pyloric valve to become partially or fully constricted, effectively preventing the passage of gas by flatulence or burping. Large gas collections cause gastric dilatation (bloat) and, in some cases, a volvulus (twisting of the stomach). Volvulus results from gross distention caused by gas pressure when the stomach and spleen rotate, rupturing attaching ligaments. The condition of dilatation with or without volvulus can often be lethal.

The nervous and hormonal systems control digestive processes. Any negative emotion affects the nervous system, inhibiting gastric secretions. Inadequate quantities of gastric secretions result in an upset digestive process. It is possible for appetite depression to progress to a point where food intake is drastically reduced or curtailed. Pleasurable sensations aid the process of digestion. It is of paramount importance, therefore, that a pregnant or lactating matron be maintained in a pleasant and emotionally supportive environment so her regular food intake is not disrupted.

Pregnant bitches, puppies and working dogs require a higher volume of food intake than the average middle-aged or elderly animal. The optimum total required caloric intake needs to be broken down into multiple smaller feedings throughout the day, as some matrons heavy in whelp are incapable of ingesting normal multiple feedings.

The quality of the food is critical throughout pregnancy and lactation. Some breeds such as Dalmatians normally require a low-protein diet to be maintained in sound condition. There are dogs whose required fat intake is accelerated from the norm, and some others require low fat but high protein to be healthy. Interactive with each dog's type is the animal's metabolism, environment and weather conditions. Dogs with low metabolisms such as Arctic types are not unlike people of the same environment, requiring little food in proportion to their ideal body weight.

Some dogs appearing to be low in metabolism yet within the "normal" range are actually hypothyroid (low thyroid). These animals gain weight easily and rapidly, and are less energetic than dogs of the same age and breed which are not hypothyroid. While not life-threatening, the life of the animal can be shortened from the effects of hypothyroidism if left untreated. Dogs tested for this condition by a veterinarian and placed on a corrective therapy very often exhibit improved estral cycles and pregnancy successes, and may lead longer productive lives.

The dam's environment plays an important role throughout puppies' development. If under considerable stress or nervous in temperament, she will require a higher caloric volume. Dogs under stress, normal or unusual, produce a variety of chemical reactions to the stimuli. These chemical reactions can, in some cases, have a negative effect on the puppies' development. Aside from nutritional and assimilation factors, it is highly important to the unborn puppies' well-being that their dam is content.

COMMERCIAL DIETS

Commercially made dog food is derived from a variety of sources and processing. Not only is the food source critical to the dam and her developing offspring, but the type of processing also helps determine digestibility. It is important, therefore, to read and understand the ingredients of the food you offer your dog. The first ingredient listed on the label is the largest by volume. For example, if corn is listed first, then corn is the main ingredient, even though the label on the package front shows chicken, beef or lamb. Also often listed are wheat and wheat middlings. Some commercially processed foods, wet or dry, do not list meat and meat by-products (and not necessarily in this order) until third or as an even later ingredient.

Wild canids such as wolves and feral dogs derive a balanced diet by first eating their prey's organs, the stomach and upper intestinal contents and the liver before muscle tissues. Dogs inherently are carnivores; rarely is grain required as a main food source. Had nature intended dogs to primarily eat grains, their teeth would have evolved differently, with a prevalence of grinding rather than rending surfaces. Most dogs require amino acids, which are derived from a variety of sources, including meat and meat by-products.

Artificial coloring added to food makes it more palatable in appearance to the owner. Dogs are not particular about the color of their food: as long as it smells good (that all-important first sense), it is good to eat. Many dogs are sensitive to artificial food coloring, a known cause of many tear-duct inflammations. This condition appears as weepy, drippy, allergy eyes. The eyes do not appear rheumy, they are clear, but matter often collects on the inner corner and tear stains may run down the muzzle. Debris thus produced by the irritated eyes may partially occlude tear ducts. (Note: The appearance of eyes in this condition can also, however, be indicative of other illnesses.)

Some biscuits and dry foods expand considerably when moistened, increasing five and ten times the size of the original nugget. These brands require soaking before feeding to insure expansion occurs in the bowl and not in a dog's stomach. While important to soak this type of food for the normal eater, it becomes especially important to do so for the greedy guzzlers. Baked biscuits normally expand less when moistened; some simply disintegrate into mush. These latter types have faster gastric emptying times than expanding foods. Biscuits which expand in the stomach must first reach a certain volume of size before they can be broken down by the digestive process. This added time allows the fermentation process to begin.

Dry food products that do not expand are usually slightly more expensive to purchase. In the long run, however, because they almost always have a higher nutritional value through digestibility and assimilation, the dog produces less stool. High-fiber foods also reduce the risk of some diseases. This translates simply: a better brand of food with more digestibility offers greater nutritional value through increased assimilation. Because the food is better assimilated, there is less waste and fewer stools (of a reduced size) to be picked up from the yard.

Dry food as a "complete" diet does not always meet the advertised criteria. Studies of dogs working under stress have shown that meat, in addition to other supplements, is required to maintain the animal in an optimum physical condition. Pregnant dogs especially require a well-rounded, balanced diet in order to produce vigorous puppies and whelp more easily. Meat protein is part of the well-balanced diet.

Commercially available fresh or canned meats are usually lamb, poultry and beef. Lamb is the most easily digested meat, then poultry and beef. Whether fresh, frozen or canned, meat should always be fed lean, not fatty. There is a wide variety of commercially prepared canned meat on the market. The best products developed as complementary additions for biscuit are meat and meat by-products. The ingredients' list will show little or no cereal content, and no food coloring additives. Make certain that the fresh meat you feed is low in fat. Place the meat in a bowl, allowing it to stand until it reaches room temperature, then knead it as if mixing a meat loaf. Is the residue on your fingers only slightly oily or fatty, just enough to give your fingers a little "shine"? Or are there actual large globules of fat on and between your fingers? If the former is the case, you have a good quality meat. If you find your fingers encased with the latter condition, change your brand of dog meat.

Commercially canned and some fresh and fresh-frozen meat for pets contain additives. Usually charcoal, a natural ingredient aiding digestion, is found among these additives. Meat purchased directly from the butcher is normally meat alone, meat trimmings and, in less reputable establishments, floor sweepings. The meat you add to your dog's diet should be a balanced product by itself. Even a mediocre canned dog food will contain a higher nutritional value than bad, fatty meat. Dogs living in very cold climates require additional fat in the diet to produce a high caloric output. Calories processed by the body produce heat.

Check the color and odor of your dog's meat. Whatever type (fresh or defrosted frozen), it should be moderately bright in color. It should not appear darkened, black or crusty. Nor should the meat appear weakly colored, or look as though food coloring had been added, making it artificially red. Place the meat on a dish and check the "blood" collected at the bottom. The meat should be richly dark in color with an invitingly fresh scent, not rancid of odor. If the meat you feed does not meet these standards, find another brand. It takes but one hour for bacteria to grow, producing toxins that cause food poisoning.

Simply because a canned food is expensive does not necessarily mean it is good. Meat should be palatable and nutritious. Some readily available products have little nutritional value. Foods that look palatable to you, and that your dog relishes, are not always the best to feed. Some of these canned products list, for example, carrots, peas and corn, which unprocessed are completely undigestible. Cooked or raw, these vegetables exit your dog's system in the same recognizable form by which they entered. Also try to avoid those cans that have a high amount of cereal content, artificial food coloring and water. Some canned foods are approximately 70 percent water! This narrows your choice on your grocer's shelf. Generally select the commercially prepared foods packaged by reputable companies which are available nationwide.

Dogs, like small children and older folk, require easily assimilated foods in their diets. Meat should not only be palatable but nutritious. Stay away from those tinned foods designed for the owners' palate, such as canned doggie stews. Doggie stews are only good for diets because the corn, peas and carrots, of no real food value for your dog, take up room in the stomach to make your dog feel full.

Cottage and other cheeses are also excellent sources of protein. If you live near a dairy distributing center, you normally can purchase day-old (past the expiration date) cheese at a terrific cost reduction. Cheese purchased in bulk can be frozen. Almost all dogs find frozen cheese a real treat during the hot "dog days" of summer! Cold weather requires that a dog's caloric intake be increased. Calories are used to produce heat, keeping the dog warm. The nutritional support offered a pregnant bitch is first utilized to keep her warm. "Leftovers" are then turned into nutritional care for the puppies. If a bitch's feeding is insufficient in quality, and/or volume, she will lose body conditioning through prenatally supplying her offspring with nutritional support.

If your matron has been maintained on a premium diet from puppyhood, and her health has been excellent, there is no reason to change her food either by type or volume during her first few weeks of pregnancy. The optimum diet for your matron during her early gestation is normally the same as that which maintained her peak condition throughout her early adult months. A well-balanced diet is composed of a variety of ingredients, more than adequately nutritionally supporting the dog. Unlike the old nursery rhyme about Jack Spratt who could eat no fat, and his wife who could eat no lean, the matron's diet requires both in order to be well balanced.

There are breeds and families of dogs that do, however, require extra nutritional support from day one. Too much of any one thing can prove detrimental to the fetuses. Moderation is always a good focus when contemplating changing or supplementing diet. Some breeds require a lower protein, fat or vitamin/mineral intake than others. Providing food to a breed type or family line that has special dietary requirements can be critical to the maintenance of the unborn puppies. Objectively look at the diet you fed your matron prior to the breeding. If you question a diet's nutritional value, refer to friendly established fanciers, the breeder of your female and the stud's owner. These people would know if there is anything in either family's genetics that requires early nutritional support.

Breeds such as Bulldogs require less food when compared to other breeds of the same weight. Dogs vary in their nutritional requirements because of higher or lower activity levels and metabolic rates. Some dogs are "easy keepers" readily utilizing all they ingest, requiring therefore a smaller volume than another. Other dogs are not so "thrifty," requiring large volumes of the same diet to be maintained in a sound physical condition. Nor should the environmental or emotional state of the matron be discounted. Females of a nervous or hyperactive disposition, no matter what breed, require stronger dietary support than their sedentary sisters.

In summary: feed your dog a good portion of meat in the diet. The amount depends basically upon your breed. The individual animal should always determine the final amount required to keep in top condition. Some dogs require more food than others, even when they are the same size. Environmental conditions play a role in the need to increase or decrease calories by volume. The immediate environment and emotional state of the matron also plays an important role in her well-being and that of her puppies. Emotionally "fractured" females divert food necessary for their fetuses in order to maintain an existence level in their own excited state. Dogs are not unlike people—some burn more energy sleeping than do others awake. Because there are basic metabolic differences between one breed and one dog and another, there are no hard rules or exact amounts to feed any specific breed, sex or size of dog: there are only sound guidelines. The owners of each dog must determine through objective analysis, evaluation and consultation exactly how much of what is required to maintain their matron in peak condition.

PRENATAL CARE: DIETARY SUPPORT SUPPLEMENTS

Your brood matron requires well-rounded support throughout all her motherhood stages. You must focus attention on her diet (including vitamin/mineral supplements), exercise program and changing emotional outlook. Her needs are integrated and complex. Each aspect is important to insure a physically and emotionally stable matron, one ready for motherhood. Your response to her requirements can make the difference between a poor or indifferent matron and one truly excellent. Never minimize motherhood duties. They go far beyond carrying to term and delivering genetically well-bred offspring.

Each dam is an individual. Some have waited all their lives for the "call of the whelping box." Special emotional support needs to be given these supermatrons once permanently relieved of whelping box duties. Given the opportunity, they can become later in life efficient and doting "aunties." They can also develop envy of other matrons and suffer real depressions. Your dog's whelping box performance is oftentimes more dependent on your attitude than genetics. As her "world," she looks to you for approbation of all her life's roles. Your support and approval are critical to puppies' physical well-being and emotional development. Motherhood duties can become onerous for the owner if the matron lacks a sound attitude. How she accepts her role and the environment in which she raises her puppies are reflected through her nurturing abilities. Her offsprings' attitude (temperament) is also directly affected by her nurturing abilities. All aspects of her requirements must be met. If she is unbalanced through her physical environment or through dietary insufficiency by volume or quality, she could prove incapable of providing her offspring with adequate nutrition.

A few mother-dogs never grow up, taking toys to the box and playing while the puppies nurse. Humans also share canine counterparts of neglectful mothers, those whose interest in their offsprings' welfare proves inadequate. Like people, not every dam has the instinct for motherhood. Serious consideration must be given to never again breeding matrons lacking the nurturing instinct when the nutritional and environmental support has been optimum.

If her requirements for emotional stability are not met through no genetic fault, she could develop sullen, withdrawn and fear-biting temperaments. The stresses of first and subsequent matronly duties demand optimum and nutritional emotional support. She is at this time more than ever acutely aware of every aspect of her environment and physical changes.

During the time your dog was growing up, you should have become familiar with certain brands of vitamin/mineral supplements and, for many breeds, dicalcium phosphate. Normal adult dogs under other stresses such as shows, field trials and working conditions also require dietary support therapies. Household pets, although not obviously stressed, also require supplements during seasonal changes, as they shed and grow new coats and as they develop and continue into their geriatric years.

Do not wait to determine a pregnancy before initiating moderate supplementation. Some bitches, especially those never before pregnant, may carry their puppies high and forward under their rib cage. A small litter may make it hard to discern a pregnancy until late in the term. Other females exhibit signs of gestation almost within days of being bred, if not by physiological changes, by attitude. Whether or not a pregnancy is displayed, supplementation should begin as a normal precautionary measure. When dosed conservatively if the breeding has not taken, you have done your female no harm. Conversely, if she is not supplemented until late in term and she is carrying a large litter either by size or numbers, irreparable harm may occur to the fetuses and whelping difficulties may be created for the dam.

A considerable number of bitches suffer a temporary loss of appetite as hormonal changes first occur. It is important directly from the beginning of a pregnancy that a female not be allowed a hunger strike. While a missed meal is not detrimental, two meals missed can be indicative of other problems. As with some human counterparts, basic dietary changes may be required immediately. Food products may no longer be tempting. Occasionally it becomes necessary to resort to bribery, tempting the matron with a favorite delicacy. Small amounts of chopped raw beef liver mixed in her food bribe almost every matron to eat with gusto. If she continues to refuse all food by her second meal, however, schedule an immediate appointment with her veterinarian. Chopped raw beef liver was considered excellent as the earliest dietary supplement. Now it is recommended as a flavor enhancer only for the poor eater. The amount to be fed varies with each individual. Too much causes an overabundance of phosphorus (and not enough calcium). This imbalance can cause delivery problems. Too much liver also causes diarrhea, resulting in a loss of critical body fluids and electrolytes. Toys and other small dogs may be safely given as little as a fraction of an ounce while large matrons may require ingestion of several ounces daily. This supplement should be continued through lactation until the puppies are fully weaned.

Many experienced "old time" breeders are strong advocates of raspberry leaves in their matrons' diets. The addition of these finely chopped leaves is supposed to help matrons sustain adequate contractions throughout their deliveries (providing all other nutritional requirements including supplementations are met). Dried raspberry leaves or raspberry tea can be found in any health food store or health food section of supermarkets.

Vitamins and Minerals

Once a pregnancy has been determined, or by the fourth week of gestation, vitamin/mineral supplements and a balanced di-calcium phosphate need to be added in moderation to the matron's diet. Pet suppliers, veterinary hospitals, feed stores and some grocers stock vitamin/mineral and di-calcium phosphate supplements developed specifically for brood matrons and puppies. These prenatal supplements have been thoroughly laboratory-tested before marketing. Each bottle's label has specific instructions for the amounts required, based on the weight and age of each dog.

Supplements are manufactured as powders and tablets. One form is not better than another; the preference is strictly individualistic between the owner and pet. Because Toys and other small breeds may have limited chewing capabilities, it is easiest to add a powder to their food. Some, however, would rather push the food around in their dishes and go hungry than eat anything powdered. The objection for many is caused by the change in their regular diet's flavor. They are not spoiled pets acting out, trying to bamboozle their owner. A number, like their larger counterparts, prefer a tablet. While tablets can be broken into small pieces, the measured dosage is not always accurate by this means.

Many dogs enjoy vitamin/mineral tablets as a special treat. Even dogs that do not anticipate their supplements usually eat them when placed on top of their meals. The dosage amount of tablets is easily monitored: there is no wondering about "heaping full" or "level" tea- or tablespoons. If an owner becomes distracted while measuring, the tablets are readily counted.

Any supplementation should begin conservatively when the diet is normally well balanced. *If overdone, supplementation can be detrimental.* As a good rule of thumb, start at a level intended for a smaller dog, then gradually increase amounts each week until the fully recommended level has been reached. For example, if the instructions indicate a matron should get five vitamin/mineral tablets daily, start the dosage at one tablet each day by the third week following the breeding. Each week thereafter, increase the dose by one tablet daily. The advantages of a conservative approach can never be overly stressed. Overdosing

50

a matron on a well-balanced diet or under-dosing a matron with a large litter or one maintained on a poor diet can, in some instances, have an adverse effect on fetal development. If the matron does not have adequate opportunity for optimum nutritional balance (including supplementation) required to maintain her health, her offsprings' genetic potential cannot be insured.

Physiological factors through multiple births determine the delicacy of a matron in gestation, parturition (whelping) and lactation stages. Unless all nutritional requirements are optimumly met, matrons strongly display evidence of their physical deterioration. An unthrifty condition is exhibited as extreme leanness, or as emaciation in more extreme cases of dietary inadequacy and insufficiency. A gaunt mother cannot feed puppies adequately, either in utero or after birth. With the widespread availability of sound diets, there is no excuse for a breeder's matron to appear unthrifty. Throughout gestation and lactation the best-cared-for matrons appear vibrantly healthy and robust.

Overweight matrons often have difficulties in whelping. One problem, "inertia," occurs when the matron is incapable of producing enough "whelping hormones" (pituitary oxytocin) to maintain strong contractions. The cause appears to be a failure to properly sensitize the uterus. Some matrons never produce enough to deliver on their own. Others may suffer inertia when whelping a large litter over a prolonged period of time. A matron may suffer inadequate and insignificant contractions to effect normal whelping.

Inertia is the greatest cause of whelping stillborn puppies. Many puppies die needlessly because the matron is overweight, in poor physical condition, lacking muscle tone or incapable of sustaining contractions because of hormonal or dietary inadequacy. Bitches incapable of whelping normally for whatever reason must be seen immediately by the veterinarian for a possible cesarean section delivery. The reason for this is that during inertia when the dam is unable to sustain contractions by strength or time, puppies can die by suffocation when the placenta (afterbirth) has already separated from the uterine horn's wall. The placenta, which usually separates after delivery, is attached to the puppy by the umbilical cord and normally contains enough oxygen for a puppy's successful trip. If the birth is slowed through contraction inadequacy, the puppy can suffocate from lack of oxygen. Thus a female suffering from overweight or malnutrition will suffer needlessly during whelping, and her inadequate condition can prove fatal to her offspring.

If in a normally sound condition, a matron's total caloric intake should not be increased until close to halfway through her term. At this time her food intake may be safely increased slowly. If a matron normally ingests two cups of food per day, she can be safely increased to three cups daily by four weeks in whelp. If, by the size of the matron, the litter promises to be a large one, her intake may need to increase as much as threefold. It must be noted that the majority of puppy growth is made during the last two weeks of gestation. Prior to that time changes occur more in the support tissues. Under normal conditions then, giving approximately twice the amount of food than usually ingested by the week of parturition is an excellent regimen to follow.

A matron can be safely maintained at this volume level during the first

CALORIC REQUIREMENTS FOR ADULT DOGS BASED ON PHYSICAL ACTIVITY AND BREED SIZE*

	Mature Weight		House Dog†	Active Dog‡	Working Dog§
	Kg	Lb	Calories	Calories	Calories
	2.3	5	200	250	300
	4.5	10	400	500	600
Small Breeds	6.8	15	600	750	900
	9.1	20	800	1000	1200
	9.1	20	560	700	840
	11.4	25	700	875	1050
	13.6	30	840	1050	1260
	15.9	35	930	1225	1470
	18.2	40	1120	1400	1680
Medium Breeds	20.5	45	1260	1575	1890
	22.7	50	1400	1750	2100
	25.0	55	1540	1925	2310
	27.3	60	1680	2100	2520
	29.5	65	1820	2275	2730
	31.8	70	1980	2450	2940
	34.1	75	2100	2625	3150
	34.1	75	1800	2250	2700
	36.4	80	1980	2400	2880
	38.6	85	2040	2550	3060
	40.9	90	2160	2700	3240
	43.2	95	2280	2850	3420
	45.5	100	2400	3000	3600
	47.7	105	2520	3150	3780
Large Breeds	50.0	110	2640	3300	3960
	52.3	115	2760	3450	4140
	54.5	120	2880	3600	4320
	56.8	125	3000	3750	4500
	59.1	130	3120	3900	4680
	61.4	135	3240	4050	4860
	63.6	140	3360	4200	5040
	65.9	145	3480	4350	5220
	68.2	150	3600	4500	5400

*These are average daily requirements. Animal requirements may vary according to age, breed, body and environmental temperature, temperament, and degree of activity. Owing to temperament, there is some overlap between the largest animals of some breeds and the smallest of others.

†Caloric requirements of house dogs = adult dogs maintained in laboratory cages.

‡Active dogs = adult dogs allowed to free run in outside pens, 125 to 480 square feet, proportionate to breed size.

§Working dogs = adult dogs running at 5 mph on a 6 per cent incline for 4 hours each day.

Data courtesy of Ralston Purina Company, St. Louis, Missouri.

From Kirk, R. W., and Bistner, S. I.: *Handbook of Veterinary Procedures and Emergency Treatment*, 4th ed. Philadelphia: W.B. Saunders, 1985.

week following whelping. If her litter is large, her caloric intake needs continuous adjusting as the puppies grow, during which time they receive sustenance solely through her milk production. Some matrons of very large breeds and/or very large litters require three (and occasionally more) times the volume of their normal food intake. Such vast amounts are generally too much, however, for very small and Toy breeds. Volume by itself is never an answer. Calories may

52

be "empty," inadequate for the dam's support during her critical lactation period. All brood matrons require several meals daily after whelping. Some require as many as four per day to maintain their own vigorous health while producing adequate quantities and quality of milk for their offspring.

Manufacturers' prenatal vitamin instructions offer product guidelines based on the matron's normal body weight. The best products offer a total balance of vitamins, minerals and amino acids. Labeling instructions are not written in stone: used as guidelines only, your approach should be conservative. Most products' instructions list dosage increases through the matron's pregnancy. Appropriate supportive amounts are also indicated for her lactation and later weaning periods. These products also suggest how much the puppies require directly after weaning. If the product you selected lacks definitive instructions, start your matron at a minimum level. Each dog's assimilation is its own. Some utilize almost everything ingested. Others that are not such thrifty keepers require large amounts of nutritional support. A conservative approach toward supplementation allows you to determine safely the best regimen for your matron, gradually increasing until the recommended level is met, about one-and-a-half weeks before she is due to whelp.

If you suspect your female is having any problems with a supplement, contact your veterinarian immediately. Signs of problems can be, but are not limited to, a discharge from her vulva, diarrhea, a loss of interest in her food and a dull, lethargic attitude. Your matron-elect may be unable to assimilate her diet as established and a change may be necessary. Remember, your matron's attitude may be a reflection of her immediate environment as well as a response to other stimuli. Candidly discuss all aspects of your matron's life with her other best friend, her veterinarian.

Puppies from conception to the onset of weaning derive their entire sustenance from their dam. She must produce sufficient quantities of quality milk to establish the puppies with a sound start in life, a start promising an opportunity to reach their genetic potential. A matron's sound diet supported by vitamin/mineral supplements alone may prove inadequate.

Di-calcium Phosphate

All breeds require di-calcium phosphate after whelping and throughout puppy-care stages. Very large breeds also often require this support late in pregnancy. Di-calcium phosphate is critical for a matron's ability to whelp successfully. This supplementation must continue through lactation, helping to insure healthy milk production. Puppies' skeletal structures can be detrimentally affected if their dam suffers a di-calcium phosphate insufficiency through pregnancy and lactation. If the dam suffers from inadequate di-calcium support, she will "steal" her own temporary calcium to balance the puppies' needs. During the period puppies are nutritionally sustained solely through their dam's milk, she requires ever-increasing amounts of di-calcium phosphate until weaning begins. Too much, too little or an improperly balanced di-calcium phosphate may also cause skeletal anomalies such as stunted growth. Di-calcium phosphate is not cumulative within the body. When not directly utilized, it is eliminated through the kidneys. It is of critical import to the dam and puppies, therefore, that a proper supportive dose therapy be managed daily.

The brand chosen should be of a low milligram dosage by tablet or teaspoon. There are nationally available brands offering doses too high, hundreds of milligrams per tablet or teaspoon. There are also products less expensive to purchase, which seem like a good deal. Moderation demands selecting perhaps a slightly more expensive brand, one with a lower dose from a reliable and easily digested source. To remove guesswork from safe measurements, all supplementation must be carefully monitored and increases made only as necessary for a sane and conservative approach to dietary support.

Abnormal calcium levels from inadequate di-calcium phosphate by either dietary insufficiency or assimilation may cause a condition known as "eclampsia." The onset of eclampsia can occur late in a pregnancy or during whelping and early lactation. While the exact cause is unknown, administration of adequate di-calcium phosphate and vitamin/mineral supplementation to a nutritionally supportive diet will, in almost all cases, prevent the occurrence of this condition. Once eclampsia occurs, however, the matron must have immediate veterinary support therapy.

The earliest signs leading to eclampsia may be noted by a loss in appetite and stiffness of movement resulting from slight-to-moderate pain. If eclampsia is allowed to progress, the dam will exhibit restlessness and an increased respiratory rate. This aspect of eclampsia is often confused with normal signs of whelping. Whenever in doubt, call your veterinarian immediately. Eclampsia is life-threatening. It does not get better by itself, it requires fast medical intervention to effect a possible reversal.

An advanced case of eclampsia may cause the dam's collapse to a position of "opisthotonos": a form of spasm where the spine bends backward, bringing the head back toward the tail, the abdomen and chest thrust forward. Convulsions initially observed as muscle spasms increase by intensity while any interim periods of quiet decrease. If left unchecked, the convulsions become increasingly violent. The matron retains consciousness throughout an episode of eclampsia. Her temperature will usually show an elevation above 103 degrees. With the condition's progression, temperatures have been known to climb above 108 degrees, by which time the dam and unborn puppies can suffer major, irreversible or fatal effects. The overall aspect of this condition closely resembles heat prostration. The clue for the owner and veterinarian, however, is the matron's engorged mammaries and environment immediately prior to the onset of the condition.

The onset of eclampsia may occur in rare instances as early as two weeks prior to whelping. It is most often noted, however, in matrons nursing large litters, two to three weeks following delivery. Eclampsia is also common to nursing matrons that are not in peak condition because of dietary insufficiency through quantity or qualitative support. If left untreated, cases of eclampsia in almost every instance end fatally.

Eclampsia is in most cases preventable. Should a matron develop eclampsia, however, she can be supported with care at home *after having been seen, diganosed and treated by the veterinarian*. At-home support to prevent a recurrence of eclampsia is helped by administration of increased di-calcium phosphate doses at twelve-hour intervals. The matron's environment following recovery from an episode must be emotionally supportive. She will need to be kept warm and quiet, in an environment without any distractions or disturbances. Once a female exhibits a predisposition for the condition of eclampsia, she must be carefully monitored thereafter. Serious consideration needs to be given if considering any future breeding plans. Puppies should not be allowed to nurse during either the acute stage or immediately following an episode of eclampsia. If at all possible by timing, either all or some of the litter should be weaned to help prevent a recurrence. If it is not possible to wean the puppies, supplementary support feedings should be initiated.

Studies have long proven that calcium alone is insufficient by nature to adequately support a pregnant or lactating matron. She requires optimum daily doses of di-calcium phosphate, doses which are closely monitored for quantity ingested. Administration of di-calcium phosphate during pregnancy has been clinically proven as a deterrent to the condition of eclampsia.

Your matron's emotional support requirements are complexly interrelated by environment and nutrition.

Artist: Jan Walker

6

Attitudes, Owners and the Brood Bitch

ANIMALS are not always as adaptable as people to environmental influences. A matron's early hormonal changes can upset the dog and her owner. She may periodically appear uneasy and restless, or demonstrate other minor personality changes. Your matron's demonstrated behaviors in response to hormonal changes are affected by and dependent upon your attitude toward her.

Some prospective mothers are predisposed toward withdrawal and inactivity as a response to hormonal changes. As long as her appetite is good and her elimination is normal, there is no cause for alarm. Treat her as you do normally, and given a few days, she should recover from her slump. A persistent withdrawal of a normally exuberant dog can be, however, a sign of depression. Extra attention of a quietly loving, rather than raucous, supportive nature will help her to recover. At times an extra car ride or a walk is enough to enable her recovery. Do not hesitate to consult with her veterinarian, however, should her depressed behaviors persist and her appetite or waste material exhibit changes.

Some matrons exhibit signs of short-tempered resentment to a normal routine, environment, other household pets and even, on occasion, the owner. Exhibition of behaviors deviating from the norm requires careful examination of the matron's complete environment to discern the cause of her upset. Usually negative behaviors as a response to increased hormonal activities last a few days to a week.

57

Most matrons make selfish demands while pregnant. They become very loving, demanding extra affection from all they encounter. Fortunate dogs that have a supportive, trusting relationship with their owners become much "more" during their prenatal period. They are usually more loving, more demanding and/ or more vocal during this time. Some retain the exaggerated affectionate poses acquired during a pregnancy.

No matron (or other dog) should be subjected to harassment of any form— by other dogs, children or adults. Even the most benignly tempered dogs have limits. A matron's limits may be shorter. If subjected to emotional or physical abuse, she will exhibit signs of her intolerance, attempting escape by moving to another part of the house or yard. She could feel threatened and exhibit signs of undue excitability and resentment if her escape attempts are thwarted. It is not at all unusual that in an altered state of excitement she would "grump" her displeasure through a warning/complaining type of growl. Warning signs of discomfort should always be heeded. A bitch displaying this personality trait requires a safe place of her own, quiet and away from noise and confusion. A matron feeling trapped and panicky could display overt signs of aggression.

Abnormal pregnancy responses may be exhibited behaviors such as with-drawal from voluntary family interaction, depressed inactivity or intolerance by growling or snappishness displayed toward two- and four-legged family members. Demonstrations of these behavioral aberrations either by themselves or together can be indicative of real physiological or psychological problems. These signals may constitute warnings of pregnancy problems. Pregnancy problems are not determined by simple observation alone. Sometimes the dog's behaviors point to symptoms, warning of conditions hidden from the lay person, and are not "normal" temporary personality aberrations resulting from hormonal changes. Such negative behavioral changes should be brought to the veterinarian's attention immediately. Your veterinarian may not always have an immediate answer to aberrational behaviors exhibited by your female. Certain responses are often innate within family lines. Contact the breeder of your female and the owner of the grandmother. Request information regarding the behaviors of these dogs during their pregnancies. If these direct contacts are unavailable, continue your pursuit of information through another reputable person. Breeders with years of successful experience may have been confronted by problems similar to those your bitch displays. Never hesitate to contact an expert who can quickly assist you with knowledgeable advice.

Blissfully ignorant, too few owners have developed a highly intuitive relationship with their pets. Our dogs inform us through their attitudes of nascent problems by exhibitions of personality deviations from the norm. Your matron's behavioral responses communicate situations, which were formerly not irritating, that have become suddenly intolerable. As the primary investigator you must evaluate any changes, if your dog is uncomfortable, intolerant or unhappy with her environment.

HEREDITY VS. ENVIRONMENT

A pedigree alone does not make a dog. Poor parental temperaments are usually indicative of inherited character traits rather than environmental responses alone. Dogs often displaying intolerance should not be considered for a breeding program. There is no point to the reproduction of unstable, unsound temperaments. Although the responses to stimuli may be acquired, the predisposition to react to stimuli in that manner is inherited. If, after careful and honest evaluation, you conclude that your dog's personality is unstable, do yourself and your chosen breed a service: withhold her from a breeding program. Spay her to prevent any possibility of reproducing undesirable behavior that would be genetically reproduced through her offspring. Breeders of dogs possessing unsound temperaments are open to censure. Undesirable personality traits are carried inherently through successive generations.

There are always, however, exceptions. Dogs not inherently "mean" can be made so by destructive environments. Negative environmental influences include but are not exclusive to teasing, a high-density multiple animal household, lack of "doggie etiquette" (education), overt or covert physical abuse and overt or covert emotional abuse. Condoning a proviso for breeding these dogs is that their other qualities "demand" inclusion in the breed's gene pool.

Reassessment of these animals must occur in a totally new and completely supportive environment. Even minor stress conditions, however, may cause reversion to former behaviors. Redeemable dogs normally stabilize satisfactorily to a positive environment once the element of trust has been established. Care must be taken with the redeemed dog that repetitions of negative environmental factors do not recur, causing the dog to suffer a relapse. Once a dog has relapsed to former unacceptable behaviors, it is far harder, if at all possible, to reestablish a sound working trust level.

MOTHER KNOWS BEST

New matrons focused on their puppies' care are usually by nature incapable of overt responses to an owner's affection during their first days of motherhood. Although undemonstrated, the owner's approach to the whelping box is generally anticipated. During the time the matron "ignores" her owner, it must be understood that her focus is by nature strictly with her offspring. It is critical at this time that you display overt approval of her new role. Like some women, there are dogs that are uncomfortable during pregnancy and lactation, displaying a certain amount of irritability. Remove all external stress from her area to help her relax. Reassure her verbally and physically, lavish her with your affections and special treats periodically throughout your hours together.

Realize that her "den" is her whelping box. Instincts demand that she protect her puppies from the world in general, not her owner specifically. A severe rift in your relationship could be caused should you treat her roughly through a lack of compassion and understanding for minor behavioral infractions during this period. Suspicious of you, she will become so with others as well. Let her know very gently that you will hurt neither her nor her offspring. Keep her confidence high in you by telling her how proud you are of her and the job she has performed.

Mother dogs are almost always highly possessive of their newborns. The owner may be met with resistance when touching or picking up a puppy. In certain cases they may raise a lip or even growl at their owner's approach. A new mother often will curl her body around her newborns, laying her head and neck across as many as possible. Be patient with your matron, but do not back down to her attitude. Sit quietly by the edge of her box and speak to her in soothing dulcet tones. Should she be resistant to having the puppies handled, leave them alone, keeping your focus on her. Do not attempt initially to force the issue. Rub her ears and stroke her in an easy, hypnotic, soothing manner. Casually, then, stroke the puppies one by one before returning your attentions to her.

Your attitude toward her newborns is critically important to the matron. If you want to handle the puppies, sit at the side of the whelping box and stroke each puppy in turn. Picking one up carefully, hold it directly in front of her muzzle so she will have the opportunity to realize that you are not going to take it away. Replace the puppy at her side in such a manner that she is able to watch you and the puppy at all moments. Any sudden movements you might make could set her on the defensive. Remember to act, talk, walk and behave always in a smooth and soothing manner around your matron and her new offspring. Your bitch demonstrates her trust level when she allows you to handle her puppies. Never harangue or subject a dam to corporal punishment. Aside from damaging her physically, she could interpret your attitude as aggression and, feeling threatened, act in self-defense on behalf of her newborns. Or, she could interpret your actions as displeasure toward her puppies. Having interpreted their owner's actions in this manner, some dams have minimized their offsprings' care because of the strength of the bond between owner and dog.

An unhappy matron will prove to be incapable of nourishing her offspring. Her environment must at all costs be supportive in the manner she requires. Away from a noisy household and foot traffic, she should remain part of the family, but as an observer. In a place of observation, she will desire through habit to continue her "Nosy Parker" attitude, wanting to know what her two-legged family is doing. The effect of an unhappy matron can be devastating to the physical well-being of puppies. Unless she is content, the matron will be incapable of producing prolactin, the milk-releasing hormone produced by her brain's pituitary system. Matrons in a state of anxiety are incapable of releasing prolactin. Without this critically essential hormonal release she becomes physically incapable by her altered state of providing her offspring with adequate nutritional support.

EXERCISE FOR THE BROOD MATRON

As your brood matron's "obstetrician," you help her pregnancy and delivery by making certain she is in peak condition physically and emotionally. If your brood-elect has been an indolent house pet, one whose sole exercise has been responding to an opened refrigerator door, she must be toned up as soon as possible. Indolent dogs are less healthy than those kept on even a mild regimen. Beginning and maintaining an exercise program is not hard or time-consuming, nor does it require special or expensive equipment.

The ideal time to begin an exercise program is prior to a breeding. However, a mild program may safely be initiated any time prior to the seventh week of your matron's pregnancy. The best exercise program is daily walks. During the walks you have the opportunity of developing a closer bond between you. No special, extraordinary equipment or training is necessary. Just put on a pair of shoes, get her lead and go.

If your exercising routine has been neglected, do not begin with an overzealous effort. Moderation is the best approach for both of you. If walking or jogging daily with your bitch has not been part of your regimen, conceptualize your walks now as a training program. You are training her muscles to be in good tone. Small dogs may be toned with a half mile daily, and the larger matrons by one mile, minimum. Besides toning her up, the companionship developed will bring your relationship to an even closer bonding. Beyond building and toning her physique, the sharing of a common recreation is good for her psyche, emotional development and worldly socialization.

Although jogging is great for some people and their dogs, it is not for everyone. It is not necessary to incorporate jogging into your exercise program. Walking alone is sufficient. Start your daily walks during the cooler hours of the warmer months, the warmer hours of the colder months. Each time of year has its own special dangers—and advantages. Begin your walks at a half-mile level. One-qurater mile out, one-quarter mile back. Increase the distance the following week to a half mile out and a half mile back. Once you have reached the half-mile level you may jog with your matron for brief periods, a few minutes at a time. Then walk again before jogging an equal amount of time. Continue on this program until you are walking at least one mile daily.

Hot weather poses special problems for dogs. Dogs' bodies are closer to heat reflected from paved surfaces, having a greater surface area exposed to the ground. Dogs, like small children and infants, are incapable of regulating their body temperatures beyond a certain point. Care and forethought must be given to exercising during any periods of hot weather. Dogs "sweat" through their pads and tongue. If your dog appears too hot visually with heaving sides, glazed eyes and a lolling tongue, she could be in serious physical endangerment. Dogs literally will die to please their owners. Thermometer "tapes" are now commonly available, inexpensive to purchase and fit easily into the smallest pocket. When placed on a dog's groin, the temperature readout is almost instantaneous.

If you are sensitive to your bitch, she may be felt while you closely observe her. Check for excessive heat in her groin (inguinal area), the "armpits" of her forelegs and her inner ear leather. If she feels more than mildly warm, she could be heading into trouble. If she feels hot, you are in trouble. Get her to the nearest water, such as a hosebib from a nearby house, and wet her down. Soak her underbody, particularly between her legs, and dampen her ear leather. Take care not to splash water inside her ears.

If she "flops down" or exhibits even the most minor of tremors the moment she stops walking, she is suffering from heat prostration. Get to a telephone immediately! Call a friend or a taxi to pick you up. Barring these possibilities, walk her home slowly and conservatively. Walk her in the shade and off the pavement as much as possible—and take breaks often. As soon as you get home, call your veterinarian. Get to the hospital immediately for further observation and evaluation.

Cold weather has its own problems. Never leave a warm house and begin jogging right away. Muscles must first be stretched and warmed up to prevent injury, lameness or soreness. Winter months in areas of snow can be dangerous. Aside from the possibility of slipping and falling, certain sites are often spread with slip retardants such as sand, salt or other chemicals. The salt and chemicals are harmful to the dog's footpads. If you have no choice during the winter of exercising in areas free from chemicals, purchase water/chemical-proof booties through any well-supplied pet shop or catalog sales. Barring the purchase of booties, always rinse your dog's feet thoroughly after returning home.

In either hot or cold weather, inspect your dog's feet daily. Check the pads and the soft-tissue areas between the pads for damage such as rawness, swelling, splitting or discoloration. Discoloration of the hair can be indicative of incipient damage. Check the nails also for signs of splitting. If the nails appear cracked or splitting, trim back the rough edges. Not a cosmetic measure, keeping the nails trimmed and smooth helps to prevent toes from becoming snagged and injured, or your clothing and other household fabrics from being torn.

There is no reason in the world for a normally active and healthy matron-elect to have her physical activities restricted. Such restrictions could prove harmful to her delivery through lack of muscle tone. Restriction from normal activities can create an emotionally discontented atmosphere. Her attitude can affect her puppies in utero and later after whelping.

The dog that lives for car rides may continue to do so until close to the end of her term. As labels state, "Certain restrictions apply." Be smart and restrict her rides to short trips on smooth roads as she begins to show her condition. Car rides have been known to induce some matrons' labor. As a result of this possibility, rides should cease altogether as she approaches the end of her term, by her eighth week. For the car fanatic, often a ride around the block when she is "big and fat" at the end of her term (eighth and ninth weeks) will keep her happy.

If your female is used to playing with children, let her continue to do so *at her own discretion.* Explain to young children that your dog can no longer roughhouse once she physically displays signs of her pregnancy or her attitude

62

The ideal time to begin an exercise program is prior to a breeding. A moderate program may be safely, slowly initiated following a breeding.

Artist: Jan Walker

says no. Tell the children in terms they can easily understand if they play too roughly with her. Fetch is fine—wrestling is out. A blow to her side could dislodge a placenta from the uterine horn wall. Once dislodged, the puppy dies. No roughhousing.

If she simply wants to lay around the yard as an observer, watching activities without participating, instruct the children and other guests to leave her alone. Watch her interaction with the children. Does she gladly accept their petting? If so, show the children how to pet her, sitting quietly on the ground next to her. Children are easily caught up with adult imagination. Get them involved in your fantasy of puppies. Teach them how to be quiet and gentle, when formerly they had wrestled with their buddy. Have the children stroke her, telling her stories, and whispering "sweet puppy nothings."

If your matron becomes uncomfortable or resentful with company, provide her with a place of her own, one where she can get away from noisy children and other activities that she finds disturbing. Always let her know of your devotion to her, through your actions, voice and tonal quality, and by comforting words with which she is familiar.

7

Equipment

ADOPT the Scouts' motto: "Be prepared!" Have all your supplies purchased and ready no less than a week prior to the due date. Like your bitch, you must also rest in preparation for the long job ahead. Formerly dogs whelped wherever: in the barn, under the porch. Today's breeder has a real vested interest in a brood matron, one of time, energy, money and no less importantly, an emotional investment. It is essential that your matron and puppies be given the very best care possible. Care beyond meeting nutritional and emotional support requires detailed attention to the environment you provide during parturition (whelping) and later. Not only is the whelping place paramount to the physical and emotional well-being of the matron and offspring, but the "layette" you assemble to assist in the whelping and care is of equal importance.

The **whelping box** is the largest and most obvious piece of equipment. No absolute dimensions can be given as a generalization because of breed and matron size variations. Manufactured whelping boxes constructed of sturdy plastic may be purchased. One can also be homemade with a few basic carpentry skills, exterior plywood, 8 right angles, 16 nuts and bolts and railing material.

The whelping box must be sturdy, allowing the dam to go in and out with ease. It should be square, as four equal sides allow the dam to comfortably position herself anywhere in the box while keeping the litter in front of her. The box should allow her to lie fully extended, from the crown of her head to just past her rump, with her legs comfortably extended. Bigger is not better: the box should not be so enormous that the newborn whelps become disoriented, or "lost" from their dam. The whelping box floor must be level with adequate support throughout. It must not rock or in any manner feel insecure as the bitch moves around. One of the four sides should be constructed low enough for her to walk over without scraping her distended abdomen or forcing her to hop in. Constructing this side with opposing end brackets allows the addition of a small board, or a hinged board may be used instead. This effectively raises the side, confining the puppies once they become mobile. The other three sides are permanently constructed slightly higher.

Measure the distance from the lowest point of your matron's abdomen to the floor. The shortest side should be no higher than this point. Next, measure the distance from your dog's point of shoulder to the floor while your matron reclines. Her position should be one with her forelegs outstretched, hindlegs tucked to one side. You may also measure from her spinal column to the box floor as she fully reclines on her side. This is the point where a railing should be installed around the entire inner circumference of the box. Railings may be removable or stationary according to the breeder's preference. Depending upon the breed, railings may vary in size from a three-quarter-inch dowel for Toys, to a two-by-four or to a two-by-six-inch board for large and heavy breeds, such as the Newfoundland or St. Bernard. A three- or four-inch railing is usually sufficient for medium and big dogs such as Dalmations and Alaskan Malamutes. While board railings are secured to the box's side by brackets and bolts, dowel

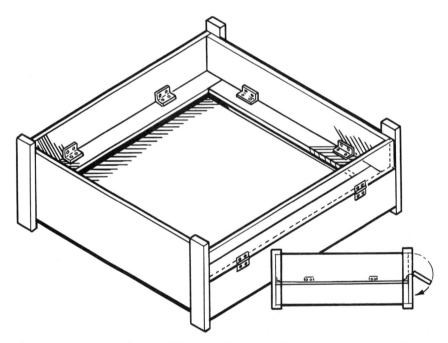

Constructing one side of the whelping box with a hinge allows the dam to walk into the box without scraping her abdomen. This is particularly important to low-stationed breeds such as the Dachshund and Bassett Hound. Once the puppies become mobile, the side can be raised.

Measure the distance from the dam's spinal column to the box floor. Place the safety bumper railing at this point. The railing's depth should be equal in distance to the breadth of a month-old puppy.   *Rottweiler: breeder Karyn Lupton*

safety railings are mounted through holes drilled in all opposite sides, then secured exterior to the box by pegs or bolts. Safety is best effected when the railing's depth on the whelping box's side is equal in distance to the breadth of a month-old puppy.

Dams of small litters have an easier time keeping their puppies before them as they move about in their whelping box. Large litters are more difficult for a matron to arrange when changing positions. Not every matron has the instinct of "nosing" her puppies to the box's center for safety. Railings are a necessary measure, preventing the matron from accidentally lying on a puppy that managed to slip behind her. Few dams have the ability to "count" offspring. Puppies lost behind the matron may be tragically smothered or crushed. Although the dam may hear a puppy's cries initially, she can become confused by the litter before her. Matrons are able to lean securely against a protective railing when it is placed at a proper height near her point of shoulder or level of spine as she lies extended on her side. Should a puppy get caught behind her, it cannot be smothered or crushed. You may think that you will always be able to hear a puppy cry, therefore making a railing unnecessary. Hearing enfeebled cries from a smothering puppy is not always possible. Nor is it possible for a puppy that is being crushed to cry out. Cries of young puppies may be too muffled to be heard. You could be elsewhere in the house should a puppy initially cry lustily. A new matron will usually whine anxiously in response to her offspring's troubled cry. In her confusion, she may not respond appropriately to the cries. With a little extra effort and a few cents more, your whelping box can be built with railings, helping to insure the safety of your long-awaited puppies.

Commercially manufactured whelping boxes are usually constructed of nonporous, easily disinfected surfaces. Wood whelping boxes may safely be left unfinished if the wood is untreated by chemical substances. Any paint used to finish a box should be lead-free and washable. Paint touted as safe enough for an infant's crib is an excellent choice.

Prior to use the whelping box requires several, thorough antiseptic scrubbings with a surgical-type disinfectant. Growth of bacteria and fungus during occupancy is prevented by daily scrubbings with this disinfectant for whelping boxes of any construction. You can purchase this disinfectant from your veterinarian or a catalog.

The whelping box should be ready for occupancy about two weeks prior to the litter's due date. Acclimate your matron to the whelping box as her "personal territory" prior to whelping. Make her bed in the box with old clean towels, a blanket or sheet and newspapers that she may shred. Let her become

Some breeders prefer to use a nonporous whelping box because it is easily disinfected. This breeder uses a child's wading pool which nicely conforms to her bitch's body.

Bulldog: breeder Patty Rungo

accustomed to getting in and out. If necessary, feed her in the box if she refuses to sleep or rest there.

A matron unaccustomed to her whelping box may refuse to use it, especially if she has whelped elsewhere. She may attempt to carry her offspring to another location. She may also try carrying her puppies elsewhere if the box is in a heavy traffic area. Exterior doors of a room chosen for your litter should be kept closed and traffic rerouted during the earliest portion of the puppies' lives. Newly whelped puppies like other newborns need a draft-free environment and one of consistent temperature.

The area established for the bitch and litter should be large enough for the box, her food and water and a place to occasionally rest away from her puppies. Many new mothers suffer from temporary incontinence. As a result, they require provision of an emergency elimination area near the box, one well covered by newspapers. A movable doorway barrier such as those employed for toddlers is ideal for a matron's confinement to a specific room. Exercise pens, portable fences made of rigid-wire paneling, are slightly more expensive to purchase and handily used anywhere in the home. These items can be purchased through well-equipped pet suppliers and catalog sales.

Be prepared to give up a portion of your home for no less than three weeks. Small and medium-sized puppies generally present no management difficulties over a prolonged time period because they require moderately little space in which to be raised. Large and active breeds pose their own problems, as these puppies grow rapidly. Puppies can be moved once they are mobile—able to clamber out of the whelping box, endowed with strong visual capabilities and eating independently from a dish. The selection of their new location should be as conducive to rearing physically and emotionally stable youngsters as was the whelping box's site.

Some breeders keep their puppies and matron in the garage. A garage can be dangerous. Although cars may no longer be parked there, residual toxic fumes often remain in this enclosed area. Dogs' sense of scent is 600 times greater than that of mankind. If use of a garage is planned, adequate preparations must be made no less than a week prior to puppy occupancy.

All refuse must be removed. Storage items such as yard tools should be placed safely behind a solid barrier, away from inquisitive puppies and dam. The floor requires preparation by repeated moppings with the same antibacterial and antifungal disinfectant used on the whelping box. Deadly toxic oil, antifreeze and other vehicular discharge on the garage floor must be completely eliminated. Previously opened cans also may emit toxic fumes unnoticed by human scenting abilities. All paint, oil, yard sprays and cleansing and waxing materials must be removed prior to the puppies' relocation.

Expect your life-style to be disrupted when you raise a litter. Most puppies, like babies, "opt" for the odd hours in which to be born. You could miss the birth of your litter if your matron is kept by herself when close to term. Importantly, your matron might "scatter," neglecting puppies in excited confusion of her first and subsequent births. It has happened: unattended matrons have whelped puppies in widely scattered locations. As a result some puppies have not been discovered until too late to save them. Your matron does not inherently know the intended use of a whelping box when her time arrives. She learns its use only through a positive association.

Save **newspapers printed with black ink** only. Do not save colored newsprint! Ink used in colored newsprint is often toxic. Black-ink newspapers are useful in the whelping box while the matron is in parturition. Thickly layer the box for the first puppies' arrivals. The scent of amniotic fluid (enveloping each puppy), the surrounding sac and afterbirth (on newspapers) helps to awaken dormant instincts of nurturing in the matron. Your brood matron may become confused if her papers are completely changed immediately after the first birth. Instinctively she could feel a puppy had been stolen, that she had just whelped more than one. It is a real possibility that she could abandon her new whelp to search through soiled papers in her efforts to locate her ''missing'' offspring.

During deliveries the whelping box and all contents become soaked from the amniotic fluid-filled sac breaking and passage of the afterbirth (placenta). Completely change soiled papers immediately after the *second and subsequent* puppies have been whelped. Do not disturb your matron, forcing her to move for paper-changing. Most matrons rise and move restlessly in the box, preparing for the next imminent birth. Her preoccupation is your best opportunity to quickly change soiled papers. During the interim period tear and remove the papers from around the matron, replacing them with fresh ones. Keep these papers flat. Immediately place all soiled papers in a handy large sealable receptacle.

The **puppy box** for the first few arrivals is an absolute necessity that helps to ensure puppies' vigor. Correct and timely use of the puppy box keeps siblings from repeatedly being soaked and chilled with every delivery. Puppies left in the whelping box with a delivering dam can suffer irreparable or even fatal injury. During contractions a dam may possess the urge to tear material. Danger is also present as the dam rises and turns. Puppies can be stepped on or chewed accidentally during these intense moments.

Puppy boxes are simple to make. They can be manufactured from any sturdy material, including a bureau drawer or cardboard carton. The puppy box size depends upon your breed and normal expected litter size. It should be large enough to hold one or two heating pads placed absolutely flat on the bottom. Giant breeds and those whelping large litters (by size and numbers of puppies) may require two boxes and heating pads rather than one. The puppy box should be a minimum of ten inches deep to produce a proper environment with the heating pad. Place the heating pad *flat* at the bottom of the box. Remove one lower box corner through which to pass the heating pad's cord. Do not make the aperture so large that a puppy could slip a head or leg through, getting caught. Wrap the heating pad in a medium-weight cotton towel or diaper. Drape a heavier towel over the open box top. Set the thermostat heat on medium from the time your matron goes into labor. You have now created a simple and safe ''incubator.'' When monitored, the air inside the box will feel warm to your hand, as will the towel wrapping the heating pad. Neither the heating pad nor the air inside the box should ever feel more than slightly warm! By means of this controlled constant environment, the incubator protects "older" puppies, allowing the matron to concentrate fully on her delivery and cleaning of the next littermate. Keep the puppy box directly by the whelping box, or in a corner next to the mother. While having contractions for the next puppy, the dam is able to put her head on the puppy box's edge, keeping an eye on her offspring.

The **heating pad** you purchase should be square or slightly rectangular, be waterproof, have a protective cover and be free of any strings or ribbons. It must also be of the type that has a variety of temperature control settings: low, medium, high and off, at least. Some have infinite thermostatic controls between low and high. These may be safely set and left on at a medium-low temperature. It is important that the heating pad be warm and ready for the puppies' births. Turn the heating pad on when the matron first exhibits signs of labor. Set the heat control to medium directly prior to the birth of the first puppy, when the matron is in hard labor. If necessary, reset the thermometer to low when she is ready to deliver her second puppy. If the puppies move about crying, they are either too hot or too cold. If they are sleeping quietly, you have the environment just right. If the puppies are "bobbing" their heads and crying, they are hungry. Be ready to put them on the dam as soon as it is feasible.

Both owner and brood bitch should be prepared for the new arrivals.   *Artist: Jan Walker*

A large stack of soft **clean towels** is another absolute necessity. Large litters may use as many as two or three dozen towels. Towels donated to the litter should be old. Do not use the good ones Aunt Sophie gave you for Christmas. Whelping puppies is a messy job. The towels will receive a substantial amount of blood and may as a result become permanently stained from the whelping. After each new puppy's arrival and the dam's first cleaning, finish drying the puppy off by *briskly* toweling it with a clean towel or diaper. Sometimes two or more towels (or diapers) may be required to effectively clean and dry each puppy.

You also need to have on hand: **sterile hemostats** *or* **sterilized blunt-end scissors**; **heavy sterile silk sewing thread, dental floss,** *or* **heavy sterile silk sutures**; **petroleum** *or* **lubricating jelly**; **several pairs of sterile surgical gloves**; **a rubber pediatric bulb syringe**; **surgical antiseptic scrub** *for your hands;* **ink pen** *and* **note pad**. Do not use cotton thread: cotton acts like a wick to moisture and stays damp, inviting bacterial infection. Hemostats, suture material and sterile surgical gloves may be purchased through your veterinarian or a surgical-supply house.

Make a trial run with your telephone cord. Be certain that it is long enough to place the phone by the whelping box. Dry and some breech deliveries can be difficult. Should difficulties be encountered, proper help can save a puppy's life. A telephone call to your veterinarian is invaluable. More than one veterinarian has given step-by-step instructions to an owner who "assisted" a delivery via the telephone.

The well-equipped "doggie midwife" will also have on hand a **tube feeder** and **syringe**. These items can be purchased from the veterinarian or a well-stocked pet supplier. Tube-feeder diameters are of various sizes. The size appropriate for one breed is not always suitable for another. If you are purchasing a tube feeder for the first time, it is best to do so through your veterinarian. Your veterinarian will also be able to supply you with the proper syringe size for the tube feeder.

Bitch's milk replacement is frequently used for supplementing or feeding orphan puppies. When fed to the matron as a dietary supplement, the replacement aids in her lactating sufficient quantities of milk. If your bitch is incapable of feeding her offspring adequately, you have a ready-to-use base. Mix the formula with water, a raw egg yolk and a few drops of bland syrup sweetener. *Do not use honey.* Raw and processed honey can contain certain bacteria lethal to infants and puppies. Use a product such as Karo syrup (or sugar) when mixing. Bitches often become dry and thirsty during a prolonged whelping period. This formula helps to keep their electrolytes in balance, their energy level strong, and it assuages thirst during whelping.

A small **scale** is requisite for recording and supervision of accurate birth weights. The scale purchased for medium- and large-breed puppies should be graduated, measuring ounces to several pounds. Small-breed scales should have weight gradations from grams to a few pounds. The trays should be scoop-shaped rather than flat, and removable for washing. Scales can be purchased through

WHELPING CHART

SIRE _____ DAM _____

DATES BRED_____ DATE WHELPED_____

LABOR STARTS_____

HARD LABOR STARTS_____

	TIME	AFTER BIRTH	SEX	COLOR/MARKINGS	WEIGHT	OK?
PUPPY 1						
PUPPY 2						
PUPPY 3						
PUPPY 4						
PUPPY 5						
PUPPY 6						
REMARKS						

Note the arrival time, sex, weight, color and markings (if any) for each puppy.

gourmet food stores, some supermarkets, health food shops, medical supply houses, hardware stores and large chain stores. Most models are relatively inexpensive, costing but a few dollars.

Accurate records of birth weights and subsequent gains of each puppy allow you to track each puppy, insuring each has had adequate nursing opportunities and is gaining well. If a gain ratio is not closely proportionate for each puppy, you may be noting an early signal of trouble. Call your veterinarian immediately. Your recorded observations can help uncover potential litter or specific puppy problems.

Place a sturdy couch or **cot** by the whelping box. Some matrons prefer to snuggle when in early labor. She might ''insist'' on having her abdomen stroked. Stroking has a calming effect, and appears to ease contraction pains. Having a bed handy allows you to rest, napping with the matron during her early labor and between deliveries.

The normal gestation period for a litter is 58 to 65 days (the average is 63 days). This is plenty of time to purchase, build and assemble everything required for the health and comfort of your matron and puppies. Once assembled, keep all the supplies clean and directly by the whelping box.

A **heat lamp** above the whelping box is necessary if an area is chilly, subject to drafts and temperature variations. Dependent upon the breed, the heat lamp should be hung no less than three feet above the box. The lamp must not be suspended so low that the dam can touch or become uncomfortable beneath it. Be certain the cord is well out of the way when hanging the lamp. Aim the heat to cover only the box's center area: the dam and puppies will lie within the lamp's range if warmth is desired. They will also be able to lie outside the range if too warm.

Place a protective aluminum shield around the heat lamp's basket. If your heat lamp has no protective basket, construct the shield from a heavy grade aluminum foil. The shield resembling a balloon should be approximately six inches from the lamp. This aluminum balloon should touch neither the light bulb nor the electrical receptacle. Should the lamp be touched accidentally, the balloon shield protects the light, keeping it from exploding. Using a pin or sewing needle, pierce the aluminum shield many times; this will diffuse the light and heat. The diffusion allows the heat lamp's continued use later by protecting puppies' delicate ophthalmic (eye) tissues.

8

The Whelping

THE AVERAGE gestation period is 58 to 65 days following conception, not a breeding. Because sperm remains viable three to five days following coitus, breeding and conception do not always occur at the same time. Nor is it entirely rare for a matron to whelp as early as 58 days from conception; or as late as 67 days from the time of a breeding.

With their first pregnancy, bitches may not exhibit external signs until late in term. Within days of her due date her abdominal muscles will appear to distend suddenly, sagging "overnight." Her vulva will significantly enlarge during the last week, and within 48 hours prior to whelping it will soften noticeably. Some matrons have also produced enough colostrum and milk by this time that nipples can be easily expressed. This latter condition, however, is not necessarily indicative of an imminent whelping, as abdominal pressure of a pregnancy may preclude accuracy of this test.

The time-tested method of taking the brood matron's temperature is somewhat controversial. A canine's temperature normally registers between 100.5 degrees and 102 degrees. The classic temperature drop of 2 or 3 degrees, believed by many to be indicative of impending birth, is not always accurate. Many matrons are prone to erratic temperatures a few days to a week before whelping.

If you rely on the "temperature method," keep an accurate record of your brood matron's temperature as her due date nears. Use a heavy rectal thermometer and take her temperature twice daily, morning and evening, keeping a graph of any fluctuations from her fifty-eighth day onward. A rise in temperature above 102 degrees can be a harbinger of trouble: call your veterinarian immediately.

As whelping becomes imminent, your matron's temperature will drop.

The dam's vulva swells significantly and softens measureably within 48 hours of whelping.
Dalmatian: Joanne Nash

This may occur several days in advance of the whelping. Other females exhibit a lowered temperature only a few hours before parturition. A temperature reading of 99 degrees, or as in some cases even 97.5 degrees, is almost always indicative of an imminent whelping. Although her temperature is lowered, her external signs should be vital and alert. A steep drop in temperature (plus other signs) is indicative of shock. If her temperature drops suddenly or too low, more than 3 degrees from her norm, call your veterinarian without delay.

Alert your veterinarian when you are certain your bitch is about to whelp. Make sure the answering service is alerted for your call should an emergency occur. Never call late at night unless you suspect an emergency.

Keep the veterinarian informed of your brood matron's progress and if her temperature drops below 98 degrees. While this temperature is normal for some matrons directly prior to whelping, it can also be a sign of impending trouble—not puppies. Such an extremely low temperature might be but the first obvious sign in a series that the matron is in distress and needs help quickly. This could also possibly be the only external sign a new breeder might recognize. There are not multiple hours to expend before getting help for a matron in distress. Every minute can mean the difference between her life and death and that of the litter. Too often ignorant people allow their matron to suffer needless agonizing distress for hours before calling for emergency veterinary assistance. A distressed whelping bitch cannot wait for help: it must be forthcoming immediately.

Most matrons also suffer a loss of appetite shortly before whelping. Or, if having eaten, they may suddenly regurgitate their earlier meal. Often they exhibit tremendous lethargy, to the point of appearing drugged, succumbing to very deep sleeping periods. Again, these are additional signs that the puppies' arrivals are not too far away.

LABOR

If your female takes an hour or slightly longer between puppies once whelping begins or she appears to lack the adequate muscular control needed to push the puppies out, she could be suffering from inertia. Apparent inertia may be counteracted at times by a moderate amount of exercise such as walking around the yard, a glass of milk as a calcium source or a ride around the block in the car. If none of these combined methods show resuls within 30 minutes, contact your veterinarian immediately.

The veterinarian may determine that your matron requires a higher dose of pituitary oxytocin to that which she is already producing. The administration of a booster shot of pituitary oxytocin will help to stimulate her contractions after some of the puppies are born. A whelping matron's response to the injection occurs within minutes if it is to occur at all. Some require help of a deeper professional nature. Not every matron's uterus is responsive to the presence of natural hormones or oxytocin. For those cases when natural milk, exercise and pituitary oxytocin are ineffectual, a cesarean section may be required.

Before any shots are given or invasive therapies undertaken, the veterinarian will physically examine the bitch, checking for obstructions and the presence and position of a puppy in the birth canal. Occasionally a puppy stuck in the birth canal will simply require repositioning. Often the first puppy being the largest impedes the litter's natural arrival. Usually it is possible to reposition this puppy by digital vaginal manipulation. Sometimes an additional physical push forward on the abdomen effects a relatively normal delivery. At times this is all that is required to get the puppies on their way naturally.

Labor is hard work. Dogs that have been in sustained labor over a long time period may end up being candidates for inertia. Should all other therapies fail, the matron will require surgical assistance. Some breeds, such as the brachy-cephalics (Bulldogs, Boston Terriers, French Bulldogs, for example), are routinely scheduled for cesarean sections for nearly every anticipated litter.

A trouble sign is a steady straining by the matron, contractions with no immediately resulting puppy. Get to the phone without delay and contact your veterinarian. If all the hospital lines are busy, call the operator and say you have an emergency call that must be put through immediately!

Whelping bitches often go through intermittent periods of labor and occasional minor contractions over several hours before intense contractions occur in rapid succession, producing a puppy. Normally the matron will visibly pant rapidly, may rend papers and cloths, will move restlessly and whine and will intermittently sleep deeply throughout the whelping. Once deliveries begin, most

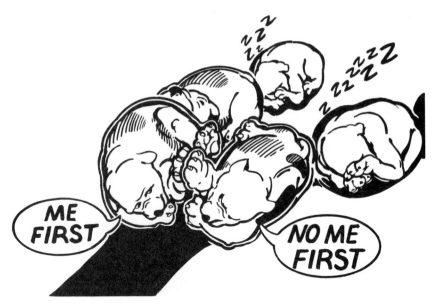

Puppies are lined up in a uterine horn not unlike peas in a pod.

puppies arrive anywhere from a few minutes to an hour apart. Two hours without producing a puppy can be a harbinger of trouble, three hours with no puppy produced could mean dire trouble. Call your veterinarian without delay.

Whelping essentially follows hereditary predilections and, in most cases, occurs successfully without professional medical intervention. Whelping is always, however, a calculated risk. Breeders often request pituitary oxytocin, believing this drug will cause their matron to sustain successful contractions. This drug is restricted to use only at certain times and never indiscriminately. Only trained medical personnel have the knowledge to make the determination if and when this drug may be used. Ill-advised use of pituitary oxytocin can cause a matron's uterus to rupture and cause her death or puppy fatality.

Before any drugs are ever administered or surgery initiated, the breeder must be absolutely certain of the matron's due date. It has happened more than once that veterinarians initiating surgery have found incompletely developed puppies! The breeder had written down the wrong breeding and due dates and the puppies were not ready for birth. Of course, if the bitch is in labor, then no mistakes can be made.

As your matron's delivery time momentarily approaches, she will become restless and may dig. Disdaining the box, she might attempt to nest or "den" elsewhere, such as on the kitchen floor, under a coffee table or at the back of a closet. Some matrons incapable of comprehending their rapid biological changes and being well house-trained fear soiling their master's home even at this time. If she wants to go outside for relief, allow her into the backyard only on lead. Arctics and certain other breed types are known champion diggers. During their pregnancies many of these dogs have the strong instinct of preparing a den for their puppies. By whelping day some dogs' yards look as though they have been under enemy fire from shell bombardment! Arctic types in particular have been known to dig colossal dens: ramps six feet and longer, with whelping dens five feet in diameter. Coaxing and bribery have little effect in moving a bitch once she feels secure in her site. Keep this type of dam on lead when outside directly prior to whelping. Prevent her or the first puppy from sustaining injury.

Your attitude toward your matron over the next few hours can help make the difference between a litter's succesful delivery and a nightmarish experience. She might whine in complaint and grunt in dissatisfaction at not finding a comfortable resting place. She might also energetically shred anything and everything in her whelping box and reach. Allowing her to shred newspapers and old towels helps her to relieve certain nesting instincts, and are perfectly natural reactions to her pain and primal urges.

Notify your veterinarian that your matron is in actual hard labor when she reaches the heavy panting stage interspersed with brief pauses. The attitude of many matrons during these moments is highly alert, almost as if listening specifically to something beyond our capabilities. Your first puppy should arrive within minutes of this behavior. If no puppy is forthcoming and she has been in labor for three hours, call your veterinarian again: insist that she be thoroughly checked.

Fortunately most whelpings occur naturally, although a first-time matron is often worrisome to the owner. A matron can whine piteously if alarmed by her pain of contractions and physical changes. Here you can offer your matron some real psychological support through physical assistance. Firmly but gently stroke her sides and abdomen from her last rib toward her hips. An adaptation of an old Native American midwifery custom, this type of stroking appears hypnotic, emotionally and physically soothing most matrons. Many females rise into a half-crouching or standing position as they give birth. At other times the same matron may "sit" with her rear quarters extended to one side. Do not be alarmed if she yelps, half-barks or makes some other real guttural "comment" at the actual moment of a puppy's presentation. Some matrons say nothing at all, others are vociferously vocal. A matron may express varying levels of vocal response from the delivery of one puppy to another. These are entirely normal reactions during moments of great strain.

With some bitches a single strong contraction may be all that is visible; others may have two, three or even four strong contractions before presentation of a puppy. Any apparent contractions and straining after that number can be indicative that the matron is in real trouble. If such is the case, quickly, without any delay whatsoever, dial your veterinarian's number. If the answering service picks up the line, insist that you be put through immediately while you stay on the line.

Usually the hardest birth is that of the first puppy. Subsequent siblings are normally born without difficulties. If a matron apparently tires during whelping, she may not be able to effect a delivery, and it is necessary to help the matron. A breeder's integrated assistance during the actual birth process, while not rare, is the more uncommon delivery. The majority of matrons are "free whelpers," with neither surgical intervention nor manual assistance required to effect deliveries.

THE UMBILICAL CORD

Usually the umbilical cord dries and falls off the puppies between two and three days after birth. Never pull or cut an umbilical cord! Some puppies born later in the litter may not drop their cords for another day or so. There is no cause for worry; nature dictates the cord's drying and dropping: you do nothing.

A number of people have the misconception that the umbilical cord attaches directly to the uterine horn wall and that the placenta is just the afterbirth. But it is the placenta that is attached to the uterine wall and the puppy is attached to the placenta by the umbilical cord. In the dog, the surface of the uterus erodes down to the blood vessels, and the placenta "packs itself" around them. Food, waste materials and gases are exchanged between the fetal circulation and the maternal circulation across very thin membranes *separating* the two blood flows. The two blood flows do not often mix.

The circulatory system is named by its relationship to the puppy. The umbilical artery conveys the puppy's blood away from its heart, carrying "used" blood with the wastes. The umbilical vein carries the cleansed blood conveying nutrients and oxygen back to the puppy.

A puppy begins the birth process in its sac protected by the surrounding amniotic fluid. At the time of disconnection from the uterine horn wall, there is enough oxygen left in the puppy's life-support system to see it through the journey down the birth canal. Different puppies take varying lengths of time to make this passage. It is crucial to remove the puppy from the sac as quickly as possible and get it breathing, as there is only a very limited oxygen supply available to the whelp en route to the world. This is one reason why a bitch encountering whelping difficulties (inertia is an example) will have a higher percentage of stillborn puppies.

A puppy's umbilical cord often remains linked to the placenta at birth. At this time the brood matron crushes the umbilical cord, grinding it between her jaws before severing it one to three inches from the puppy's abdomen. Crushing the cord stems blood flow from the puppy and prevents bacterial access. While normal, this ideal scenario does not always happen. Not every dam adequately clamps each puppy's umbilical cord at an appropriate length of one to three inches. Problems can also occur if a matron fails to adequately crush the cord or sever it short, above the crushed site. The cord can be severed too short so that stemming the blood flow becomes problematic. The opposite may be such that the crawling puppy actually "steps" on its own umbilical cord, irritating it. Either condition of an umbilical cord too short or too long can be safely remedied.

As the "midwife," your simple precautionary measures help prevent infection. Hemostats are used to clamp an umbilical cord at the appropriate length for

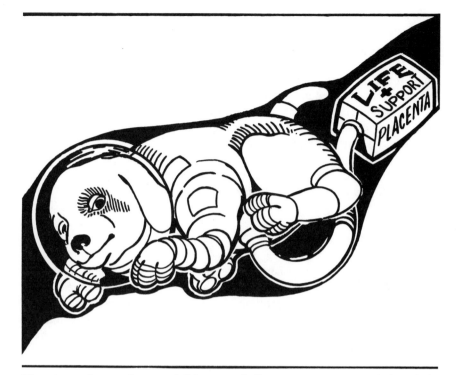

There is usually enough oxygen left in a puppy's life-support system to see it through the journey down the birth canal. However, there is only a very limited oxygen supply available.

each puppy, staunching seepage by crushing and sealing. If you do not have a pair of hemostats, your scissors can be jury-rigged with tape and gauze, temporarily changing the shears from slicing to crushing. Wrap several layers of tape midway around each blade of the scissors. Follow this with several turns of sterile gauze over the tape. When crushing the cord, do not attempt to bring the blade edges firmly together. Should you do so, the tape and gauze will be severed by the scissor-blades' sharp edges.

It may take several repeated applications of the hemostats to permanently seal an umbilical cord. In a rare case, the licking, washing actions of the mother can stimulate the cord into reopening, causing profuse and fatal bleeding. Crush a cord by clamping the hemostats one to three inches from the puppy's abdomen. The desired length of umbilical cord is dependent upon the puppy's size. The cord should be of a length that the puppy is incapable of clawing and irritating the cord, freshening a wound. If you do not have hemostats, initially tie the cord with sterile suture (or thread), or pinch the cord firmly, then crush it with the taped scissors or between your fingers. Once the blood flow has been slowed, tie the umbilical cord's end with sterile thread, suture or dental floss. Make a loop first, before placing the thread around the cord. Pull the loop closed tautly, enough to crush the cord and stem seepage, then knot it. Tie a second firm knot on the other side of the cord. Cut the thread, suture or dental floss adjacent to the knots, as well as ragged and excess length of the umbilical cord, with the sterile blunt scissors. The dam may attempt removal of the umbilical cord and thread if excess length is left attached. Do not be afraid: the puppy cannot be hurt by severing ragged or excess cord and tying thread tautly.

Sometimes an umbilical cord is severed too closely to a puppy's abdomen. Here, effective use of the hemostats becomes crucial. If you have none, scissors wrapped with tape and sterile gauze, your fingers or even your teeth will do. Unless the puppy is subject to evisceration, there is enough umbilical length to crush the tip. If possible, also tie the end with the sterile thread, suture or dental floss as far from the puppy's abdomen as can be managed.

NORMAL DELIVERIES

A matron's instinct to nurture engages with her first puppy's delivery. Praising her throughout labor and delivery gives your matron the impetus and approval she requires. Any expression of disgust, fear or overexcitement by the breeder can have a deleterious effect on the matron's attitude. Should you fail to offer your matron adequate emotional support, she could, in the rarer cases, refuse care of her litter.

First seen in a normal birth is the partial emergence of a grayish blue (slimy-looking) sac from the bitch's vulva. Usually the matron is able to deliver the sac containing the puppy onto the whelping box floor by her second or third strong contraction. Although your hands may be shaking, do not lose your calm demeanor at this point. Your attitude just now can prove crucial to the matron's acceptance and care of her offspring. Usually but not always the matron delivers the placenta (afterbirth) directly after each puppy. To the novice breeder (and even some experienced hands), this may first appear as though the matron has delivered a second whelp. Pay attention to her first delivery—first. Some matrons turn to eat the placenta first. Then they go on to eat the sac, tearing it from around the puppy. As the matron ingests all evidence of the fresh birth, she will inadvertently shake the new whelp still attached to the placenta by its umbilical cord.

Three events are occurring simultaneously. First, age-old instincts demand that all strongly-scented bloody evidence of a fresh birth be destroyed. Such evidence would, by its very nature, attract predators to a whelping den's site were the dog wild. Second, the placenta contains certain nutrients vital to the matron, helping to nourish her during a time when her strength is sorely taxed. Included among these nutrients are those assisting the whelping matron to maintain strong contractions. Finally, during the moments the matron ingests the sac and afterbirth, she stimulates the puppy to an independent life, toward breathing on its own.

Manually tear the sac from the puppy's head if the matron tends to the

82

First seen in a normal birth is the partial emergence of a grayish-blue (slimy-looking) sac from the dam's vulva. Close observation shows that this puppy is arriving head first.

Photographer: Margaret Cleek, Ph.D.

placenta first. Do not attempt to remove the puppy from its proximity to the dam. In the excitement of a birth, and by the thickness of the membrane composing the sac, it may be hard to tell which end of the puppy is which. You will know as soon as you begin to tear the sac. Once the sac is torn, ease it over the puppy's body starting from the head. Carefully pick the puppy up, holding it a few inches off the whelping box floor to make it easier for the dam to crush and sever the cord. If a large-breed puppy, wrap your fingers around the entire rear quarters, including legs. Envelop the head and forelegs with your other hand, leaving the abdomen (and umbilical cord) exposed. A small-breed puppy may be enveloped in one hand. As the dam severs the cord, your fingers protect the puppy's legs from becoming mangled.

Allow the dam to gnaw the umbilical cord. The grinding-crunching sound heard is that of the dam severing the cord from the placenta. Keep one or two fingers between the puppy's abdomen and her mouth. This prevents her from severing the cord too closely to the puppy's body or accidentally biting a leg. The matron should sever the cord within a few minutes of the birth. If she does not, clamp the cord with sterilized hemostats approximately two inches from the puppy's abdomen.

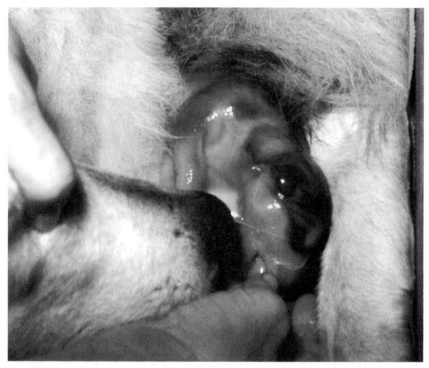

The delivery of the first puppy takes the longest amount of time. If the dam continues to have strong contractions and the puppy is not withdrawn in between them, tear the sac from the pup's head and clear the mouth of amniotic fluid.   *Photographer: Margaret Cleek, Ph.D.*

It takes but a few moments for her to dispose of the placenta and sac surrounding the puppy. It may at first appear as though the matron is "eating" her puppy (especially to a new breeder). Cannibalism rarely occurs, particularly with matrons that are well supported emotionally and physically. A new mother dog could, however, panic and kill or accidentally ingest a puppy if an attempt is made to remove it from her during these first intense moments. Your demeanor at this time is often critical to the dam's acceptance of her puppies.

Allow the matron to eat the first four placentas, then at least every alternate placenta as they arrive. By this time having the rhythm of your matron's whelping pattern, you should be able to scoop up alternating afterbirths. Hold the afterbirth either in a towel or a piece of newspaper until the matron has finished removing the sac and severing the cord from the puppy. Count and make certain the matron delivers one placenta for each puppy whelped. Make a notation on your pad of the time and sex of each puppy born and if the placentas were also delivered. Some bitches retain, or fail to pass, entire placentas. It is very important that the number of placentas be counted, that one arrives for each puppy whelped. At times one or several placentas may be

Everything seems to happen very fast. Usually, but not always, the dam delivers the placenta directly after each puppy. Some bitches eat the placenta before returning to the newborn pup. As long as the puppy's color is good and it is breathing well, do not worry while the dam instinctively cares for herself and her youngster.   *Photographer: Margaret Cleek, Ph.D.*

temporarily retained and arrive later. There is a one-to-one ratio: one puppy, one placenta. If any are retained following parturition, uterine inflammation and serious infection can result. Your veterinarian may administer a pituitary oxytocin "clean-out" shot following the whelping if the matron fails to deliver entire placentas for each puppy born.

Clear Passages

Puppies are frequently born with amniotic fluid present in their lungs. With their first breaths they may inhale any amniotic fluid left in the oral cavities, mouth and nasal passages. As a result, these first critical breaths will be neither lusty nor vigorous. A puppy with fluid in its airway and lungs will gurgle and bubble, being incapable of a lusty cry. Therefore, *always hold the newly born puppy at a head-down angle. Never position the puppy's head higher than its lungs before hearing a vigorous cry!* Do not attempt to remove the puppy from its proximity to the mother. Depress the bulb of the syringe and gently insert the tube portion into the puppy's mouth. Slowly release the bulb, withdrawing any fluids accumulated from the puppy's oral cavity. If amniotic fluid is present, you may have to repeat this procedure two or three times. Follow this by gently

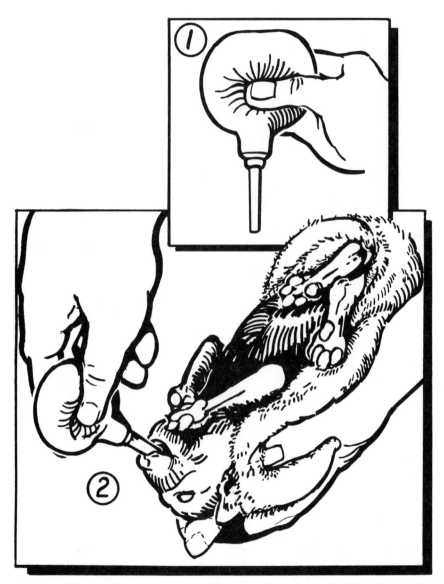

Puppies are frequently born with amniotic fluid present in the lungs. With their first breaths they may inhale the fluid from the mouth and nasal passages. Hold the newborn at a head-down angle. Depress the bulb of the pediatric syringe and gently insert the tube into the puppy's mouth. Slowly release the bulb to withdraw fluid from the puppy's mouth.

swabbing the mouth with a thin clean towel, sterile diaper or cotton swab. As soon as the puppy is free of ties to the placenta, briskly rub it with toweling—still in the head-down position. This brisk stimulation helps the puppy's circulation, causing it to take deep life-giving breaths.

Fast remedial steps are necessary if a puppy's first breaths are still gurgling, indicative of potentially serious trouble. Gently open the puppy's mouth. Make sure there are no obstructions, including a tongue rolled back into the throat. Quickly again, use the bulb syringe and briskly rub the puppy down. Are there any little bubbles coming from its nostrils? Hold the puppy near your ear and listen carefully. How does it sound? If the cry is not lustily clear-sounding, and you continue to hear an abnormal gurgling breathing, you must "shake the puppy down," in order to clear its lungs and trachea.

Learning to shake a puppy down is easy. Wrap the puppy in a towel to get a secure grip and hold the puppy head-down firmly in both hands. The puppy's spine should be along your fingers, its stomach facing your abdomen. One hand firmly supports the head, neck and shoulders of a large-breed puppy. The other hand, directly behind the first, supports the remainder of the puppy's spine down

Shaking the puppy down to clear its airway is easy. Stand slightly straddle-legged and think of the puppy as a delicate but large thermometer which you must shake down in fluid motions, in an even, one-two cadence.

past its hips. Stand slightly straddle-legged and think of the puppy as a *delicate* but large thermometer that you must shake down in fluid motions. Now you are ready.

Neither too fast nor too slow, in an even one-two cadence, swing the puppy in an arc from slightly below the level of your shoulders. Then continuing the arc, rapidly lower the puppy until you are slightly bent over. Stop the arc abruptly when the puppy's muzzle faces the floor. Its head should be even with or between your legs. Do not bend over so low that the puppy is in any position but that of head-down.

Shaking the puppy down in this manner helps to clear the lungs, trachea, throat and nasal passages of any accumulated fluids. Do not be surprised to see a small spray of amniotic fluid fly out of the puppy's mouth and nose when it is shaken down in this manner. After shaking the puppy down two or three times, stop. Listen to the puppy's breathing. It should sound much clearer. If it does not, repeat use of the bulb syringe and shaking the puppy down. Briskly rub the puppy with a towel before once again listening to its breathing. Continue to repeat the procedure over several minutes, as necessary. The puppy will let you know when it has had enough. All of a sudden the life-threatening gurgles will change to a loud, clear-sounding lusty cry. Be alert, however, because fluid from the stomach is often regurgitated to refill the throat.

Resuscitation

If a puppy's progress is impeded, staying too long in the birth canal, it may be apparently lifeless. Some of these puppies may have a faint heartbeat but no respiratory response; others may exhibit neither condition of life. A few apparently stillborn puppies will respond to efforts of resuscitation. The following method of resuscitation combined with shaking a puppy down has happily revived many whelps born lifeless.

Never blow into a gurgling puppy's mouth! Never blow into a puppy's mouth and nose before it has first been shaken-down. Should you fail to shake a puppy down before resuscitation measures are attempted on an apparently stillborn puppy, you will force all amniotic fluid present into its lungs. The puppy will die of asphyxiation, ironically drowning in its own life fluid. Prepare an apparent stillborn for resuscitation by first using the bulb syringe and shaking-down method several times to clear the airway as much as possible.

Wrap your hand around the puppy's chest, your fingertips against the rib cage just behind the elbow. Pump your fingers two or three times in rapid succession to stimulate the heart. This action will expel any oxygen in the puppy's lungs. Quickly follow the pumping by covering the puppy's muzzle, mouth and nose with your mouth, and blow gently. This is tricky: *do not blow too hard or you could rupture the newborn's delicate lung tissues. Do not blow air you have exhaled! Use your cheeks only to gently push fresh air into the puppy's lungs.* Give the puppy four breaths, then repeat the finger-pumping action over the lungs and heart. It is frequently necessary to repeat these resuscitation measures of breathing and pumping for as long as 20 or 30 minutes before the puppy may respond sturdily on its own.

Check the puppy's color quickly after four or five minutes of resuscitation. Are the pads and gums pink or blue? If the gums are white or bluish white, it may be too late to save this particular puppy. If the gums or pads on the paws were pink at birth, and pink in response to your ministrations, there is a sound chance the puppy can be revived without the aid of drugs.

Once resuscitated and breathing well on its own, give the puppy a final brisk toweling. Thoroughly dry the puppy, causing it to cry and use its lungs. Then give the puppy back to its anxious mother. Now take a quick breather before noting the puppy's arrival time, sex and markings, if any.

IDENTIFYING LOOK-ALIKES

Puppies of some breeds are all born the same color. These puppies may be easily identified by the application of nail polish to their toenails. For example, the right front foot toenails of one puppy may be painted red, another puppy's painted in pink. This leaves the left forepaws on two others, and the hind toenails on four additional siblings. Thus with but two colors, eight puppies of the same sex and color may be readily identified from birth onward.

Some puppies of breeds born one color change as they mature. Dalmatian puppies, for example, are born solid white. By the time the youngsters are several weeks old, their colors and spotting begin to appear identifiable and in a pattern. At this time they no longer require identification by nail polish. The coloring of some other breeds changes rapidly, at times within hours of birth. The color of these puppies should not be entered in the notebook until they are several hours old and fully dry, and their coloring readily identifiable.

GETTING PUPPIES STARTED

It is best for puppies to begin nursing as soon as possible. Some puppies born vigorous have from the time of birth a tremendously strong instinct of where to go and how to suckle. Others take time to begin suckling and may require assistance. The sooner a puppy nurses, the less chance there is of losing it.

Puppies are born incompletely developed, their ears and eyes sealed as protective measures. Their only "developed" sense is scent. Although newborns are unaware of siblings, there is a primal level of awareness. It is this primal awareness that drives the newborn puppies to vie with each other, seeking heat and life-giving colostrum and milk from the dam. Early nursing is highly important because colostrum antibodies are absorbed during only the first two days. The dam also receives direct benefit from the first puppies' nursing opportunities: nursing action aids uterine contractions, helping her to deliver subsequent siblings.

Because of the dam's abdominal distention, the first one or two puppies

It is important to get the puppies started nursing as soon as possible. The sooner a puppy nurses, the less chance of losing it. A nursing puppy also helps to stimulate the dam's uterine contractions. *Photographer: Margaret Cleek, Ph.D.*

may not be able to nurse right away. A dam's breasts are often taut during whelping. This distention and tautness are created through internal pressure from unborn whelps behind the mammaries. Nursing can be extremely difficult until pressure impeding the dam's flow eases and the glands become relatively flaccid. Normally by the third puppy's birth, enough pressure has been relieved in the dam of a large litter that sufficient nursing may begin, aiding her uterine contractions. Dams of small litters do not often appear to encounter this problem.

If a puppy fails to nurse right away but continues to ''nose around'' aimlessly, you will need to help nature along. Many puppies through instinct and scent head directly back to the area from which they originally met the world. Put the puppy to one of the dam's teats and express a small amount of colostrum (milk). This may be all the assistance required. Other puppies need a stronger hint of what to do and how to get started. Open the mouth of a puppy requiring a firmer ''suggestion'' to initiate suckling. Express some colostrum from one of the dam's mammaries and rub a small amount on and around her nipple area. Gently insert her nipple into the puppy's mouth while expressing additional

90

colostrum/milk. Usually this is sufficient to get a puppy started. Do not worry if the puppy, being one of the first born, still refuses to nurse. Puppies can go one or two hours without nursing and remain healthy.

Not every puppy is born ravenous. Sometimes it takes sibling rivalry to stimulate a newborn. If a puppy is reluctant to nurse two hours after birth, one or two tube feedings may be necessary to prevent dehydration. Any instinctive behavioral aberrations from the norm should be reported to your veterinarian. The puppy could have an unnoticeable birth defect preventing an ability to nurse. Such puppies should be mercifully and humanely put to sleep as soon as possible.

A puppy with a normal palate, both soft and hard tissues, will have a complete and ridged roof to its mouth. A newborn's palate is relatively low, aiding adequate suction. If a puppy has a high roof (or so it appears), it may have trouble such as a cleft palate. If upon opening the puppy's mouth the palate appears to have an aperture, you most likely have a cleft-palate puppy. The condition of cleft palate means that the mouth roof is open to the nasal cavities. Most unexamined cleft-palate puppies appear normal at birth and will attempt nursing. A sign of this condition may be noted by bubbles of milk issuing from the puppy's nose as it nurses, and the accompanying warning signs of gurgling and complaining cries.

It is possible to keep a cleft-palate and some other abnormal puppies alive by tube feeding. It is not fair, however, to the puppy because it can never live a normal life. An apparent abnormal condition may also (but not always) be indicative of other unseen, internal problems in the puppy's development. Often

Nursing puppies help to stimulate the dam's contractions.   *Alaskan Malamutes: D. Biss*

the obvious defect accompanies other hidden defects. Euthanasia, although sounding cruel, is far more benevolent than forcing an animal to live, incapable of growing and enjoying normal pleasures of life. How much more merciful it is to allow such a puppy to go quietly and humanely "to sleep" rather than spend a life in distress.

Birth defects are not necessarily either congenital or hereditary. In some cases, they can be caused by an insufficiency or surplus in diet. Even when conditions are apparently optimum, a lack of assimilation of certain nutrients essential to the formation of vigorously healthy and normal puppies can occur. Two beautiful and healthy dogs can be brought to a union that looks good, genetically speaking, on paper. While genetics is a science, it is not exact. Because both desirable and undesirable genes are passed inevitably from one generation to the next, one can never be certain what will be presented in a litter. There is always some risk in breeding. Breeding is not for the fainthearted or for those not willing to devote a lot of time, money and energy.

DIFFICULT DELIVERIES

Most puppies have a normal presentation at birth. They need little more than a bit of brisk toweling from you and a lot of "TLC" from their mother to help them get started. There are those times and few puppies, however, that require assistance. Usually the hardest birth is the first puppy. Delivery of a dry or overly large puppy can take longer than normal and may affect the next puppy's birth. This next puppy may be stillborn or have more fluid in the trachea and lungs. Subsequent siblings are normally born without difficulties.

Occasionally a puppy is born apparently devoid of life if, for example, its progress has been impeded in the birth canal. A few of these puppies may have a faint heartbeat but no respiratory response; others may exhibit neither. Some of these puppies respond positively to resuscitatory efforts. Never give a puppy up until resuscitation has been attempted.

Not every stillborn puppy or difficult delivery is the result of a brood mare suffering inertia. However, this problem will often cause a higher percentage of stillborn offspring. Puppies are normally vigorous while attached to the uterine wall; once "freed," however, they have limited time in which to arrive.

Time is crucial. Tear the sac from around the puppy. Rub the whelp briskly while it is in a head-down position. Use the pediatric bulb syringe to suction the puppy's oral cavity. Then clear the trachea and lungs by shaking the puppy down as described earlier. Each direction of the arc's swing should take approximately three seconds. Repeat these procedures several times until the oral and tracheal passages are cleared as much as possible.

Check the puppy's gums and paw pads for color should your efforts fail to elicit a response. It is hard, if indeed possible, to bring puppies back to life that appear dead-white or blue-white of color. Always exert efforts on behalf of those puppies whose pads and gums appear pink. Repetitions of rubbing the

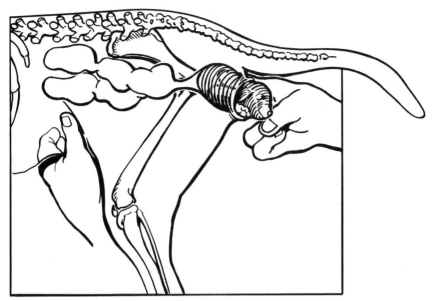

Time is crucial in assisted deliveries. Place one hand in the dam's inguinal area to prevent the puppy from being withdrawn back into the birth canal. Don sterile gloves and gently insert one or two fingers into the dam's vagina when it is necessary to reposition a puppy that is "stuck."

puppy briskly, applications of the bulb syringe and shaking down are usually effective. Once tracheal passages are cleared, and if no response has been stimulated, resuscitation must be attempted as a final effort. Follow steps for resuscitation as described earlier.

Dry Delivery

Some other deliveries can present whelping difficulties that if unaided can result in a loss of puppy life. Timely aid may save a life without injury to the dam or whelp. A dry delivery, when the puppy's protective sac breaks inside the birth canal, can be such an event. This delivery may be either a head-first or breech presentation (rear quarters first). While breech is a normal canine birth position, a dry breech delivery can be dangerous to a puppy.

The puppy is presented entirely or partially free of a sac in a dry delivery. In some cases a puppy's progress is impeded by having one or two legs stuck, its head turned back blocking passage or even its body turned sideways in the birth canal, with neither end presented. Under these circumstances the dam cannot deliver without assistance. Petroleum or another antiseptic vaginal jelly facilitates the dry delivery. Cooking oil may be substituted as a last resort if no other lubricant is available.

While it is imperative to get a puppy breathing on its own as quickly as possible, *the puppy must never be pulled indiscriminately*, no matter how excited

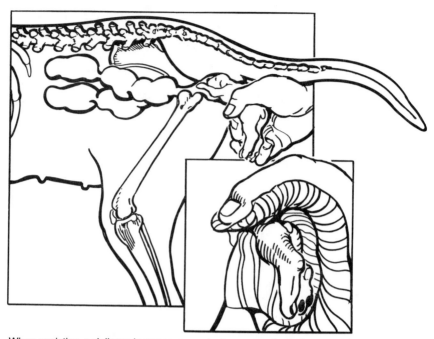

When assisting a delivery is necessary, grip the puppy firmly (yet gently) with a towel to prevent it from being withdrawn back into the birth canal between the dam's contractions. **Never pull a puppy!**

you become, or how piercingly the matron may yelp. While time is crucial, the delivery must be effected without injury to the puppy or dam. You need to work with the dam's contractions. Place one hand in the dam's inguinal area directly behind the puppy's position in the birth canal and exert a slight pressure to help prevent backward slipping. Gripping the puppy firmly with a towel in the other hand prevents it from being withdrawn. Wait for the next contraction and exert a slight, steady pulling pressure downward toward the dam's feet. One or two contractions are usually enough to effect a birth.

Should a matron encounter delivery difficulties, the problem must be correctly diagnosed before remedial measures are made. Your hands must be scrubbed, your nails trimmed and filed smooth in case adjusting the puppy's position proves necessary. Don sterile surgical gloves (or dip your bare hands in surgical antiseptic). Using a very small amount of lubricant, gently insert one or two fingers into the matron's vagina. The puppy should be palpable, presented facing the dam's feet. You will be able to feel if the puppy is still confined or if the sac has been broken under pressure of delivery. If the puppy is still in the sac, additional lubricant will not prove beneficial.

If the puppy's head is foremost, its legs will need to be gently eased into the correct birth position. This head-first position can "jam" a puppy against the vaginal opening. Gently and carefully, push the puppy a few slight millimeters

94

back into the birth canal. Only then may the puppy be repositioned with the forelegs extended first, protecting the matron and whelp from damage during birth. The dam should then incur little difficulty expressing the puppy with one or two more contractions. A small amount of additional lubricant may be required around the puppy and just inside the vagina. You will need to firmly and gently hold the puppy as it is presented and withdrawn back inside the birth canal at the end of contractions. If presented head-first, keep the puppy's face down toward the dam's feet. If the delivery is breech, hold the puppy's hind feet "facing" the dam's paws. Never hold a puppy face-up or straight toward you during a birth. If the puppy is presented differently, it may require repositioning.

Wet Delivery

Allow the matron to do her work while you gently but firmly grip the puppy's sac (in a wet delivery) with the aid of a towel or diaper. Holding the puppy in a position of presentation prevents it from being withdrawn into the birth canal. Each contraction brings the puppy closer to birth. Your job is simply to hold the puppy, preventing withdrawal and allowing Nature to work.

If you are unable to grip the puppy's sac and the head is definitely presented first, break the sac free from around the puppy's head. Although not fully delivered, immediately use the pediatric bulb syringe to suction amniotic fluid from the puppy's mouth.

It often takes more than two or three contractions to deliver a particularly difficult or large puppy. Generally speaking, there should be no more than four contractions. There may be a problem if, after this number, the puppy is not fully presented. If a puppy's progress is impeded, a leg could be stuck behind the vaginal opening or possibly insufficient lubricant was applied. Delicately feel the puppy's position. Telephone your veterinarian immediately to obtain expert assistance if the puppy's position feels normal and the matron proves incapable of a presentation.

A breech delivery puppy is presented rear-foremost. The hindlegs are tucked against the puppy's abdomen in the direction of the head. Normally the puppy is still in the sac and problems do not occur. Although entirely common, a breech delivery is usually slightly more difficult for the dam than a head-first presentation because the puppy's largest area arrives first. There are exceptions to this, however, as with brachycephalics: notably Boxers, Bostons, Bulldogs, Pugs and other short-faced breeds. It is easier for a brachycephalic bitch to effect a normal delivery when the presentation is breech because the heads of these breeds are larger in circumference than are the bodies. Many brachycephalic breeders, particularly Bulldog and Boston, expect and avoid delivery complications by routinely scheduling cesarean sections.

A breech delivery is difficult to assist when a puppy is confined in the slippery sac. Surgical gloves are better than human skin for securely holding anything slippery. Gauze pads (available at all pharmacies and supermarkets) make a second good choice; a thin towel is an adequate third choice. If you have none of these items, you must work with your fingers. Gently secure a grip (this is the tricky part) on each side of the puppy without applying undue pressure. As each contraction occurs, aid the puppy and matron by applying a steady, firm pressure, preventing the puppy from slipping back inside the birth canal. Do not pull! Unless absolutely critical for a grip, do not break the sac of a breech delivery! Recheck the puppy's position if passage is not facilitated with one or two additional contractions. Run your finger around the puppy's sac, just inside the vulva, making sure nothing is obstructing the delivery. Occasionally it may take several contractions to deliver a puppy from this position. Remember to keep the puppy's rear quarters pointing toward the dam's feet until the breech presentation has been completed. Once breathing well on its own, give the whelp a final brisk thorough toweling causing the pup to cry.

A number of breeders were advocates of alternately dipping puppies in hot and cold water to ''shock them to life.'' Hot and cold dipping, however, critically threatens any chances for the puppy's survival.

9

Orphan, Premature and Unthrifty Puppies

THE ENTIRE LITTER needs to be checked by your veterinarian as soon as whelping is completed. At this time weak or other problem puppies can be identified. If the decision is made to try and save them, your veterinarian can help detail the special care required. In certain cases of very weak or deformed puppies the hard decision of euthanasia may be recommended, especially if the litter is large, and is one that will challenge the bitch and your abilities for optimum care.

The most common birth defects are facial and palate clefts, missing toes, deformed legs and hernias. Umbilical hernias can be aggravated when the dam drags a newborn by the cord. Less common but still not rare is the abdominothoracic fissure (incomplete closure of the body cavity). At birth these puppies appear eviscerated and must be quickly and mercifully euthanized. While the bitch cleans this puppy licking the viscera, she may ingest it as she instinctively chews the umbilical cord. This can lead to cannibalism. Newborns should also be examined for prolapsed anus, spina bifida and other breed abnormalities.

EARLY NEONATAL CARE

Some bitches become nervous, bewildered or even terrified with the advent of their first litter. The manner in which a matron accepts or rejects her offspring is often in direct response to the breeder's attitude or whelping box site.

Normal puppies are plump and firm at birth. They have good muscle and skin tones. This is when many breeders like to first grade their litter. These puppies feel firm and tense when held in hand. The skin on the abdomen, feet and mouth is a healthy pink, the legs and back are straight. If puppies cry continuously or constantly squirm and crawl, these are signs of infant puppy distress and if left untreated are harbingers of serious trouble. Well-nourished, healthy puppies are warm, quiet and sleep most of the time. As they develop they yawn at awakening. After their first few weeks they engage in short periods of play before eating and sleeping again.

Excessive handling of newborns is unwise. Excessive handling of newborns by more than one caretaker is extremely unwise and can be dangerous to the puppies. It may cause certain mothers to reject a puppy or mercilessly pick on it, and can also lead to the transmission of infections to the newborn.

UNTHRIFTY PUPPIES

Unthrifty puppies have poor muscle tone. They show obvious signs of discomfort by initially high activity levels and crying almost unceasingly. If left untreated, the high activity and crying levels soon cease and the puppies become comatose.

Unthrifty or abnormal puppies are identified not only by their activities but also physically. They appear thinner than siblings and rather limp to touch because of poor muscle and skin tones. Often the skin of these puppies is flaccid and wrinkled; they may feel cold to your touch or, at the very least, cooler than do the thrifty siblings. The skin over these puppies' abdomens, feet and mouth interiors (oral mucosa) may appear reddish purple in color or paled when compared to that of the littermates.

Usually these puppies are incapable of sustained nursing, readily losing nipple contact with the dam. They become easily chilled and disoriented in the box. If these puppies manage to survive somehow for a few weeks without assistance, they will after this period of time appear bloated (potbellied), and have splayed and flattened feet and toes and crooked legs. Such unthrifty puppies generally respond positively to a few milliliters of raw liver juice fed daily for their first few weeks. Supplementary tube or bottle feeding for three or four days on a four-hour (around the clock) schedule may also be necessary to help these puppies become established and thrive.

Any weak, unthrifty puppies should be removed from the litter and maintained in the puppy box. They need to be placed back on their dam under your watchful supervision at regular intervals. The dam is able to ''stay in touch,'' stimulating elimination, cleaning and nurturing them at this time. The puppies are also stimulated by vigorous littermates. This regular periodic tactile reinforcement helps avoid *failure-to-thrive syndrome*. Severely debilitated puppies should not be placed with the dam for any feeding unless carefully held by the breeder. In spite of being maintained on sheepskin in the puppy box, these puppies require

Puppies continuously receive stimulation from the dam and siblings through positive tactile reinforcement. Stimulation is crucial to the healthy development of a puppy, to avoid Failure to Thrive Syndrome. *Samoyed: Gail & Debbie Spieker*

periodic stimulation and turning to avoid "bed sores" when they are incapable of adequate independent movement.

PREMATURE PUPPIES

Premature puppies require special care. The first 24 hours are critical to their survival. They *must* be maintained on an *hourly* schedule. The next 48 hours these puppies must be maintained every 2 hours around the clock. The following 48 hours the puppies can be stretched to a 3-hour schedule around the clock. By their fifth day, they can be changed to 4-hour intervals. When these puppies have reached one week, the night feedings *only* can be set to a 6-hour schedule, resuming the 4-hour intervals during the day. This highly intense schedule must be maintained until the puppies are ready for their first semisolid foods at about 13 days of age, *after* their eyes have opened and they have developed some visual acuity and independent physical mobility.

Premature puppies are born incompletely developed. Many lack the strength, ability and instinct to suckle. These puppies must be fed by a catheter tube until their nursing reflex engages. This reflex miraculously engages on or close to the date they were due in the world. They may lack a strong respiratory ability, and may arrive with only a rudimentary coat. They are weak and vulnerable. Their ability to survive rests solely on the breeder's dedicated efforts.

An incubator maintained at 90 degrees Fahrenheit until three or four days *after* the due date (*not* whelping date) helps to boost the survival rate of these delicate infant puppies. A premature puppy incubator can be set up using the puppy box as the foundation. Leave the heating pad covered by a towel on a medium setting. Place washable (fake) sheepskin on top of the heating pad and towel, and place a thin towel over the box's top to help maintain the warm environment. If desired, place a small encased thermometer on the sheepskin, away from the puppies, for temperature readings. Sheepskin can be found through medical-supply houses, well-stocked pet suppliers, wholesale catalogs and some veterinary offices.

Importantly, the puppies also require the oxygen level of their incubator to be boosted. Small oxygen tanks can be rented or purchased through medical-supply companies and almost any general rental company. Rent or purchase one or two back-up oxygen tanks. Cut a small hole in another corner of the incubator box (away from the heating pad's cord), and insert the tip of the oxygen catheter. Leave the setting on the lowest measurable amount: too high an oxygen level setting can contribute to ophthalmic (vision) problems later. By the time the puppies' due date arrives, they should be well developed enough that additional oxygen is no longer necessary. *Never smoke around premature puppies and oxygen; never smoke near puppies at all.*

While tube feeding is easiest and less time consuming for the breeder, it does not satisfy puppies' need for suckling. Ideally, tube feeding is utilized as a temporary measure only, for early supplementation or initial maintenance of unthrifty or premature puppies. Puppies *absolutely require* the closeness of nursing, the tactile reinforcement of snuggling and being held. Without adequate positive tactile reinforcement, premature puppies can suffer failure-to-thrive syndrome.

GAVAGE (TUBE FEEDING)

Learning correct tube feeding procedure (gavage) is not difficult when the right materials are used. The tube feeder is a soft pliable catheter that will not injure a puppy when used correctly. The tube feeder is best purchased through your veterinarian, who will equip you with the correct diameter catheter and syringe size for your breed. Both catheter and syringe are sterilized between early feedings. The syringe should have clearly graduated markings on the side so an accurate record of puppies' intake can be made. You also need a bowl or large measuring cup for warm water, a candy thermometer and a nontoxic indelible pen or dull knife.

Place water heated to 100 degrees Fahrenheit in the bowl or measuring cup. Heat the formula separately (also to 100 degrees Fahrenheit) using the candy thermometer to regulate the temperatures of both liquids. Put the thermometer, syringe, catheter and warmed formula into the bowl of water for transport to the "nursery."

While the litter may be relatively uniform in size, each puppy's physique

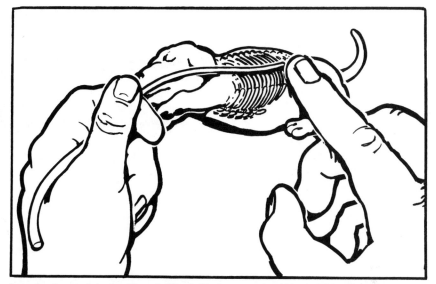

Learning how to tube feed is not difficult. Each puppy should be individually measured with the catheter from the tip, held just behind the last rib, along the side of the chest and throat, to directly in front of the muzzle.   *Artist: John Kirkpatrick*

may vary slightly. Every puppy should be *individually measured* for gavage feeding. Correct measurement is crucial to the puppies' well-being. Have a nontoxic indelible pen or moderately dull knife handy. Lay each puppy flat on its side on a towel, and carefully measure the catheter from the rounded tip held at a point just behind the puppy's last rib, along the side of the chest and throat, to just in front of the puppy's muzzle. There should be plenty of catheter left over. Mark the spot of the puppy's muzzle on the catheter with the pen or by scoring very lightly with the dull knife. Too short a catheter measurement can allow formula to be aspirated by the puppy. A catheter measured and introduced that is too long can puncture through the newborn's delicate stomach wall. Have your veterinarian ''walk you through'' the exact procedure.

The end of the catheter may be too wide to allow attachment to the syringe. Severing the catheter directly behind the beginning of the flute allows secure attachment to the syringe. After attaching the syringe, place the catheter end into the warmed formula and withdraw the syringe from the plunger. Always fill the syringe a few milliliters over the amount directed by your veterinarian. Once filled, *keep the catheter tip pointed downward*, preventing air from getting in.

Place the puppy on a towel in your lap, head elevated in a slightly inclined position. Wrap one hand around the back of the puppy's head, palm against the back of the skull. Gently stroke the puppy with your thumb and opposing fingers respectively on each side of the muzzle by the lip corners. The puppy usually responds by opening its mouth, sometimes yawning! *Always* keep the syringe elevated and the catheter end pointing downward as you approach introduction.

101

You want minute amounts of formula to slowly drip from the catheter's tip, preventing air from getting in. You may want to hold the plunger end of the syringe in your mouth until you acquire dexterity.

Before the catheter is introduced into the puppy, slightly depress the syringe plunger, forcing a small amount of formula out of the end. Carefully note the extreme force with which it is expelled through the small aperture. This may surprise you. It demonstrates that great care must be taken when feeding these most delicate of all newborns, to *very slowly depress the plunger* to avoid perforation of a fragile stomach wall.

Directly and gently introduce the tube through the *front* of the puppy's mouth. *Never* approach tube feeding at an angle. Pause for a moment when the catheter is inserted to a point just past the uvula (the pendent fleshy lobe in the middle of the posterior border of the soft palate). If at this point you encounter resistance to the tube's insertion, *stop. Never force a catheter down a puppy's throat!* If forced, the tube does not enter the esophagus (alimentary canal) leading to the stomach, but instead the trachea (windpipe) leading to the puppy's lungs, in which case the puppy drowns.

Do not be alarmed when the puppy first struggles at the catheter's introduction. Do not push against resistance if the catheter does not slip easily down the esophagus; it might be against the trachea. Don't panic. Withdraw the catheter and try again. Very gently apply a small amount of steady pressure to the catheter against the puppy's resistance; the puppy will reflexively swallow against the pressure. Suddenly you find passage has opened, and the tube slides down easily. The catheter is in position when the mark you made is just slightly beyond the tip of the puppy's muzzle. You are now ready to begin feeding.

Slowly depress the syringe plunger. The amount fed is determined by each puppy's capacity. *Never* feed a puppy until its abdomen is distended and hard. Nor have you fed enough if the puppy's abdomen remains flaccid. Ideally, the puppy's abdomen appears full and rounded, slightly turgid to your touch. Overfeeding the newborn can cause fatality. Feed only half the formula, then withdraw the tube to burp the puppy. Replace the syringe and catheter into the warm water, leaving the tube's tip exposed to prevent water from mixing with the formula while the puppy is being burped. It is hard to avoid getting air into a puppy's stomach when feeding by catheter. It is not an easy task to hold a squirming puppy by the head and the catheter firmly in one hand, while holding onto the syringe with your other hand. Until practice has allowed you some dexterity with this process, you may feel as though you need four hands to coordinate your efforts between tube, syringe and puppy. (See Burping.)

If you remain insecure with the prospect of gavage (tube feeding) and are still not positive the catheter is going into the puppy's stomach, try this check first with a few drops of water, previously boiled and cooled to warm. If the esophagus is missed and the catheter is introduced into the trachea, the puppy immediately and reflexively coughs. If the tube is properly situated, nothing happens and you can proceed with tube feeding as instructed.

Each breed and puppy has different required intake amounts. Initiate tube feeding by offering only a small amount of formula. Carefully watch and gently *feel* the swelling of the puppy's abdomen. If overfed, the puppy distresses immediately, indicating this condition by struggling or crying. Another contraindication is if the puppy regurgitates a portion of the feeding, or the abdomen exhibits signs of being distended. The puppy's abdomen should *never* feel hard, nor ever appear collapsed, tucked up, wrinkled or flaccid. If the latter occurs, you have not fed enough or possibly not often enough. The well-fed puppy has a slightly rotund appearance.

You must figure each puppy's individual feeding intake requirements by breed and weight. A puppy strictly fed by tube or bottle must ingest several proportionate ounces every few hours around the clock. Charts on premature and orphan formula cans offer feeding guidelines: your puppies may require slightly more or less than the suggested amounts. If a puppy's intake deviates more than just slightly from the suggested guideline's norm, consult with your veterinarian immediately.

ORPHANED INFANTS:
INTENSIVE, CRITICAL-CARE PUPPIES

Orphaned puppies can be successfully reared only if the breeder is totally dedicated to them on a 24-hour-a-day, 7-day-a-week basis for the first few weeks of their lives. Rearing orphaned puppies is the most challenging, taxing and heroically critical-care task any breeder could undertake. Not everyone is a hero.

The puppies must be maintained in an incubator environment with a temperature of at least initially 90 degrees Fahrenheit. After three or four successful days have passed and the puppies are stable, thrifty and robust, the temperature may be slowly declined by small increments. Between the fourth and eighth day the temperature can be reduced to 85 degrees (but no less during this period); after a week the temperatures may be slowly eased down to 80 degrees Fahrenheit. The support environment should be maintained at this level until the puppies are about three to four weeks of age. After four weeks the temperature may be reduced further, to about 75 degrees Fahrenheit.

Logic must prevail, the temperature is determined essentially by puppy responses and breed. Arctics, for example, thrive better after the first week or ten days on conservatively lower temperatures. It is to be remembered, however, that all orphaned puppies require at least initially a slightly warmer environment than nonorphaned puppies.

Because orphans have no dam to snuggle up against, deriving body warmth and just as importantly stimuli and tactile reinforcement, they become prime candidates for failure-to-thrive syndrome (FTT) when stimulation is not present. The newborn puppy continuously receives stimuli from the dam and siblings through positive tactile reinforcement. Under normal conditions the puppy is bumped and shoved, instinctively vying with littermates. This dam and sibling interactive stimulation insures that the puppy uses its body, pushing toward the dam's teats, pushing in rivalry against littermates. The puppy kneads as it nurses, further stimulating the dam's flow of milk; she vigorously washes her offspring, cleaning the puppy and bringing about the process of elimination.

Stimulation is crucial to the development of a strong healthy puppy to avoid FTT. The breeder is able to effect stimulation by gentle periodic stroking with one or two fingers, awakening the puppies directly prior to feeding. It is beneficial for these puppies to be snuggled and fondled over extended periods of time during feeding intervals. Stimulation of this nature offers puppies small measures as surrogate dam positive reinforcement.

ELIMINATION OF BODY WASTES

There is far more to caring for orphan and critical-care puppies than tube or bottle feeding alone. If for any reason the dam is physically incapable of caring for her offspring, it becomes critical for you to substitute her role. A dam's licking her offspring is a complicated innate response to motherhood. At birth, puppies are physically incomplete. Their sealed eyes are not well enough developed to greet light; their tear ducts are inoperable for approximately two weeks after whelping. Nor is their muscle development complete, being incapable of autonomous elimination. When the dam licks her offspring's genitalia, she stimulates an elimination response. Only by this means of stimulation is a puppy able to eliminate body waste. As a surrogate, the breeder must also stimulate puppies to elimination on the same regular basis as feeding intervals.

The most effective way to stimulate a puppy's response is with cotton batting. Lightly dampen a soft cotton ball in warm water and gently stroke the puppy's genitalia in an action reminiscent of the dam's tongue, in one direction only. Do not rub. The stroke used should be steady and moderate. If no response is immediately forthcoming, change direction and try again with short gentle strokes. If there is still no response, wait a few minutes before trying once more. The puppy must be stimulated to urinate and defecate at each feeding interval until able to independently perform these functions. Not every puppy will respond to stimulations before *and* after each feeding. One or the other may be enough, but both periods should be attempted for the puppy's comfort and health. While other materials may also be effective, newborn tissues are delicate, and repeated stroking for elimination, then wiping for cleaning, with anything but dampened cotton batting can cause a puppy to bleed. This site quickly becomes subject to infection. If elimination is incomplete or irregularly maintained, puppies become toxic and die.

Careful and exact attention to the details of each puppy's bodily functions must be scrupulously maintained in an organized manner. Keep a notepad and pen handy in the "nursery." *Any deviation* from the norm, quantity of formula ingested, urinary or excretory output, needs to be noted each time on the chart. These critical-care puppies also need to have their weight noted no less than three times daily indicating a steady growth average, insuring their continued optimum condition. Once the puppies approach ten days, and if vigorous, the weight may be checked twice daily. After the eyes open and they have sturdy mobility, their weight should be checked every few days. If a puppy's weight levels off or declines at any time, the veterinarian must be called immediately.

ORPHAN PUPPY DIET

One of the greatest problems faced by a breeder in rearing orphans is finding and maintaining the correct formula balance required by the breed, age and stage of development. Your veterinarian and other breeders experienced in this area will prove immeasurably helpful.

Many formulas are far from ideal because they are too low in fat and total caloric value, containing too much lactose and other sugars that cause diarrhea. As the result of an inadequate formula, puppies become underfed, rapidly dehydrating. Commercially premade liquid and powdered formulas are available. It is best and easiest to start these puppies on the liquid diet. These are good, however, as a formula base only when rearing orphan and other critical-care puppy infants.

When needed, puppy formula can be homemade or purchased. A supplemental feeding formula base such as Esbilac liquid or powder is readily obtained through your veterinarian and pet supplier. These "heat and eat" orphan formulas are marketed as complete. Some puppies do not fare well on these formulas alone, developing a negative reaction resulting in permanent blindness. Diluted, these specially prepared diets may be made safe for sensitive (and all) puppies. Sensitivity to these "complete" formulas remains, unfortunately, unknown until weeks have passed, when puppies open their eyes and gain visual acuity.

Formulas are made safe for all puppies with the addition of goat's milk and acidophilus: one-third prepared formula and one-third each goat's milk and acidophilus. Health food stores and major supermarket health food sections carry both of these latter items. To this formula base is added a few drops of Karo syrup (molasses or sorghum), a drop or two of liquid puppy vitamins, amoxicillin (under the veterinarian's direction when necessary) and a raw egg yolk (only *after* the puppies are a week old).

Never add an entire raw egg to a dog's diet no matter what age the pet may be. Raw eggs, while being very high in protein, also contain the enzyme avidin, which ties and destroys biotin, a vitamin necessary for normal body functions. Puppies fed entire raw eggs are prone to suffer poor growth rates. Older dogs will exhibit hair loss and poor skin quality.

Do *not* substitute honey, which even in the processed form can contain a bacteria lethal to newborns. Nor is cow's milk recommended because of high lactose concentration. In an emergency situation canned milk or the top portion (less than one-half) of *un*homogenized cow's milk may be used when carefully removed from an unshaken quart. Whatever you and your veterinarian decide is best to optimumly support your puppies, be certain the formula is heated to 100 degrees Fahrenheit before feeding.

While *bottle feeding is better for puppies through tactile reinforcement,*

105

COMPOSITION OF MATERNAL
MILK AND SUBSTITUTES

	Kcal Per ml	% Solids	Fat	Protein	Carbohydrate
Bitch milk	1.5	24.0	44.1	33.2	15.8
Esbilac powder*†	1.0	98.4	44.1	33.2	15.8
Esbilac liquid*	0.9	15.3	44.1	33.2	15.8
Cow milk	0.7	12.0	30.0	25.6	38.5
Evaporated milk‡	1.2	14.0	15.8	13.9	19.5

*Manufactured by Pet-Vet Products, Borden Chemical Company, Borden, Inc., Norfolk, Virginia 23501.

†1 volume to 3 volumes water.

‡4 volumes to 1 volumes water.

From Kirk, R. W., and Bistner, S. I.: *Handbook of Veterinary Procedures and Emergency Treatment*, 4th ed. Philadelphia: W. B. Saunders, 1985.

Nutrient	Per Lb	Per Kg	Nutrient	Per Lb	Per Kg
Protein (gm)	2.25	5.0	Vitamins		
Fat (gm)	0.70	1.5	Vitamin A (IU)	50	110
Linoleic acid (gm)	0.1	0.22	Vitamin D (IU)	5	11
Carbohydrate†	-	-	Vitamin E (μg)	0.55	1.2
			Thiamine (μg)	11.0	24
Minerals			Riboflavin (μg)	22.0	48
Calcium (mg)	120	265	Pyridoxine (μg)	11.0	24
Phosphorus (mg)	100	220	Pantothenic acid (μg)	100	220
Potassium (mg)	65	144	Niacin (μg)	114	250
Sodium chloride (mg)	91	200	Folic acid (μg)	1.8	4
Magnesium (mg)	6.4	14	Vitamin B_{12} (μg)	0.5	1.1
Iron (mg)	0.6	1.32	Biotin (μg)	1.0	2.2
Copper (mg)	0.07	0.16	Choline (mg)	11.8	26
Manganese (mg)	0.05	0.11			
Zinc (mg)	1.0	2.2			
Iodine (mg)	0.015	0.033			
Selenium (mg)	1.1	2.42			

* 1977 modification by Cornell Research Laboratory ...; data taken from NAS- NRC Publication No.8, Nutrient Requirements of Dogs, 1974.

**Carbohydrate as such has not been shown to be required. As a common ingredient of dog foods, it serves as an excellent source of energy and may be required for reproduction.

From Sheffy, B.E.: Nutrition and nutritional disorders. Vet. Clin. North Am. 8:10, 1978

From Kirk, R.W. (ed.): Current Veterinary Therapy X, Small Animal Practice. W.B. Saunders Co., 1989

premature and some orphaned puppies may not initially have a fully developed sucking reflex. These puppies must be nutritionally supported by tube and syringe until the instinctive reflex engages, usually taking only one or two days.

Orphan puppies whelped at their due time are initially fed (and genitals stimulated successfully) *every two hours around the clock*. This schedule is ideally maintained for the first two days. Feeding and genital stimulation can be stretched to every three hours around the clock on the third day, providing the puppies are normal, vigorous and gaining steadily. Preferably maintain the puppies on the three-hour schedule for two days, but no less than 24 hours. After this time and providing the puppies are developing well, gaining weight and not under stress, the time interval may then be stretched to every four hours around the clock. Continue the puppies on their four-hour schedule of feeding and elimination for their first two weeks of their lives. After ten days or two weeks (depending on the puppies' development), they can go for a *single* six-hour stretch between feedings *at night only*. By this time they also begin independent elimination. Absolute consistency coupled with optimum care is primary to being a successful surrogate mother.

The amount fed daily to each puppy is calculated by each puppy's current weight. A rule-of-thumb guideline is contained in the following chart. Always check with your veterinarian before establishing your puppies' dietary criteria.

Recommended Caloric Intake

Week	Cal/Lb/Day
1	60–69
2	70–79
3	80–89
Subsequently	90–100

Some professionals may advocate slightly higher caloric levels. It should be remembered that a high environmental temperature averaging 85 degrees Fahrenheit is being provided, and as a result, the puppies require fewer calories to maintain normal body temperatures. The very slightly reduced caloric intake also reduces risk of digestive upset.

Referring to the chart as a guideline, it is seen that a two-day-old puppy, weighing two thirds of a pound, requires (2/3 × 60) 40 calories per day at that weight. Figuring that the formula provides 1 calorie per gram, the amount needed is 40 grams, about one and a half ounces. As the puppy thrives gaining weight, the caloric intake is adjusted accordingly.

It is crucially important to the health of the puppies that all utensils be kept scrupulously clean. If they are not, a bacterial enteritis can result from unsanitary conditions, either in the food or the utensils. Dispose of all unused portions of formula or gruel. As a result, the formula should always be mixed in small batches, keeping unoffered portions well refrigerated, and only small amounts prepared for each feeding interval.

By the time orphan puppies are three weeks old they can be started on gruel from a shallow pan. At this time many breeders also teach the puppies to lap formula from a bowl. As an initial introduction to drinking, this is fine. The tactile reinforcement and nurturing offered through bottle nursing, coupled with consistent handling, is best continued for the puppies until normal weaning time. (See Chapter 13, Weaning the Puppies.)

BOTTLE FEEDING

"Orphan puppy" nursing bottles useful for Toys and other small breeds may be obtained through the veterinarian, pet supplier or wholesale catalog. Large-breed puppies nurse best on regular baby bottles and nipples. Purchasing several nipple styles proves helpful if you have never bottle-fed puppies. Today's competitive market demands a variety of products. Stay with the basics, keep your selection simple to best meet your purposes. Obtain a nipple shape close to that of your matron. Most puppies fare better on regular, rather than ''preemie'' nipples. Single, large, many-holed or cross-top nipples all prove helpful depending on the breed.

Puppies can get colicky like babies. Make certain never to allow a puppy to ingest air when either tube or bottle feeding. It is easy to avoid ingestion of air when bottle feeding by always turning the bottle, nipple end down, before offering it the puppy. All the air in the bottle rises to the solid end. You are able to tell if the puppy is nursing freely by watching the rise of bubbles in the bottle. The bubble flow should be rather rapid, small and uniform in size, rising in even response to the puppy's nursing. If the bubbles are large the puppy may also be ingesting air, in which case check the nipple cap.

Many hungry puppies suck so hard and steadily that they do not allow passage of air back into the bottle, thereby creating a vacuum. The vacuum collapses the nipple, making it harder and frustrating for a puppy to nurse. Occasionally remove the bottle from the puppy's mouth to allow a return passage

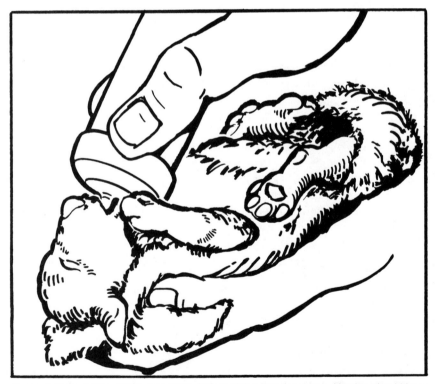

Always turn the bottle, nipple end down, before giving it to the puppy. Nursing should be a rewarding experience. *Artist: John Kirkpatrick*

108

of air back into the bottle, either through the nipple release when turning the bottle upright, or by momentarily loosening the cap. Never abruptly pull the bottle from a puppy's mouth. Placing a finger in the corner of the puppy's lip breaks the nursing vacuum, making removal easy. Remember to replace the cap securely before giving the bottle back to the puppy.

Always check the nipple's flow, making sure a puppy's suckling is rewarded by enough, yet not too much milk, before initiating feeding. Pinch the lower portion of the nipple, expressing a small amount of milk to check the flow. A puppy should be able to actively suckle without choking. If the rising bubbles are not uniform and are large, the cap is not secured tightly enough. The nipple's holes may also be too large, in which case the puppy draws milk too quickly and chokes. If the cap is set correctly then changing to a nipple with fewer holes becomes necessary. Nursing should always be a rewarding experience for the puppy. When flow is restricted so the puppy is incapable of obtaining milk quickly enough, the nursing experience becomes frustrating. The puppy is then ready to graduate to a nipple of increased flowing capacity such as one with multiple holes or cross-top.

Puppies do not take to a bottle as a duckling takes to water. No matter how hungry, some puppies instinctively resist anything unnatural such as a manufactured nipple. There is an art to starting the resistant puppy on bottle feeding. If the dam is available, rub the bottle and nipple and a towel over her mammaries. Drape this towel across your stomach and lap. Hold the puppy on your lap against your abdomen. Although the puppy's ears are sealed, it can feel the rhythm of your breathing and respond to your touch.

Express a small amount of formula from the bottle and wipe it over the nipple. As you introduce the bottle's nipple to the puppy's mouth, move your legs slightly, jiggling your lap. With tiny motions also jiggle the bottle up and down in the puppy's mouth. These movements re-create the dam's breathing and puppy's nursing position on the dam, causing the puppy to instinctively and reflexively latch onto the nipple. Acquiring dexterity with the bottle is always hardest with the first puppy. All you need is the patience of Job over the next few weeks!

Burping

Puppies, like infants, must be burped after each feeding, without fail. Each puppy is an individual and most require burping halfway through their bottle or tube feeding in order to finish the formula, or else the space is taken up by air. Some puppies greedily drain their bottle. Always make certain that you do *not* allow a puppy to suck the bottle dry. The ingestion of any air can cause a puppy to become colicky just as it can with a baby. Puppies at this age will not overfeed (unless they are starving) from one feeding to the next. If you have been staying on schedule, you can trust your puppy's responses, exactly how much (or little) it should take from the bottle.

If the puppy is very tiny you can burp it by making small spiraling, circular motions with your fingers from just above the puppy's hips, forward to its shoulders. You may have to repeat this action quite a few times before the puppy burps or quietly expels any excess air. Be quiet in order to listen for the puppy's tiny burp or quiet air expulsion. An alternative method to traditional burping is to "sit" the puppy in the palm of your hand and massage the abdomen gently, or even gently bounce the pup. When the puppy is older, bigger and more vigorous, it may be placed against the palm of your hand for burping, and eventually against your shoulder like a newborn human baby.

Always keep the puppy's head elevated as the catheter is withdrawn when gavage feeding. Always be very gentle. The premature puppy is very delicate with a newborn baby's fragile skin although it is covered with soft downy fur. Once the puppy has burped, resume feeding as before, taking care to allow formula to drip from the end of the catheter or nipple before reintroduction. Continue to feed the puppy by ratio of weight, or until the puppy's stomach shows that it is full. It takes surprisingly little to fill a premature (or on-time) newborn's belly. That will begin to change within a day or two as the puppy gains strength. Eventually the feeding intervals increase from hourly, to two, three, then four hours, with the puppy taking increased amounts at each feeding interval.

HELPING THE DAM'S MILK PRODUCTION

Some matrons are incapable of sustaining a sufficient or nutritionally adequate supply of milk to optimumly support their offspring. Milk production can often be augmented by supplementation with a bitch's milk replacement, mentioned earlier.

While the supplement may be offered shortly before the matron is due, it should be fed regularly throughout her lactation period. This milk helps matrons maintain their strength throughout parturition when offered between deliveries. Add Karo syrup and a raw egg yolk to each batch of milk replacement made. The raw yolk is high in a nutritional value dogs are able to digest and utilize: the albumen (white) when raw cancels the yolk's value. If you want to feed your dog an entire egg, hard-boil it.

Mix the milk according to directions on the label, adding the raw egg yolk and a teaspoon or tablespoon (depending on your breed size) of Karo syrup, molasses or sorghum. The sweetener helps support the matron's strength and electrolyte balance throughout whelping. While raw honey is excellent for instant energy and electrolytes, it can be dangerous to newborns and may contain bacteria lethal to newborns, bacteria that passes through the dam's digestive system to her milk and offspring.

NEWBORN PUPPY CHECKLIST

Head and neck: check mobility, rooting reflex and position at rest and during movement.

Skull: check size, shape and the fontanelle.

Ears: check size and position.

Eyes, eyelids: check for neonatal ophthalmia. Eyelids may open early: observe carefully for signs of inadequate tear (duct) production.

Nose: check nostrils' shape; presence of fluids (clear discharge, milk, mucus, blood, pus).

Mouth: check for cleft palate (puppies usually cannot nurse effectively and milk exudes from the nostrils and mouth, and the puppy cries plaintively). An undetected cleft palate will usually result in aspiration of milk or slow death by starvation. Check the color of mucous membranes; dehydration may be noted by a bright pink or red color; cyanosis (lack of oxygen) causes membranes, pads and toes to turn a bluish color. Check suckling reflex and for any bedding in the mouth that will interfere with nursing.

Skin: check for wounds caused by an overexcited dam; hydration, gently pinching the skin directly behind the occiput (the skin wrinkles when the puppy is dehydrated); the coat and weight for indications of a premature birth (incomplete hair cover); paws for bedding irritation or deformity.

Legs and joints: check for deformity, soft tissue and joint swelling indicative of injury; freedom of mobility range.

Tail: check for deformity, length and mobility.

Spine: check for deformity, body length appropriate to breed; watch for range of motion.

Abdomen: check the skin color, which should be pinkish. Pallor can be indicative of internal trauma or hemorrhaging; check umbilicus for signs of infection (swelling or discharge). The abdomen should be enlarged after nursing and while resting. A restive or crying puppy, or one with an enlarged abdomen and weakness, may be indicative of infection or swallowed air.

Chest: listen carefully for breathing difficulties; check nursing ability, muscle tone and activity level.

Rectum: check for redness, swelling, diarrhea (which could be signs of infection, overeating or environmental sensitivity). Observe the dam for signs of excessive attention.

Genitalia: check appearance and position; watch for inflammation from excessive maternal attention or inappropriate sibling nursing.

Profile view of a normal Malamute puppy.   *Canadian Veterinary Journal*

Profile view of a chondrodysplastic puppy.   *Canadian Veterinary Journal*

10

Medical Problems

THIS PORTION is not written as the definitive dictionary of all possible disorders and birth defects. The advent of multiple births can geometrically increase chances of anomalies. Some defects have been clearly proven to be hereditary, occurring more frequently in some breeds and lines than others.

Birth anomalies can be separated into three major categories: skeletal, soft tissue and organ. They include nervous systems disorders, coat and skin conditions and increased susceptibility through congenitally lowered resistance. Among *developmental* skeletal *disorders are* those which are *caused by nutritional factors* resulting from dietary inadequacy, assimilation problems, and those which are of inheritable origin. Not every line or every dog is subject to producing birth anomalies. It is possible that the careful breeder rarely encounters any major problems.

Chronic or genetic problems require diagnosis and supervision by a veterinarian for either long-term cure or short-term alleviation of symptoms. It is crucial that a proper evaluation and diagnosis of any condition be made as soon as possible, determining whether causal factors are environmental or genetic. While it is important to treat animals with genetically linked medical problems, improving their life quality, they should be removed from any potential breeding program.

Abdominal hernia is a protrusion of a portion of the abdominal contents through an opening in the abdominal wall. In certain cases the diaphragm may be herniated. The *predisposition* to inguinal or umbilical hernia is *inherited.* Affected animals should not be considered in breeding plans. Some hernias commonly arise from congenital defects of the inguinal ring or umbilicus. Increased abdominal pressure, blows with blunt instruments and severe exertion, as well as parturition, may lead to hernias.

Abdominothoracic fissure is an incomplete closure of the body cavity (abdomen and chest) that occurs during the early *developmental* stage, prior to birth. These puppies appear eviscerated from the moment of birth. When a dam licks, cleans and severs her puppy's umbilical cord, she may accidentally ingest the exposed internal organs. This act can, on occasion, lead to cannibalism.

Acromegaly is the defective or incomplete development of skeletal extremities (e.g., nose, jaws, toes), and is most often marked by progressive enlargement of these portions of the anatomy. This condition is most commonly found in St. Bernards, Rottweilers, Newfoundlands, Irish Wolfhounds, Great Danes and Bloodhounds.

Anconeal dysplasia, often mistakenly referred to as elbow dysplasia, is the *un*united anconeal process of three small bones in dogs' elbows that normally unite as puppies grow. The exact cause of this developmental abnormality is unknown. Clinical signs include a history of intermittent progressive lameness affecting one or both forelegs. The condition is neither necessarily continuous nor simultaneous. Lameness is usually exhibited following exercise. The elbow of an affected dog does not fully extend as the dog gaits. Usually some swelling is present in the area between the elbow and humerus. Crepitation is rarely palpable until arthritic changes occur in the joint or complete nonunion of the anconeal process is present. Diagnosis of this condition may be confirmed only by radiographs. Pain can be alleviated and gait improved by surgical removal of the anconeal process. Arthritic changes to the joint seldom occur after surgery. Corticosteroids are of little or no value without surgical correction.

Anoxia is the lack of oxygen in puppies that may be especially observed when a dam is obese beyond the normal boundaries of pregnancy. Obesity can cause a delayed and otherwise difficult delivery. Anoxia is, to some degree, a normal part of the birth process, between the placenta separating from the uterine wall and the puppy's first breaths. In difficult deliveries this time is often prolonged, causing stillbirths from the lack of oxygen. Also, resultant problems and irreversible changes associated with low oxygen during whelping can be convulsions and death within a few hours of birth.

Canine herpes, often referred to as *fading puppy syndrome*, affects puppies between one and three weeks of age. A formerly healthy puppy becomes acutely ill, crying and not nursing. The onset is sudden, fever may not always be present and death can occur within hours. Affected bitches may have nodules on the vagina, accompanied by inflammation. Recovering puppies remain carriers for months. Treatment is by supportive care.

Cardiac defects of a wide variety are prevalent among certain breeds. Causal cardiac factors can be hereditary, traumatic, toxic, and normal aging processes. The heart is a complex organ involving valves, arteries, veins, ventricles, sinuses, chambers and walls. Included in cardiac problems are abnormal sounds including murmurs, arrhythmias, fibrillation, flutter, rate disturbances (brachycardia and tachycardia) and congestive failure. Interatrial and interventricular septal defects are, however, among the most common congenital cardiac anomalies.

Central progressive retinal atrophy, often called **CPRA,** is a condition of central atrophy of the retina. The condition most often affects dogs between four and eight years of age. Affected dogs may exhibit difficulty in avoiding close obstacles while distant vision appears to be unimpaired. Affected dogs exhibit a slowed and incomplete pupillary light reaction by the time signs of reduced vision are noticed by an owner. Only qualified veterinary ophthalmologists should make the determination of this condition. Transmission of this condition is believed to be an autosomal recessive factor. As the result of inheritance, any dog with this condition should be withdrawn from a breeding program.

Chondrodysplasia, commonly known as "dwarfism," is found only in Alaskan Malamutes. The condition, except in more severely affected cases, may go unnoticed or be misdiagnosed as rickets. Severely affected dogs may exhibit a Bassett Hound–type of conformation. Not all such conformations are dwarfs. Such malformation may result from other reasons, generally of nutritional origin. The mode of inheritance is a simple recessive gene producing the condition.

Bilateral stunting of variable severity is exhibited by lateral deviation of the foot, carpal enlargement, bowing of the forelimbs caused by early closure of the epiphyseal plates and exhibition of a forward-sloping topline. Lameness is seldom exhibited in the mature animal, with exercise being self-limited by the degree of affectedness. Some chondrodysplastics closely resemble their normal counterparts. Determination of this condition by a qualified veterinarian is reliable between six and twelve weeks of age through radiology of one or both foreleg carpal areas. Radiographs are not definitive after this time, and diagnosis is made through specific blood tests. Affected and suspect dogs should not be bred outside the test-breeding program established by the Alaskan Malamute Club of America's Chondrodysplasia Study Program. Few animals are so severely affected that euthanization is required.

Chondrodystrophy, characterized by abnormal cartilage development, is found most often in Dachshunds, Bassett Hounds, French Bulldogs, Bulldogs, Pekingese and Clumber and Tibetan Spaniels.

Clefts—Lip clefts—of the upper jaw are among the most common congenital lip abnormalities. Lower lip clefts are rare. Commonly known as "harelip" (cheiloschisis), the condition is caused by failure of the processes making up the jaws and face during embryonic development. Aside from *nutritional deficiencies, imbalances and stress factors* during pregnancy of the matron, the defect is also believed to be *hereditary*. However, the exact mode of transmission is presently unknown.

Lip clefts are often associated with other serious birth anomalies such as cleft palates. If the defect is not overwhelming, surgical correction can be instrumented during the first few days of life. Because lip clefts create marked nursing difficulties the affected puppy must be hand-fed until correction is made. Successful surgical intervention does *not* render these puppies suitable for any

115

future breeding program. Those exhibiting gross defects should be euthanized quickly and humanely.

Clefts—Palate clefts (palatoschisis)—may involve solely the palate or, in more severe instances, may extend from the lip through to the hard and soft palates. Palate clefts of this nature are also often associated with other abnormalities. While heredity is believed to be the primary cause, faulty nutrition of the dam during pregnancy or other interference with fetal skeletal development have also been known to be factors.

Generally this type of cleft is not first obvious at birth unless a deliberate examination is made or until the puppy begins nursing. A nursing cleft palate puppy regurgitates milk through the nose. If not humanely euthanized, such puppies will die of starvation or a secondary infection. In some few cases surgical intervention may be successful. Normally, however, such strategies are not satisfactory and humane euthanization is advisable.

Coat defects are common to many breeds, and while not grave, they remain aberrations according to the individual breed Standards.

Colic, generally rare in nursing puppies, can also occur in young dogs. It is usually the result of a viral infection such as hepatitis or herpes virus infection, or another form of septicemia. Sudden dietary changes or ingestion of large amounts of indigestible material can also cause the condition's onset. Signs can be bloating and vomiting, fluid and fetid feces. Prompt veterinary attention will prevent advanced dehydration through measures of support therapy.

Colitis is a condition that has been ascribed to a variety of disorders including defective autoimmune mechanism. Signs of such abnormality may include repetitions of constipation followed by diarrhea. As the condition progresses, diarrhea becomes more frequent and resistant to treatment. The feces are marked as watery and foul-smelling. More advanced cases contain mucus, blood and pus. Diagnosed by the veterinarian, treatment is usually best effected by confining the animal to a warm, dry area and curtailing exercise. The diet should be changed to include a vitamin/mineral support and be of a low residue: e.g., lean meat, gelatin, cooked cereal, eggs and sugar. These meals should be fed in small amounts, in multiple feedings (four or five times) daily.

Coprophagy, the eating of feces, has been noted as a ''vice'' most often exhibited by puppies and adults that are confined to small (and often unclean) areas. The predilection toward coprophagy is especially noted among certain Sporting and Working breeds. The onset is often attributed to boredom. When one animal in a multiple dog environment acquires the habit, others may soon follow suit. Nutritional deficiencies have also been touted as partly responsible for coprophagic behaviors. A change of diet and/or environment is indicated when such behavior occurs. Refer to a successful breeder and/or veterinarian. Runs at 90-degree angles to others encourage exercise and relief of boredom. Frequent removal of feces and daily thorough cleaning can also successfully arrest this behavior.

Deafness is usually the result of disease or aging in the dog. Total or partial hearing loss may also be the result of a defect in the external, middle or inner

116

ear portions or of the nerve supply. Total deafness is sometimes seen in *all-white dogs*, specifically those breeds where white alone is a breed Standard disqualification. Deafness has been severe among Dalmations. It is strongly urged that all Dalmatian puppies be thoroughly hearing-tested by a qualified technician before being placed in a home.

Deafness can range from minor to complete impairment. Some affected animals appear to lack intelligence, being unresponsive to commands. They may make nuisances of themselves through constant barking. Many affected dogs develop acuteness of other senses. While careful breeding has already eliminated deafness from certain breeds such as the Bull Terrier, individually affected animals must be withdrawn from a breeding program.

Diabetes in dogs is divided into two main categories, obese and nonobese, and is comparable to juvenile-onset diabetes in humans. The condition usually develops in the middle-aged animal. An owner may first note this condition when the dog eats well but steadily loses weight. The dog exhibits increased thirst and urinates frequently. Diabetes can cause secondary problems in dogs also. One effect is dogs of this condition are prone to developing cataracts. A complete physical by the veterinarian will reveal the presence of diabetes in the suspect animal. Treatment is daily doses of insulin and dietary control. Dogs of any breed may develop diabetes. There is a stronger prevalence of this condition among Poodles, Miniature Schnauzers and all Dachshund varieties.

Epilepsy is a functional disorder of the brain characterized by symptoms related to the nervous system (which remains structurally unaltered). Convulsions, hysteria, aggression and other unusual behavior patterns can also occur as a result of parasites or toxic chemical exposure, as well as *hereditary factors*. Clinical signs of a *petit mal* type seizure are manifested by the dog convulsing for approximately two minutes, with or without loss of consciousness. Seizures occur at decreasing intervals and will be of increased duration. Recurrent episodes often increase in frequency with advancing age. Normally the dog appears restless shortly prior to a seizure. If the seizure is *grand mal* (accompanied by unconsciousness), the dog may appear drowsy and disoriented for minutes after an attack. Dogs suffering either form of epileptic seizures are tired subsequent to an attack and require a quiet place to rest. A convulsing dog will not encounter injury during a seizure when in a "protected area": away from walls, furniture or other solid objects. Nor will a dog injure a person if left unrestrained during this period.

Medication has proven helpful in the control of seizures especially when dispensed during stressful periods (such as thunderstorms). The veterinarian should be notified of each seizure to help establish the proper level of medication. Some owners are able to prevent seizures through a heightened awareness of their pet. By recognizing prodromal behaviors, they can administer the anticonvulsant medication in a timely manner.

No dog exhibiting epilepsy should be included in a breeding program. Owners of related animals should be notified so they may become aware of their pet's possible predisposition to this disease.

Gastric dilatation and **Gastric torsion complex** is a condition that may occur in any breed, at any age. Commonly known as **bloat**, this syndrome is most often encountered among large and deep-chested breeds. The complex results from the dog's inability to pass food (or other ingesta) through the stomach into the lower intestines, or lack of capacity for emesis (vomiting) if torsion has occurred. Initial clinical signs of gastric torsion can occur suddenly, normally a few hours after a meal. The dog may become restless, excessively salivate and have unproductive attempts at vomiting. As the abdomen distends, pain manifests. Reluctant to move, the dog may also refuse to lie down. As the case advances in severity, the onset of shock becomes evident with pale mucous membranes, a rapid heartbeat (tachycardia) and a weakened pulse. A dog with this condition is headed toward a rapid and painful death. This is a true veterinary emergency.

Dogs that have survived are prone to recurrence. Studies of gas present in afflicted dogs' stomachs indicate a primary cause to be accumulated swallowed air. Gulping eager eaters appear to swallow more air than finicky, picky eaters. Exercise shortly after eating has also been associated with gastric torsion. Other factors that may produce gastric torsion can be general anesthesia, abdominal surgery, traumatic injury, spinal injury, overeating, ingestion of foreign materials, whelping, vomiting and malignant tumors.

Recurrence of the torsion complex because of dietary indiscretion is inevitable unless faulty feeding practices are amended. The dog should be fed light brothy meals three to five times daily for approximately three days before establishing a more normal diet. Relatively soft foods should be offered no less than three times daily over the following few days. When "normal" feeding resumes, the dog should be fed at least twice daily, and in small quantities each time. Raising the food dish on a platform to a level of the lower chest is also recommended, helping to reduce air intake during feeding.

There are a few points that bear emphasis with gastric torsion. The time factor in discovery and treatment by a veterinarian is critical because the dog's total collapse is imminent with this condition. An *immediate* diagnosis by a veterinarian is imperative to effect initiation of *rapid treatment* for survival. Delays in presentation, diagnosis and treatment must be avoided or the condition will prove fatal.

Once successfully treated, dogs can continue to lead normal healthy and productive lives providing daily concessions are made. Animals suffering an occurrence of this complex must lead as stress-free lives as possible. They should be fed several times daily throughout their lives. They should not be fed dry food alone: any kibble must be fed "wet." Dry food that does not swell once water and meat are added to it is recommended. Certain dogs may, however, require a special diet that is available only through the veterinarian.

Gastrointestinal defects usually lead to a delay in the passage of food, resulting in regurgitation and often pneumonia from inhalation of some food. The problems are usually caused either by a band across the esophagus and stomach that does not open properly, delaying passage of food into the stomach; an esophagus that cannot contract properly to force food into the stomach or an overactive pyloric valve through which the stomach contents pass into the duodenum, not allowing food out of the stomach into the lower intestines.

Hemeralopia, commonly known as "day blindness," is a nonprogressive genetically inherited condition that may be detected as early as seven weeks in puppies. Known as "night dogs," these dogs give evidence of better vision under low-light conditions. Indoors or during dim exterior lighting conditions such as an overcast day, the vision appears normal. Under normal daylight, however, these dogs tend to be uncertain of distances, bumping into objects. Protected dogs who have learned the hazardous positions of fences, trees and furniture can lead restricted but content lives. A strange environment can bring grief to a dog suffering hemeralopia. Suspect dogs should be checked by a veterinary ophthalmologist. *Those suffering from the condition should be withdrawn from a breeding program.* If the affected dogs have already been bred, owners of all offspring should be notified in order that their animals be checked for the presence of this condition. Owners of other closely related animals would also benefit from the courtesy of notification.

Hemolytic disease can occur if a blood transfusion is indiscriminately given to a bitch used for breeding. Blood administered to brood matrons must be cross-matched or, at the very least, *A-negative type.* Hemolytic anemia has been found in A-positive puppies born to A-negative dams that had been immunized by prior transfusions of A-positive blood. Failure of a veterinarian to take precautionary measures of cross-matching when giving breeding bitches transfusions may result in the loss of the puppies.

Puppies acquire all their A-antibodies from milk ingested during the first day of life. *Antibodies do not cross the placental barrier.* Puppies fed formula the first day to day and a half may be returned to the affected dams, because antibodies cannot be absorbed through the bitches' milk after the first 24 hours. Severely affected puppies nurse poorly. They become extremely pale within a day or two of birth. Almost all deaths that occur do so within the first 72 hours. If an affected puppy survives more than 72 hours, the prognosis improves significantly. While spontaneous recovery can occur, it is unusual. Affected puppies may be successfully treated if seen by the veterinarian as soon as indicative warning signs occur.

Hemophilia is commonly known as the "bleeder's disease," resulting from the tendency to bleed following comparatively insignificant trauma. Coagulation time is markedly increased in affected animals. (Normal newborn puppies have low-level coagulation factors.)

The clinical, hematologic and hereditary aspects of hemophilia in dogs is identical to those occurring in mankind. Various types (hemophilia A and B) are inherited sex-linked recessive traits, carried by the dam and manifested in the male offspring. Other forms of hemophilia are autosomal. Dogs that exhibit even the slightest signs of prolonged bleeding following trauma should be checked for hemophilia by a veterinarian. Known dogs and carriers (the dams) should be withdrawn from a breeding program. Owners of all offspring require notification for veterinary evaluation.

Hermaphroditism is relatively uncommon and is characterized by the presence of both sex organs within a single animal. A pseudohermaphrodite, however, possesses the gonads of one sex while the external genitalia and sexual characteristics belong to the opposite sex.

Hip dysplasia, while known to be a largely hereditary condition, may also be traumatically induced. The condition occurs when the acetabulum (hip joint socket) is too shallow to maintain stability of the joint during movement. Upon radiologic examination the femoral head may prove to have abnormal flattening in all but the most mild of cases. The neck of the head of the femur may exhibit a thickening. Arthritic changes occur in time. In more severe cases, arthritic changes may occur early in the dog's life.

Traumatically induced hip dysplasia may be present in either a unilateral or bilateral condition. There can be a wide variety of causal factors: a severe blow to a dog's rear, a lighter blow to a small dog or puppy (such as being dropped or hit by a newspaper) or raising puppies on a slick surface. *Dogs possessing the condition should be withdrawn from any breeding program.*

Controlled breeding programs and sound environments for puppies offer the only means by which occurrence of hip dysplasia may be reduced. Corticosteroids and salicylates provide a measure of relief for severely arthritic animals. New surgical advances are continually being made to alleviate the pain of this condition in severely affected animals.

Hock joint instability is most often found in those dogs lacking a proper degree of rear angulation. These dogs generally appear to have "straight" hindlegs when viewed from the side, lacking adequate development of the stifle, the lower portion of the thigh. When gently palpated, such hocks move forward in a double-jointed action. In cases of severe hock laxity (compensation for underdeveloped stifles), such animals should be withdrawn from any potential breeding program.

Hydrocephalus, known as "water on the brain," is moderately common to dogs, occurring spontaneously or by inheritance. Surgical relief for this condition involves implantation of a one-way valve and shunt from the brain, allowing excess cranial fluid to safely drain into the bloodstream. Dogs of this condition should not be bred.

Hyperthyroidism is the condition of excessive thyroid hormone secretion. Early indications can be weight loss accompanied by increased appetite. Restlessness and nervousness accompany increased heart and respiratory rates in conjunction with the elevated metabolic rate. After the dog is tested by the veterinarian for the condition, proper dosage levels of the correct medication can be made.

Hypertrophic osteodystrophy is the name given to a skeletal disease of young, growing dogs. Although puppies of the larger breeds are more prone to this condition, it may be found (but more rarely) among puppies of Standard and Toy varieties, that is, above or below a median size. The condition usually affects puppies between four and eight months of age. Swelling is obvious and readily observed at the distal portions of the ulna and radius at the pasterns on the forelegs. These swollen areas are warm to the touch and sensitive, causing playing or walking to be painful. As a result, these puppies are usually inactive,

120

preferring to lie quietly much of the time. Intermittent fevers can occur and may reach as high as 106 degrees Fahrenheit.

Some affected puppies have been fed an overabundance of vitamins and minerals. Treatment of the condition is ineffective once it occurs, but ameliorative therapy measures of aspirin and corticosteroids appear to effectively alleviate pain and fever. Ascorbic acid has been proven effective in returning blood levels to a normal range. Spontaneous improvement generally occurs when growth ceases. Once incurred, permanent deformity is usually (but not always) present.

Hypoglycemia (low blood sugar) is common in small breed neonatals. Acute stress and/or enzyme and hormonal systems that are inadequately developed at birth can be causes. Symptoms can include muscle weakness, twitching, depression and eventual collapse. Immediate veterinary attention is required. Emergency at-home treatment until the puppy can be rushed to the vet is ideally corn syrup (or as a last resort, well-refined honey), which is absorbed quickly through the oral mucosa.

Hypothyroidism is manifested by a low metabolic rate in addition to other clinical signs that can be determined only by a veterinarian. Dogs with this condition may exhibit sluggishness and are comparatively "easy keepers," requiring substantially small amounts of food relative to their size. Some clinical manifestations are more apparent than others, often occurring among older dogs. Varying in intensity with individuals, signs include but are not limited to inactivity, obesity, sparse coat and patchy hair loss. Diagnosis of hypothyroidism is made through a blood sample. Treatment is effective through replacement thyroid therapy in all but the severest cases where irreversible changes have occurred. Any dog with abnormal mating, heat or gestation should be checked for low thyroid.

Intussusception is the "telescoping" of an intestinal portion into the adjacent portion caused by irregular or excessive peristaltic movements. Intestinal parasites, enteritis, dietary indiscretions or errors and bowel tumors are some of the possible etiologies of this condition. The onset of this condition may be moderately slow and can include a depressed appetite and vomiting. Straining to defecate may be exhibited, not necessarily with evidence of pain. The stool is usually fetid, dark (or hemorrhagic), semifluid and mucoid in appearance. Early diagnosis by the veterinarian is critical to save the animal before it becomes so weakened that it cannot withstand the required life-saving surgical procedure.

Megaesophagus is most commonly seen in weaning puppies. Persistent vomiting without straining or retching of undigested food and saliva is noted with the introduction of solid foods. The interval between eating and vomiting varies with individuals and by activity. The dilated (enlarged) esophagus containing gas is determined by radiographic (enhanced by a dose of barium) or endoscopic examination. Discovery of this condition must be made before the animal becomes weakened through inadequate nutritional support.

Only rarely does a spontaneous recovery occur. Some dogs may be saved by surgery. Cases lacking severity may survive on a liquid or soft foods diet, well balanced and fortified with vitamins. Feeding should be from an elevated location, such as from a platform, chair or stool, or hand-feeding throughout the animals' lives. Elevated feeding assists swallowing in less severely affected cases. These animals must not be engaged in a breeding program.

Nervous system disorders can include a variety of problems including epilepsy and temperament types such as "sudden rage syndrome," which are known to be hereditary. *These dogs are not breeding program candidates.*

Nutritional anemia can cause the deaths of some or all of the puppies in a litter. Affected puppies usually weaken slowly, and die quietly at about ten to thirteen days of age. An external sign that a breeder may note would be pale mucous membranes. Pale mucous membranes are also indicative of other serious afflictions requiring immediate veterinary support therapy. Nutritional anemia can be prevented by feeding the pregnant bitch an optimum diet throughout her term, including adequate amounts of liver and iron.

Ophthalmis neonatorum is an acute pussy eyelid infection not uncommon to newborn puppies. Bacterial infection causes the eyelids to swell markedly. The eyelids must be treated and bathed regularly with an antibiotic ointment prescribed by the veterinarian.

Osteochondritis occurs in the developing skeleton and is most often found in rapidly growing large and giant breeds. Trauma, lack of adequate vitamins and minerals, hormonal imbalance, metabolic disease and lowered oxygen tension are some causes. The first sign of osteochondritis is normally a unilateral lameness accompanied by pain upon palpation of the affected area. Muscular atrophy may or may not be present. A history of trauma is not necessary. This condition is principally a noninfectious disease of the young when approximately 75 percent of the growth has been completed, usually appearing at between three and ten months of age. The onset is often slow with a period of time elapsing between signs. Very mild cases may pass relatively unnoticed. However, any time persistent or recurring lameness occurs, the pet should be seen by a veterinarian.

Osteochondritis dessecans usually occurs as the result of trauma and is seen most often in giant breeds, and more frequently among males. A piece of articular cartilage and attached piece of bone become detached to lie loosely within the adjacent joint space. The problem is self-limiting and treatment normally consists of rest and prevention of weight-bearing on the affected limb. Surgery is usually advised with most animals regaining satisfactory limb use by maturity. Some, however, are affected by the onset of osteoarthritis as the result of the trauma. Except for those cases of clear trauma causing this condition, affected animals should be withheld from any breeding program as the predisposition to the condition may be hereditary.

Patellar luxation can result from poor muscle tone or abnormal muscle distribution caused by improper tendon placement, or can be traumatically induced. Smaller breeds are more frequently affected than are larger breeds. Recurrent luxations are characterized by intermittent lameness. Pain is usually absent and the dog may be freely palpated. An affected leg may have a "pigeon-toed" appearance. Persistent luxations cause continuous lameness or abnormal gaits.

122

Lateral luxation is uncommon and usually the result of severe trauma. Bilateral luxation is evidenced by walking with a hopping movement and standing difficulty. Determination of this condition should be made by a veterinarian. Surgery is frequently required. The activities of affected animals should be restricted following surgery to prevent recurrence. *If a hereditary relationship can be determined, affected animals should not be used for breeding.*

Patent ductus arteriosus is a relatively common cardiac anomaly that can be usually diagnosed when a suspect puppy is 12 to 16 weeks old. If one puppy is affected, usually others in the litter are affected as well. Affected puppies exhibit signs of tiring easily, difficulty breathing (dyspnea) and lack of oxygen (cyanosis). Radiological examination exhibits an enlarged and rounded heart and a continuous murmur is noted as present. Surgical correction is possible, but it is expensive.

Persistent right aortic arch is not an uncommon occurrence, especially in Bostons and German Shepherds. Clinical signs usually first appear between four to six weeks of age, when semisolid or solid foods are first introduced to the puppies' diets. A fibrous and vascular band constricts the esophagus at the heart's level. While liquids can pass through the esophagus's constricted area, solid foods are stopped before the stricture site. This area becomes dilated as the result of food buildup. Puppies with this condition vomit persistently when fed anything other than liquids, becoming rapidly thin and weak. Solid food is promptly regurgitated without undue retching, and may have a strong foul odor or be fermented. Surgical correction is possible when performed before the esophagus becomes greatly distended from accumulation of solid foods and atonic (loss of muscle tone).

Progressive retinal atrophy is a progressive hereditary condition resulting in blindness. Known as **PRA**, the eyes of the animals are often smaller in size than others of the same breed, age and litter. Most affected dogs first exhibit clinical signs by four or five *years* of age, although younger animals may also demonstrate signs. Owners of affected animals usually report that their dogs initially exhibit reduced night vision followed by a gradual loss of day vision. When examined, the pupillary response to light is sluggish in the early stages, becoming incomplete or absent with the disease's progression. At the ultimate stage, the pupil remains widely dilated and fails to react to strong artificial illumination. Cataracts are common in generalized retinal atrophy. Transmission of this condition is believed to be by an autosomal recessive factor. *As a result, dogs exhibiting clinical manifestations of this hereditary problem must not be used in a breeding program.* Determination of this condition should always be made by a qualified veterinary ophthalmologist.

Prolapsed rectum can occur in a puppy straining to defecate, one suffering diarrhea or, less commonly, constipation. Straining by the puppy during bowel elimination causes the anal canal's lining to extrude beyond the rectal boundaries. The problem requires immediate treatment.

Place a clean, moistly cold soft cloth gently against the extruding tissue. Elevate the puppy's rear carefully and gently push the extrusion back inside the rectum. It is important to keep the delicate anal tissue moist with the application of a small amount of petroleum or K-Y jelly to prevent dryness and infection. Trim coat growth carefully from around the immediate area. Notify the veterinarian of the puppy's condition and stool type. If the prolapse recurs minor surgery may be indicated.

Pyloric stenosis is a narrowing of the distal aperture of the stomach, through which the stomach contents pass into the duodenum. Discovered early enough, the condition may be successfully treated by surgical intervention.

Rickets is a condition demonstrated by puppies having crooked legs, splayed feet, weak spines and an unthrifty, thin appearance; not to be confused with dwarfism. Diagnosis (of either condition) is made through radiographs of the distal ends of the long bones (ulna and radius). High doses of vitamin D and calcium-phosphorous supplements will normally effect a positive, prompt response. If treatment is delayed, permanent deformity can result. Dwarfism found in some breeds is inherited, and will not respond to any form of therapy.

Seborrhea is a miserably uncomfortable skin defect that can be costly to the owner during the pet's treatments. Progression of this affliction can prove fatal as the result of secondary infections if the primary cause is left medically untreated.

Skull defects range from an improper skull shape according to a breed Standard, to a serious impairment. Deviations from normal skull development can mask other serious problems. Always consult with the veterinarian if presented with any skull defect including the presence of under- or overshot jaws, missing or supernumerary teeth.

One serious example of a skull defect is the condition in which the fontanel (soft boneless area in the center of the skull that all newborns have) does not close properly. This condition may be noted by the palpation of a "soft area" through which living tissue can be felt. The site can range in size from a mere dot to a more severely involved area. This defect can eventually result in hydrocephalus.

Spina bifida (one of five forms) is a developmental anomaly characterized by a defect in the bony encasement of the spinal cord.

Stockard's syndrome is a form of paraplegia most often found in Great Danes, St. Bernards, Bloodhounds and even dogs of indeterminate origin. The onset occurs between eight and sixteen weeks of age and is caused by a triple set of dominant factors. Some affected individuals eventually learn to walk, supporting themselves weavingly over their forequarters. Atrophy of the rear is evident and the peculiar shuffling gait of this syndrome is permanent. There is no treatment for this condition, the cause of which is a progressive degeneration of the motor neurons in the lumbar portion of the spinal cord.

Swimmers are more common among the heavy-bodied breeds, being those puppies incapable of collecting their limbs beneath themselves to crawl efficiently. Another cause of this condition can be weak leg muscles unable to support the weight of the large-bodied puppy. Usually swimmers are found in whelping boxes with slippery or otherwise insecure footing. The rib cage and sternum (breastbone) are often flattened, giving the puppy a "turtle-like" appearance. An untreated puppy will continue to progress only to a certain point; eventually the lung capacity is diminished and death results.

Almost all swimmer puppies can be effectively redeemed with "hobbles." Usually hobbling the rear legs is sufficient if initiated within a few days of the condition's onset. Rarely will the forelegs require hobbling. The rear legs propel, the forelegs pull. Usually as the rear strengthens the forequarters develop concomitantly. Hobbles may be constructed by placing adhesive tape immediately below each hock. Care must be taken not to wrap the leg too tightly, impeding the blood supply. Leave a tab on each leg. Hold the puppy so the legs dangle in a natural position. Then place a connecting bar of tape between the legs. Severely affected puppies may require initial treatment with a longer, less desirable band. After two days the connecting band may be replaced with one slightly shorter. By the fourth day or week's end, the swimmer puppy's locomotor development should be close to or the same as that of the siblings. Never hesitate to consult a veterinarian.

Toxic milk syndrome causes puppies to suffer bloating, cry, have greenish diarrhea and swollen, distended red anuses. This condition indicates an incompatibility with the dam's milk. The bitch must be immediately treated by a veterinarian with hormones and antibiotics while the puppies remain at home receiving supportive care of an orphan formula.

Umbilical hernia is the presence of a protruding naval. This can be congenital or traumatically caused by too much strain on the abdomen. While common to certain breeds, it can occur in any litter. Often the condition is caused simply by delayed closure of the umbilical ring. The condition should, nevertheless, be noted by the veterinarian and, when severe, corrected by surgery.

Von Willebrand's disease (canine) is a group of related bleeding disorders caused by a specific protein deficiency. It is believed that the most common forms of the disease are mild, remaining subclinical. Certain mild forms and moderate to severe forms can contribute to life-threatening or fatal hemorrhage. Inflammatory diseases and certain physiological stresses such as parturition produce marked increases in Von Willebrand factors. Determination of VWD is made by a veterinarian. At the present time there is no cure for this disease, but affected animals should be eliminated as breeding prospects.

BREEDS KNOWN TO BE SUBJECT TO VON WILLEBRAND'S DISEASE

Afghan Hound	Bichon Frise
Airedale Terrier	Boxer
Akita	Cairn Terrier
Alaskan Malamute	Chesapeake Bay Retriever
American Cocker Spaniel	Collie, Rough and Smooth
Basset Hound	Dachshund, all varieties
Bearded Collie	Doberman Pinscher
Bernese Mountain Dog	English Cocker Spaniel

English Setter
English Springer Spaniel
Fox Terrier, Smooth
Fox Terrier, Wire
German Shepherd Dog
German Shorthaired Pointer
Golden Retriever
Great Dane
Great Pyrenees
Greyhound
Irish Setter
Irish Wolfhound
Italian Greyhound
Keeshond
Kerry Blue Terrier
Kuvasz
Labrador Retriever
Lakeland Terrier

Lhasa Apso
Manchester Terrier, Standard
  & Toy
Miniature Schnauzer
Papillon
Poodle, Miniature
Poodles
Rottweiler
Samoyed
Scottish Terrier
Shetland Sheepdog
Shih Tzu
Siberian Husky
Soft-coated Wheaten Terrier
Tibetan Terrier
Viszla
Welsh Corgi, Pembroke
Whippet
Yorkshire Terrier

Water puppies or **Walrus puppies** is a condition occurring infrequently in a variety of breeds, and occurs in certain family lines and breeds more than others. The presence is noted directly at whelping, the appearance being that of marked tissue engorgement throughout a puppy's body, although the paws usually appear normal. The body of such a puppy feels "spongy," resulting from massive water retention. The condition's onset is seen shortly prior to whelping, and because of the massive engorgement that generally increases a puppy's size threefold, it is usually impossible for the dam to successfully deliver unassisted by surgery. A dam known to produce this condition may at times be treated with a safe diuretic by the veterinarian shortly prior to her due date. A breeder can assist in prevention by decreasing (but not stopping altogether) salt intake of the matron near the end of her term. Although usually fatal, some water puppies may be saved by direct tissue massage and prompt veterinary evaluation.

Wobbler syndrome (cervical spondylopathy) is a hereditary condition that appears to be a failure of proper support around the vertebrae. Large breeds such as the Doberman Pinscher and Great Dane are afflicted, although it can be found in smaller breeds such as the Basset Hound.

Wobbler can be a fatally progressive condition affecting the spinal cord, particularly in the cervical area. An afflicted dog's head may shake with palsy, and its movement is a swaying or wobbling motion of the hindlegs. The rear legs are very weak, supporting the dog minimally at best, and eventually not at all. Wobbler is frequently accompanied by considerable pain. Signs of this condition also include progressive lack of coordination in the hindquarters. Usually, but not always, the forelimbs move normally. In the more advanced stages, the animal suffers in both the front and rear quarters. The onset generally occurs between three and twelve months, but may occur later, and has been found on rare occasion in an animal as old as two years. Wobbler can occur suddenly, with the dog becoming quadriplegic within twelve hours of the onset.

While the exact etiology is unknown, it has been suggested that the deformity and secondary displacement of the vertebrae are caused by a long neck and rapid growth. *Over*nutrition, especially from foods very high in protein, calcium and phosphorus, trauma and heredity are also believed to be influencing factors. Skilled veterinarians are able to distinguish this anomaly from other skeletal diseases by radiology. Acute cases respond best to surgery. General treatment is limited, but may respond positively to strict confinement, anti-inflammatory medications and, when appropriate, a neck brace, if tolerated by the dog.

Prognosis after surgery can be favorable, to guarded, to unfavorable, depending upon the dog's condition at the time of diagnosis, if only one or more lesions are noted for surgery and if the dog was ambulatory at the time of presentation. *Any dog diagnosed with Wobbler syndrome should be immediately withdrawn from any breeding program* and owners of related dogs notified of this condition.

Always carefully check puppies' eyes when they first open to make certain that the tear ducts are functioning properly, washing the eyes and keeping them moist. This single puppy litter is tactily reinforced with a stuffed toy. *Alaskan Malamute: Susie Richardson*

11

Postpartum Care

YOU and your brood matron have been through a physically and emotionally exhausting period. Before taking your well-deserved rest, be certain the dam and puppies are comfortable, each puppy has nursed well, the heat lamp is not too close, and the heating pad is not turned up too high. Proper environmental temperature is crucial to puppies' well-being. Large litters can pose particular problems when all the puppies may not be able to snuggle close to their dam at the same time. Because newborns are incapable of controlling their own body temperatures, chilling to any degree leaves them susceptible to infectious disease. Except for certain arctics, puppies' room temperature should be maintained at about 85 degrees Fahrenheit for at least their first few days.

Initially offer your bitch lean food such as meat alone, vitamins, di-calcium phosphate and possibly bitch's milk replacement. Many matrons are more exhausted than hungry at this time. Do not worry if she refuses one or two feedings during her first 24 hours of motherhood. Do not expect a bitch to leave her puppies to eat. Hold the food, milk and water dishes for her during her first few feedings. Place a fresh bowl of water next to the whelping box before you nap.

Ingestion of the placenta may cause diarrhea and bowel control problems during the first two or three days. The bitch's bladder can also fill during whelping if she drinks of the milk supplement you offered. Even the best house-trained dog can run into trouble at this time. One manner of preventing serious cleanup problems from arising is to place four interlocking layers of opened newspaper on the floor over heavy plastic film such as that used by painters. Unless you have tile floors, your matron and puppies are on a porous surface. Even the best linoleum brands seep a certain amount of moisture unless dried immediately.

Plastic sheeting covered by newspaper saves all flooring, is nonporous, makes any cleanup easy and is inexpensive to purchase through any hardware, painting or building outlet.

It is not necessary to discard plastic sheeting after each use. Clean it with a solution of water and disinfectant. The disinfectant should not be so strong of odor that it is overpowering, is offensive to the dam or interferes with the puppies' scenting their dam and siblings. Use the same solution to wipe the whelping box down daily. Dilute the solution until you are barely able to discern a scent. Remember dogs' scenting ability is 600 times greater than that of humans.

Do not sleep in your own bed for at least the first three or four days after the litter's birth. Keep all doors open between you and the new litter if you have not placed a cot near the whelping box. If a puppy encounters trouble, you must be able to hear any muffled cries and go to the rescue. Should you sleep too comfortably in a familiar bed, you may sleep too deeply and not hear the puppy's cries for help. Some new dams are easily confused by puppy distress cries and may whine but not respond appropriately. Dams have too often needlessly crushed or smothered puppies inadvertently. Sleep with "one ear open" during the puppies' first week, or preferably, until their eyes begin to open.

Many matrons refuse mixed food (meat and dry) the first few days following a whelping. Offer your matron meat only the first two days following parturition. By this time her appetite will have increased because of the puppies' nutritional demands upon her. If, however, your matron refuses all food and milk replacements for more than six hours following whelping, call your veterinarian. Refusal of food and reticence of drinking is a clear sign of trouble. If your matron is drinking water and the milk supplement regularly, her eliminations and temperature are normal, her tongue and gum color are good, she may safely refuse solid food for a day. It is normal for a matron to eat sparingly during the first 24 hours. The incentive of bribery by meat alone, such as a small amount of raw liver, chicken and broth, is wise, helping the bitch maintain strength and meet the increasing demands of milk production. A little kibble can usually be added to the meat by the third day, and thereafter increased daily by small amounts until double or triple her normal ration, as she demands.

The dam should be seen by a veterinarian for a postpartum examination within 24 hours of whelping. This examination is extremely important for the health and safety of the dam and puppies. Many a uterus remains distended and flabby for several hours following whelping. It is not uncommon for a dam to retain one or more placentas, large amounts of blood and other body fluids in the uterus. It is also possible that she retained one or two puppies. Unless all of these are expelled immediately, retention will predispose the dam to infection. As a result, many veterinarians are strong advocates of giving the oxytocin shot in addition to palpating the dam and examining the puppies within the first 24 hours of whelping. The oxytocin injection causes deep uterine contractions and stimulates the bitch to let down her milk and discharge any retained fluids, placental material and puppies. Should a dam retain fluids, placental material or a dead puppy, she could become toxic and die.

MAMMARY GLAND CARE

Examine your brood matron's mammary glands daily, directly prior to whelping, and throughout lactating and weaning periods. You may notice a secretion of a moderately thick liquid appearing clear or brown with streaks of white milk. Unless this discharge is bloody or yellowish of color, there is no cause for alarm. This first secretion, known as *colostrum*, is normal and present in every new mother. Colostrum as the "first milk" contains the mother's antibodies and is necessary to all newborns, particularly in the first 24 hours of life. If you are tube- or bottle-feeding, and the dam has colostrum, express some into the formula. The antibodies contained in colostrum are called *immunoglobulins*, protecting the newborns against infectious diseases to which the mother is immune. This is one important reason why it is imperative the dam be updated for prophylactic vaccinations prior to breeding.

Every matron sheds along her abdomen prior and subsequent to whelping. If heavily coated, the shedding process may be incomplete. Puppies can ingest air while nursing if hair remains around the mammaries. The resulting gaseous pains of colic are often quite severe, causing puppies to scream for hours on end in pain. Additionally, the presence of hair collects milk, thereby promoting rapid bacterial growth. While this does not initially cause the dam discomfort, it will

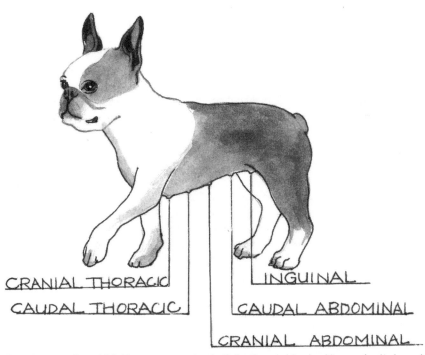

CRANIAL THORACIC
CAUDAL THORACIC
INGUINAL
CAUDAL ABDOMINAL
CRANIAL ABDOMINAL

Examine your brood bitch's mammary glands daily, thoroughly checking each nipple and teat. The glands should always feel moderately soft and pliable. *Artist: Jan Walker*

131

cause illness in puppies, which can rapidly lead to death. Hormonal changes alone may prove inadequate to hair removal, particularly with dams of long or heavy coats. Help nature along and protect your puppies by scissoring the hair away. Short-bladed, slightly curved, blunt-ended shears called mustache or nasal scissors are best for this job. Remove the coat as close to her skin as possible, around each mammary and from the entire abdomen. This latter is equally important. Moisture can gather here, creating a virtual hotbed for bacterial and secondary infections. Maggots can, in extreme cases of total neglect, be harbored in this area!

Check each teat and nipple daily. Heavy mammary glands require daily washing and thorough drying of the entire abdominal area until the puppies are weaned. Her milk glands should always feel pliable, being moderately soft although heavy and full feeling to your examination. Your matron is in serious trouble should there be any hardness either in an entire individual gland or row, visible redness and/or red streaks or yellowish or bloody discharge expressed. Not every gland may be infected. Initially only one or two will have problems. Placing a bandage over the nipple of the affected teat is usually sufficient to stop very young puppies from nursing. Use of a small amount of camphorated oil (or Vicks VapoRub) halts older puppies (eyes open) from nursing at an infected site. It is absolutely crucial to prevent puppies from nursing on an infected teat. If allowed, such nursing could cause severe dehydration resulting from diarrhea and serious illness. Call your veterinarian for an immediate appointment.

Breast infections are known as *mastitis*. Severest cases can prove fatal to the dam and puppies if left untreated. If it is not possible for the dam to be seen by a veterinarian right away, you may take safe initial steps to alleviate pain. Ease her breast congestion by expressing a small amount of milk to relieve tightness and pressure. *Discard this milk!* Milk that has been produced and *retained* within the mammary gland can have a toxic effect on the puppies.

The mammary glands can also become hardened from an overproduction of milk. Sometimes when puppies have not recently nursed, the dam's glands become overfilled, taut and painful. Because of their tightness, the puppies may be incapable of suction and will cry. Expression of milk is painful to a bitch in this condition. She may growl at her offspring and not allow them to nurse, further compounding the problem. Pack the taut swollen mammaries with damp warm towels to help alleviate the pain and soften the glands. Express enough milk from each breast until she becomes comfortable but not depleted. She will normally allow the puppies to resume nursing once the glands are pliable as normal. Should the condition recur, however, the dam must be seen by the veterinarian as soon as possible.

THE DAM'S APPETITE

The dam's appetite should become ravenous within 24 to 36 hours of whelping and peak just prior to finger-feeding the puppies. Within these first weeks, her appetite consistently progresses in intensity as the puppies grow and demand increasing milk production. The dam's feeding at this time is crucial to her well-being and that of her offspring. No matron should ever appear gaunt and poorly maintained. Should a dam be malnourished during this period, she will literally kill herself to provide adequate increasing quantities of milk for her puppies.

Your brood matron will require two to four times her normal caloric intake, dependent on her litter size and age. Some puppies may be easy keepers, having a high food assimilation factor. As a result, they require less food intake per ounce or pound than others of the same breed and age, placing fewer demands on their dam's milk production/caloric intake. Dams require multiple high-protein and fat feedings throughout the day. After having (usually) refused kibble the first few days, appetite increases to the point where a bitch will once again eat balanced meals of kibble, meat, egg yolks (or cooked whole eggs), vitamins and di-calcium phosphate, plus her bitch's milk replacement (supplement). She should be fed equal portions three to four times daily. Extra protein is required during lactation. An excellent source is cheese. Cottage cheese is also a "binder," helping prevent diarrhea, to which many are prone. If diarrhea persists for more than a day, call the veterinarian. Your dam cannot produce quantities of nutritious milk while suffering water depletion and an electrolyte imbalance.

ROUTINE HYGIENE

Your brood matron will keep her whelping box clean the first few weeks. As she stimulates her puppies to eliminate, she ingests their wastes. Because they are born incompletely developed, the matron must perform this stimulation or the puppies become toxic and die. If she has an overly large litter or is neglectful, you must help perform this function. (See Chapter 9, Orphan, Premature and Unthrifty Puppies.) Even though the dam keeps her box clean, and she may have little postpartum vaginal discharge, the whelping box must still be cleaned daily. The discharge appears as blood the first day or two following whelping. Shortly thereafter it diminishes and becomes dark, finally ceasing altogether. The discharge must *never* be profuse, overly bright, greenish or odorous. Should any of these conditions occur, call your veterinarian immediately.

Change the blankets or towels daily the first week, and twice daily thereafter. Never allow bedding to become damp, as chilling could be fatal to the puppies. Make certain that all bedding is completely flat in the box because puppies can become lost under or behind wrinkles.

Check the puppies' stools as they eliminate. Signs of trouble can be a bright or strangely colored stool: yellowish, streaked; foamy or mucoid of consistency; odorous. Constipated (hard) stools that may be accompanied by straining and crying, or loose stools of a diarrhetic condition, are indicative of life-threatening conditions. They can also be an precursor to other problems, not the trouble source itself. Normal puppy stool has form, and is not overly hard, runny or mucoid. Brown, it holds together in a soft but formed "rope."

DEWCLAWS

The Great Pyrenees breed Standard requires the presence of double dew-claws (the ''extra'' toes) on the hindlegs and single dewclaws on the forelegs. The Briard Standard also requires the presence of double dewclaws on the rearlegs, although removal of dewclaws from the forelegs is optional. Unless your breed standard specifically requires their presence, dewclaw removal is strongly recommended for health reasons: that of the dogs and their future owners.

Dewclaw removal is best performed when the puppies are three, but not more than four, days old. Required tail docking may also be done at this time. Safe removal of these appendages can be performed by several different and

Dewclaws should be removed when the puppies are three days old. Tail docks may also be performed at this time. The surgery of dewclaw removal and tail docks should only be performed on vigorous puppies. Note the presence of tails on these two-day-old Boxer puppies.   *Boxer: Jane N. Rivas*

relatively painless methods. Being surgery, it should be performed only by a doctor of veterinary medicine. Some veterinarians remove dewclaws from vigorous puppies during the matron's postpartum examination. It is more usual, however, to set up a later appointment for these surgeries. Dewclaw removal is a traumatic experience that should be performed only on vigorous puppies. If a dewclaw is not removed with the digit, a small stump may be left. There have been a few cases of apparent spontaneous regeneration of the dewclaw when surgery has been incomplete.

Most puppies cry abruptly during dewclaw removal but stop immediately after the surgery is completed. While some may whimper for a few hours, this is generally not the rule. If whimpering is prolonged, check the legs for reopening of the wound. Infection can occur within hours to days following dewclaw removal. It is first noticeable by a slight tissue swelling of the dewclaw area, then the pads of the feet. Prior to swelling, incipient infection may be determined by the presence of heat in the feet, pads and legs above that of the normal body temperature.

Usually the veterinarian employs application of silver nitrate or cauterization to stop bleeding at the site of dewclaw removal. Bleeding, when present, is almost always negligible. Application of silver nitrate or cauterization forms a scab over the removal site. The lesion heals quickly and the scab falls off in a few days to a week. A small scar may be found with careful scrutinization of the adult dog. Often there is no scar at all: the wound edges join, creating a full union.

No dam should be present when dewclaws are removed. Nor should she be held on lead in proximity to the surgical area. The instinct to protect her young is never stronger than during the earliest weeks. Even the most mildly tempered female could attack given enough provocation, such as causing her puppies to cry.

Check each puppy thoroughly at least once daily. Should a dewclaw site become reddened or swollen, indicative of infection, administer antiseptic wash (obtained from the veterinarian) with an eye dropper. Dewclaw removal makes general health care of a dog's feet easier. An active dog can accidentally rip off dewclaws when playing or working. Dewclaws are often forgotten in routine toenail care of dremmeling or clipping. Some dewclaw nails that grow long through neglect have curved to reenter the dog's flesh, thereby causing great pain and infection. Dewclaws of puppies and grown dogs have accidentally torn into other dogs as well as eyes, lips and clothing of children and adults.

Dewclaws may be safely removed from an older dog as minor surgery with but a few stitches. Literally a stitch in time prevents an accident. Removal can also be cosmetic. Some dogs' dewclaws lie close to their legs, never causing troubles. Other dogs have protruding dewclaws that are extremely dangerous to the dog and people, as well as being unsightly.

COLLARS

The *only* time the brood matron should wear a collar is when you take her out to the yard or to the vet. *Collar removal is mandatory* prior to whelping and throughout the time puppies are near their dam. A crawling puppy can get a leg or head caught in a collar, causing irreparable injury. Flea collar removal is a must when the dam is with her puppies, either in utero or after. Flea collars are composed of toxic materials absorbed through a dog's skin. Although harmless to the adult animal, flea collar chemicals are passed through the dam's system and are present in her milk, thereby having the potential of causing irreparable damage to a nursing puppy.

EARLY EYE DEVELOPMENT

The average puppy's eyes open between 12 and 15 days of age. The ear canals open about two days later. Although puppies are unable to see or hear before this time, they have been receptive to stimuli of light and dark, noise and quiet. While still sealed and shortly before the eyes open, puppies "blink" in response to light and scent. Their little noses wrinkle when confronted with a new odor. At this time and while the ears are still sealed, they also begin to move their ears in response to vibrations they can feel. Small dogs such as Toys and some miniature varieties have a tendency to develop faster than large and giant breeds. Some smaller puppies have been known to open their eyes as early as eight days. These are only guidelines to physical development and emotional maturation. Remember, there are no definitive rules governing youngsters' development from species.

Never, under any circumstances, pry open or pull apart a puppy's eyelids, during any developmental stage! Forcing a puppy's eyelids open can cause irreversible injury. The delicate eye tissues may not have matured enough to manage the impact of light. Nature protects developing immature eyes during the first week-plus of puppies' lives. When puppies are physically (and emotionally) well-enough developed for the impact of daylight, the "sealed" eyelids slowly open according to nature's dictates. This process may take as long as four or five days among some individuals. Other rapidly developing puppies may open their eyes to light's emotional and physical impact within 24 hours. In the normal course of development not every puppy opens its eyes at the same time as littermates. If, however, all but one or two puppies have their eyes open and functioning well, consult with the veterinarian about the slower developing youngsters. Multiple inseminations of a brood matron allow her eggs to be fertilized during the different breeding intervals. In most cases the slower development of certain puppies is no cause for alarm, these youngsters simply having been conceived at a later time.

When puppies' eyes first open, a small reflective "crack" becomes visible at the inner corner of one or both eyes. It is particularly important to keep the

All puppies are born with their eyes and ear canals sealed as a natural protective measure until development is completed. Puppies' eyes open between 12 and 15 days of age. *Never*, under any circumstances, pry open or pull apart a puppy's eyelids during any stage of development. *Alaskan Malamute: Monte Biss*

puppy area under subdued lighting conditions during the eye-opening period. Use a heat lamp only with caution once puppies' eyes have begun to open. Construct a large aluminum foil "basket" or "hood" around the light if continued use of the heat lamp is required. Punch numerous tiny holes in the fabric with a pin, thin, sharp pen or pencil tip.

Carefully check the eyes as they first open to ascertain if the tear ducts are functioning properly, washing the eyes and keeping them moist. These glands

Tear duct inflammation is most often first noted by brown tear stains at the inner corners of a dog's eyes. White-faced and Toy breeds appear to be more prone to tear duct inflammation. Often the problem is caused by an allergic reaction to food or environment.

Bichons Frises: Carol Haines

do not always initially function adequately. Glisteningly bright "reflective" eyes are indicative of well-functioning tear ducts. Often puppies whose eyes open early and some premature puppies do not have fully developed and functioning tear ducts. In such cases the topical application of an ophthalmic ointment is advisable. Topical medication is indicated if the eyes are dull and of a dry appearance. The ointment should be applied to the puppies' eyes five or six times daily, or according to other instructions the veterinarian may give you. While treatment of initially unproductive tear duct glands is rarely protracted (usually requiring attention only over a few days), blindness can result if left unattended. A sterile 5 percent boric ophthalmic ointment solution may be purchased from the veterinarian or a pharmacy (under the vet's direction). Place a small dab of ointment on each eye every four hours. Continue the treatment until the eyes lose the dry "flat" (nonreflective) appearance. If a dry-eyes condition persists for more than two days consult the veterinarian. The puppy could have other problems of a more serious nature.

All puppies' eyes at first opening have a protective film, bluish in coloring; this is normal whether the breed has blue, brown, or bicolored eyes. If a puppy's eyes, however, appear white or solid blue of color, again, consult the veterinarian.

Once the eyes have opened enough for them to be impacted by light, puppies may suddenly become noisy. Their first senses have been tactile response and scent. Coupling scent (and shortly later, sound) with sight occurs over several days. During this time puppies may "squeak" in sudden fear upon awakening

138

Puppies can be stimulated toward housetraining by separating the whelping box into two areas, sleeping and eliminating. Even very young puppies do not like to eliminate where they sleep, eat and play.   *Dalmatians: Rambler Dalmatians*

or having any visible perception of movement. After the first day or so the puppies no longer squeak in alarm, but instead may cry vociferously whenever the dam enters or departs their immediate area. By three weeks puppies are able to focus fairly well and have learned to associate many sights with sounds and scents.

If like most people, you are a camera bug, use extreme caution when photographing puppies between 8 and 20 days. Prior and subsequent to this time a flash may be safely employed. After the seventh day carefully examine puppies' eyes before shooting. Do not use a flash during this period. Extreme and sudden bright light can damage puppies' delicate eye tissues. Use of ASA 400 or 1000 film allows good photographs to be taken under low-light conditions. Natural bright light may also be used safely for short durations during this time period.

PUPPIES AND THEIR SURROUNDINGS

Puppies begin to generate noises shortly after their eyes open, and earliest tottering mobility around the whelping box becomes fact. Depending upon their developmental maturation between three and four weeks, puppies should have the stimulation of being moved to a safe daytime area. The new larger area physically stimulates and mentally challenges them. This area must also have good purchase (footing) in all portions. Usually a dam's instinct agrees with this move. When dogs' earliest ancestors were closely related to their wolf cousins, several den sites were utilized. The first was that of whelping, where water was in plentiful nearby supply. The second den was larger, accommodating maturing whelps, providing them with safe areas of exploration. Once large puppies initiate mobility, they require a large permanent area to clamber from the whelping box. The new area should be large enough to have clearly defined sleeping, eating, playing and toilet areas.

Theoretically a garage or basement can be ideal, helping hobby breeders rear puppies in a large area. Under certain conditions, however, these places can be dangerous or lethal. Exploration of stairwells can cause fatality or injury by falling. Basements have dangers beyond stairwells. Trapped ammonia fumes from urine are toxic. Heating systems, electrical panels and appliances require thorough checking before placing a litter nearby. A garage must be thoroughly cleaned, the floor mopped and hazardous materials removed: physical objects, items exuding noticeable odors, cleaning abrasives, stored gasoline, motors, paint. Inhalation of toxics by minute amounts can be lethal to puppies and small dogs. Even idle engines emit lethal fumes we are incapable of discerning. No litter's health is worth risking parking a vehicle in the garage.

A safe play area can be devised using a garage's side door to the yard. The areas under and around the door must be blocked from cold and damp drafts when the litter is inside during inclement weather. Their flooring should have a firm, nonslippery purchase.

Vigorously mobile puppies require sunshine in addition to a safe romping area. Inclement weather periods require special lighting and additional vitamins (including C) to give puppies what is normally received from natural sunlight. Alternatives to placing the litter outside in sunshine during winter months can be found. A playpen or exercise pen can be moved, following the sun through one or more rooms. Puppies can chill when placed too close to a window. Care must also be taken not to situate puppies where they cannot move away from heat. Puppies heat and chill quickly, lacking ability to regulate body temperatures when very young.

The whelping box should be lined initially with clean soft blankets or towels. If carpeting is used, it should be washable. Indoor/outdoor carpeting can be dangerous because manufacturing chemicals react strongly to urine. Use of this material can cause harmful burns to puppy feet and bodies. Newsprint is slick, has poor purchase for footing and also contains harmful chemicals used in the ink. Wood shavings can be inhaled or ingested, also causing fatalities.

Mobile puppies can be stimulated toward house-training by separating the whelping box into two areas, sleeping and eliminating. Even very young puppies do not like to eliminate where they sleep, eat and play. Within a few days of placing tactilely different materials in the whelping box, puppies learn to move away from their sleeping area to eliminate. Removable sides help encourage them to sleep in the whelping box, eliminating away from it. If a heat lamp is still in use, move it to cover only the sleeping and playing areas.

While the dam must have continued accessibility to her litter, she requires a "respite" area, one where she can observe activities and relax away from the puppies. A platform or barrier insures the dam's emotional and physical respite. Large-breed matrons may utilize a flat-topped dog house or picnic table.

Puppies like to sleep in a "lump sum," huddling when tired or frightened. Once out of their box, an airline shipping crate (with the door removed) makes a very effective dog house. (Some breeders use the bottom as the whelping box.) Large litters may require two crates, either directly side-by-side or, if facing, with moderately close passage in between. Early use of airline crates provides new owners with distinct advantages. The newly arrived puppy readily accepts the familiar crate as its sleeping quarters, making the adjustment to a new home substantially less traumatic.

Puppies emulating their dam before weaning will begin to lap water. Clean water must always be available regardless or whether or not they appear to partake. The water dish should be elevated and secured to prevent tipping, keeping puppies from playing in and dirtying the water, yet low enough for the puppies to drink. Puppies discovering water are funny. Some, in eagerness to explore or drink, plunge into the water past their eyes. Others bite the water. Arctic-type puppies may paw water before lapping, instinctively "breaking ice" to drink. If the puppies are of a type that like to play in water (and are more than five weeks of age), a child's sturdy plastic wading pool may be utilized during good weather.

Dogs can also learn from other dogs' behaviors. These are social and environmental acquired responses. *Alaskan Malamutes: Robin Haggard*

12

Early Puppy Care

EARLY optimum care is crucial to well-rounded puppy development. It is during this time when some breeders fail in their responsibilities, either through ignorance or lack of commitment. *The committed breeder is aware that there is no real profit in rearing a litter other than the satisfaction of doing the best job possible, including correct placement of each puppy.*

Once puppies' eyes open the real work and expense of rearing a litter begins. As puppies begin to display individual character traits their emotional and physical development relies ever more heavily upon the breeder and less with their dam. This is also when early observations can be made between the committed, conscientious breeder and one who lacks dedication. The conscientious breeder recognizes and readily assumes the responsibilities of optimumly caring for a litter and is not one who abandons them to their dam's care alone. The difference between breeder types is first discernible when the puppies are about three weeks or slightly older.

Supplementary feeding while continuing to allow the dam and offspring full access to each other is crucial to large litters, yet often is of no less import with relatively few puppies. Untimely puppy supplementation causes the dam's health to wane shortly before deprivation becomes noticeable in her offsprings' development. A brood matron should be vibrantly healthy, carrying neither excess weight nor appearing undernourished. The emotionally and physically healthy dam consistently maintains an active and lively interest in her puppies and environment.

EARLY SOCIAL CONDITIONING

Earliest puppy stimulation and socialization with the breeder begin from the moment of birth when the sac is broken. Because their first sense is that of scent, the breeder is familiar to the puppies before their eyes open. Further stimulation is given by the breeder as puppies' eyes open and they become aware of a hazy world beyond their olfactory sense. Until now they essentially became familiar with their breeder's scent through their dam's coat and learned different portions of her anatomy: where there is and is not her heavy milky scent.

Only the breeder should handle puppies during their first two weeks. While such handling is consistent with sound early puppy care practices, it does in reality limit their world. Once they react to a feathery touch on their eyelids, although their eyes are not yet open puppies are highly aware of differences in people. As a result, puppies can react violently the first time handled by anyone other than their breeder. Some struggle, screaming to be free; others may growl menacingly although the new handler implicitly follows the breeder's instructions. Reactions can be indicative of how puppies handle strange situations later in life: reactions from complacency to submission or aggressiveness, dependent upon the nature, age and socialization of puppies at first contact by a stranger. Puppies' first human bonding is through the breeder. The experiences must therefore be positive. If a puppy is incorrectly handled or handled not at all, it responds instinctively with distrust toward all humans. It is therefore crucially important that *all* early contacts be positive. Once the barrier of distrust is instilled, the puppy becomes hard to work with, and in some cases, unmanageable.

Never "swoop" a puppy quickly into your arms, or hold it at arm's length. *Never* pick a puppy up by its legs, ears, tail or scruff. Severe, even irreparable damage can result. Place your hands firmly around the puppy's body so it feels secure and comfortable in your grasp. Large-breed puppies demand slightly different treatment. Place one hand around the midsection, use the other hand to cup the rear quarters before lifting. Supporting the puppy in this manner allows it to feel secure before it is lifted from the whelping box. Snuggle the puppy closely, let it smell your familiar scent. Hold the very young puppy either against your face, neck or chest. Here scenting you best with little puppy "whuffles," they feel the wonderfully reassuring and hypnotic rhythm of your breathing and your heartbeat. Here they remain relaxed with less tendency to struggle against the restrictiveness of first being held. It is generally best not to place very young puppies in a lap until after they begin to walk because they are not afforded the same sense of security.

When handling newborns or even much older puppies it is helpful to make repetitive "kissing" sounds. The vibration of these "kisses" is felt by even the youngest puppies. These kissing sounds are also the first sounds puppies hear as their ears become receptive. Repetitious kissing offers the vibration and sounds of security and comfort because it is the sound puppies make when nursing. Well fed with warm milk and nestled in secure comfort by its dam while feeling her

Holding a puppy securely.   *Pug: Knox & Kelly*

heartbeat and breathing is one of the earliest conditionings a puppy encounters. When you emit this sound of security and comfort associated with well-being as you pick a puppy up, it responds instantly to your stimulation. Feeling secure, the puppy snuggles rather than struggles.

Puppies are never objects, no matter how many you have in a litter. Each puppy develops individual character traits that make it unique, distinguishable from siblings even within hours of birth. While puppies eventually display many parental character traits, they also learn through association with role models. Within a few weeks strong individual character traits become self-evident. Puppy conditioning beyond diet is, therefore, a highly important part of the breeder's job.

As puppies grow their coordination continues to develop almost proportionate to stimuli: perception—brain; reaction—taste or go. The good breeder spends ever-increasing positive time allotments in association with the puppies, nurturing and fostering close human bonding. Some breeds are more "people-oriented" than others by nature. Other breed types have a tendency to be somewhat stand-offish from people, either innately or by being "dog-focused" before people-oriented. These puppies require additional positive reinforcement from the breeder before being carefully placed into a suitable home.

Everything the breeder does has an effect on puppy associations. Therefore each experience in a puppy's young life must be a pleasant one. Although dogs come with their own set of "genetic instructions," which dictate many of their

Dogs come with their own set of genetic "instructions" which dictate many of their responses as with these Vizslas in the field.   *Vizslas: C. Wright*

146

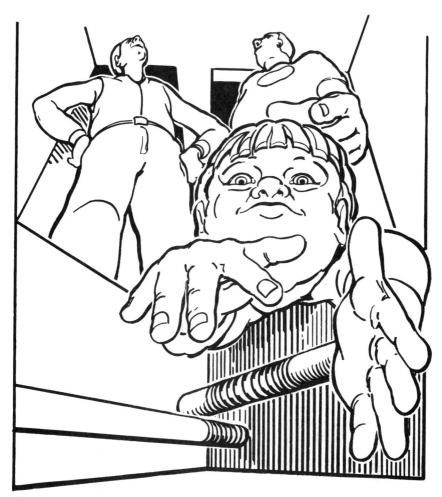

Give yourself a dog's eye view, getting a whelping box view of the world. People are giants and suddenly lifting a puppy can be intimidating for a youngster.

John Kirkpatrick

responses, dogs also learn from other dogs' behaviors. It is important that the dam greets your approach each time with happy anticipation. Her attitude has a vast influence on her offspring's personalities. Although a different structure, your interaction is no less important. Put yourself in "puppy shoes" for a few moments, getting a whelping box view of the world. Through this different perspective a puppy's world is either perceived as overwhelming and threatening or intriguing with new smells, sounds, sights and tastes awaiting explorations. If you were a puppy, obviously you would want to be the latter, happy, well adjusted and socially secure. Think for a moment from a puppy perspective. Swooping a puppy up from a standing position can be an intimidating experience not unlike having King Kong in your home, suddenly snatching you through the air. The effect can be traumatically detrimental although no harm is intended.

Older, more sophisticated puppies pose their own problems. Socially active and physically adept, they can become a danger to themselves when not handled carefully. Sit or kneel on the ground before holding a vitally energetic puppy. Simply because you want to cradle a puppy does not mean it is ready to be held. Puppies are wiggly creatures that may be apparently relaxed one moment and furry dynamos the next. A puppy cannot harm itself by suddenly leaping from your arms or lap if you are sitting on the ground. A puppy can be seriously injured if it falls from your arms as you stand, or from your lap as you sit on a chair.

When people come to see the litter, instruct them to sit on the ground if they want to hold a puppy. You have handled your puppies every day, are familiar with them and know how to manage each one. Visitors do not, no matter how experienced they may be. These are your puppies, their habits and personalities are known only to you. Carefully instruct these people in the art of puppy snuggling. If they refuse to sit in a manner safe for a puppy, do not allow them to hold one. Ultimately, the physical and emotional well-being of the litter is your responsibility alone.

ESTABLISHING HIGH TRUST LEVELS

Puppies are born with "four toward the floor." They do not like to be upside down, struggling mightily against this position from their time of birth. Even in play, the "underdog" puppy struggles to rise rather than submit passively to a littermate's assertive play. A dog on its back is like a turtle in the same position, totally vulnerable. Dogs instinctively know they are vulnerable to attack when on their backs. The secure, socially well-adjusted dog often takes this position in its own home, as a royal invitation for a belly rub and when fast asleep. These dogs have a high trust level of their environment. This social adjustment can be fostered early in a dog's life by the breeder, and later, by the owner. Placing a puppy on its back, having it totally relax, instills a tremendous trusting sense. From a household pet to top contender, trial or show dog, the conditioning and associations acquired by supine desensitization have a real and lasting benefit.

When the puppy is securely cradled on its back, in your arms or in your lap (as you would a human baby), talk soothingly and earnestly to the puppy. Repeat nonthreatening short-term eye contact, make the comforting kissing sounds while giving a belly rub, until puppy totally relaxes, thoroughly enjoying your performance. Some puppies find immediate pleasure in this contact. Some struggle, innately fearful of this position. And others struggle vigorously because they are alpha-type personalities objecting to this submissive position. A roughly playing puppy in the alpha (superior dog) position stands over a victim until the underdog's submission is complete. If they cannot run away, frightened puppies

148

display a submissive attitude by cowering, rolling onto their back and ultimately urinating, crying "uncle." Never force a vigorously struggling puppy to (initially) remain on its back for more than half a minute to one minute. The puppy's struggle will not be continuous; there will be moments of pause. Instantly encourage the puppy to relax further with your soothing voice and belly rub. Gently place the pup upright back on the ground among siblings. *Never* allow this puppy to jump from your arms when you are finished, no matter how close to the ground you may be. Repeating this action over and over again, several times daily, is called a desensitization process, which fosters human bonding. It is through this desensitization that a puppy learns there is nothing to fear from this submission; indeed, pleasure results.

Many puppies clutch the handler's arm with surprising strength when first picked up. How many people have said, "How cute! Look how the pup is holding onto me. The puppy likes me and is hugging me!" Do not believe this for a moment. When a puppy wraps its paws and grips firmly, it is innately terrified of being dropped. This is a real fear that all babies and puppies have. Trust acquired through desensitization and positive reinforcement eventually affects the puppy through all its learning scenarios. These puppies readily learn through positive reinforcement augmented by pleasurable responses, through belly rubs and dulcet tones, that trust is more than okay—trust has positive rewards. Puppies handled consistently with this early social conditioning are prepared to learn rapidly. Fear is not part of their vocabulary and does not present an obstacle that must first be overcome before training of any manner can begin. These well-socialized puppies are essentially unflappable and receptive to new stimuli.

Once the puppy relaxes in your arms each time, the next step may be taken: learning to relax upside down. Every puppy adjusted to the conditioning anticipates being picked up and held. Trust level is high. Remember, however, that the attention span is short, only momentary. If held too long they neither resent nor struggle to be free, but will most often fall asleep, confident in their security.

This acquired trusting behavior extends to litter visitors, although a puppy's initial response to a stranger's touch may be rigid panic or struggle. Once strangers hold the puppy *always* upright in their arms, the youngster soon relaxes.

You are responsible for the early conditioning of your puppies' responsive bonding to humans. When their associations with you are only positively pleasurable, they have a better opportunity to be outstanding and trusting pets. If early socialization and bonding are neglected, the dog, through ignorance and mistrust, will have barriers to overcome before becoming the pet most people want in their homes. There is far more to breeding dogs than the melding of pedigrees and sound nutritional support; there is the conditioning and socialization for a permanent effect on puppies' temperaments.

Puppies may avidly lick the corners of an adult's mouth to stimulate those salivary glands, eliciting a regurgitation response of a recently digested meal.

Greyhounds: adult & puppy: Patricia Gail Burnham, Ph.D.

13

Weaning the Puppies

METHODS for weaning puppies and drying dams are topics of controversy. Each situation is different and one humane method is not necessarily better than another. It is generally agreed that complete weaning should begin at approximately five to seven weeks. There are always exceptions. The important criteria to bear in mind are the dam's health and the puppies' physical and emotional maturation. If the dam's health is in jeopardy, or the puppies are "dog-oriented," then weaning is initiated early.

Wild canid whelps develop earlier in many respects than domestic puppies. They begin their initial weaning process shortly after their eyes open. Adult canids (dogs and wolves) carry food for their whelps back to the den in their stomachs. When these animals approach the den they are greeted by the puppies, who avidly lick the corners of the adults' mouths. In response, the adults' salivary glands (located just inside the mouth corners) become active. Tensing their stomach muscles to contract reflexively, the adults easily regurgitate their recently ingested meal. There is neither force nor straining to effect regurgitation. This first "puppy food" is the easiest meal a puppy can digest. Enzymes in the saliva and esophagus begin to break the food down before it is utilized by the adult's stomach. This first highly digestible food is mush, similar in texture to puppies' finger-fed "pablum." Regurgitation is neither common nor rare among domestic dogs. If the dam of a litter is stimulated to regurgitation and she responds accordingly, there is no cause for alarm.

Weaning by the breeder can occur over a period of time or be done somewhat quickly. By the introduction of feeding mush and finally puppy food, the weaning process has already been initiated. These early meals are a similar consistency and appeal (although not content) as canid whelps' first food. Bear in mind that your dam and litter do not understand what you are doing. Under natural conditions the dam takes a prolonged period to wean her offspring. Drying is therefore protracted and painless. By our standards, complete, early weaning of puppies from their dam's milk is necessary because prophylactic inoculations should be initiated ten days before they move into their new homes.

Making the decision of when to wean is arbitrary for many breeders, who do not fully take into account individual puppies' emotional development, or the dam's readiness to relinquish this aspect of her motherhood. Some brood matrons are never ready to give up their motherly duties while others cannot get away quickly enough. Most dams, fortunately, fall between the two poles. If you coordinate your weaning of the dam and puppies according to her natural schedule, the weaning process becomes painless and is easily accomplished. Psychologically speaking, it is best for the puppies to be kept with their dam for as long as possible: for as long as she will tolerate them. Normally the dam tires of nursing duties shortly after her puppies' razor-sharp deciduous teeth erupt. The dam, having moderate to considerable pain during ever-briefer nursing episodes, becomes more and more reluctant to nurse her offspring. Nature, in its own course, is preparing the puppies for separation.

Any dam is a candidate for mastitis if she continues copious lactation. In order to prevent this painful condition, it is important to limit her daily food intake by volume reduction at the onset of her weaning: food reduction = less milk production. Slow weaning demands sanity of method. Do not cut the matron so far back that she virtually compromises her health by continued lactation. Weaning by food reduction occurs over days, until the dam is back to her normal rations. Her calcium and vitamin/mineral support should also be decreased commensurately during this period, and stopped altogether the third or fourth day after normal food rations have been reached. Once the dam is fully dried, moderate amounts of vitamin/minerals and small amounts of dicalcium phosphate should be resumed until she has returned to her normal conditioning.

Instead of being a nerve-wracking experience, weaning can be approached successfully from another direction, leaving a family's sanity intact, and keeping good neighborhood relationships. The full weaning process should not be initiated until after the puppies begin to eat solid foods well independently. If your brood matron follows the norm, you may take cues for weaning from her behavior.

When the puppies are about six weeks old, begin reducing the mother's extra rations by small amounts, at each feeding, over a gradual basis. Reduce the dam's liquid intake the first (and ensuing days) by deleting her dam's milk supplementation. By suddenly deleting the bitch's milk supplement, troublesome distention and congestion of mammaries are usually avoided. Delete one of her meals the second day. Always continue to feed her normally proportioned rations at her regular (throughout the year) meal time. Continue to decrease her supplemental feedings over the period of a week or slightly longer. Watch the dam for episodes of gluttony during this period. Always separate her from the litter during the puppies' meals. Do not allow her to finish their leftovers. Continue to feed the orphan puppy formula to your litter on a regular basis, multiple times daily.

Weaning covers two very important functions: drying the dam and physiologically preparing the puppies for their prophylactic inoculations. During this transitional stage of puppies' emotional development, where they begin to move from dog orientation (of puppy-to-dam and puppy-to-puppy) to people orientation, the litter continues to need the crucial interaction and role modeling the dam offers.

Coating the dam's mammaries with a camphorated oil (or Vicks VapoRub) immediately prevents puppies from successful nursing attempts. The heavily pungent camphor odor is offensive to puppies' olfactory senses. They will not nurse while the odor is present. If the puppies are adequately on a nutritionally supportive and appealing diet, they will normally not engage in nursing. Although pungent to them also, some matrons thoroughly enjoy the camphorated rub because of its cooling effect on their sore and swollen mammary glands. It is highly important to continue checking each of the dam's glands thoroughly at least twice a day. A small amount of milk may be expressed, to alleviate a dam's discomfort or pain, should one or more glands become overly taut during the initial drying process.

BINDING

If any puppies persist in nursing attempts in spite of the camphor rub, or if the matron is heavy and sagging, she can be helped toward restoration of her "youthful figure" by binding. Binding is also an outstanding nursing deterrent, placing a barrier between puppy and nipple. Camphorated oil may be rubbed external onto the binding as well, further resisting nursing attempts.

T-shirts make wonderful binding material for large and giant breeds. Your matron requires four shirts in her wardrobe: two for wearing and two for washing. You also need a set of diaper safety pins. Small- and medium-sized dogs' T-shirts can be found in infants' and children's departments. Toy-sized T-shirts are found—where else of course—in the toy department! Place the shirt over your dog's head in a "normal" fashion, forelegs through the armholes. Reverse this procedure with the second shirt, placing her hindlegs through the armholes and tail end through the neck aperture. This shirt's neck portion can be gathered and pinned, and if necessary, gathered and pinned also in between her hindlegs. Pull each shirt from the hem until it fits snugly. The material has a lot of "give." As a result, even when pulled almost tautly, the material relaxes in a few minutes. Pull the hem of her top shirt down toward her hips, tug the rear shirt forward toward her shoulders, smooth out any wrinkles, then secure the overlapping hems with diaper safety pins. Gather excess material up, over the top of her rib cage, along her spine. Secure this gathered material snugly with a row of diaper pins along her spine. Pull the shirt over her abdomen up tautly (but not uncomfortably), and secure this gathered material along her spine with a row of diaper safety pins.

TRANSITIONAL BEHAVIOR AND SOCIAL ORDER

Weaning is a bilateral experience. The puppies are weaned from their dam's milk *and* nurturing. The dam is weaned from milk production *and* the company of her offspring. Under natural conditions, as the puppies move into this next transitional stage, training and socialization begin in earnest. At this time the physically and socially healthy dam generally engages in play with her litter. Through this interactive play certain behaviors are learned, primarily what constitutes acceptable social behavior and what does not.

Puppies do not all develop at a uniform rate. Within a litter some puppies are assertive, some aggressive and others passive in interaction. The different attitudes and developmental stages should be observed and remembered. It is usually during weaning that puppies rapidly progress developmentally and are ready to establish a social order. Dogs are always, to some degree, pack-oriented animals. Within each pack is a social order called a hierarchy. "Puppy packs" work hard at establishing their "pecking order," their hierarchy. One or two puppies consistently vie for dominance, some are exuberantly playful, others are independent explorers and the lowest puppies in the social order are passive followers.

An overly assertive puppy can develop permanent aggressive tendencies if the behavior displayed is allowed to continue unchecked. This bully puppy

Although eating well on their own, it is best, psychologically speaking, to keep puppies with their dam for as long as possible. During the transitional stage of weaning, the puppies require the crucial interaction and role-modeling the dam offers.

Dalmatian: Joanne Nash

Within each pack is a social order, a hierarchy. One or two puppies consistently vie for dominance within this order. Permanent aggressive tendencies can develop if the displayed behavior continues unchecked. *Alaskan Malamutes: Keven Curtis*

usually picks on the most passive littermates to consistently achieve success, further fostering this socially unacceptable behavior. Unchecked, this puppy's social development may become permanently delayed, "stuck" in this stage. The submissive, passive puppy's personality can also be ruined if it is not rescued or unable to go uninhibitedly through normal growth interactive play. When the dam is present, however, overassertiveness or puppy aggressiveness is usually placed in check because the bully also includes "attacks" on its dam. Puppy attacks on the dam normally follow a certain behavioral pattern. These attacks should not be confused by the breeder with normal interactive growth as a puppy pushes its limits and learns acceptable behaviors. The bully puppy (male or female) attacks the dam in much the same manner as more passive siblings, biting the dam's paws, ears, tail or other portions of her anatomy. The dam remains tolerant up to a point, after which the puppy is disciplined.

At first, the dam may merely issue a warning growl. If her warning growl is not heeded, she may snap the air, nose the pup away or hold its head or muzzle in her mouth. If the puppy persists, she often applies pressure with her jaws, again warning and disciplining, although not severely. If the puppy continues, the dam growls threateningly and snaps suddenly to frighen the offending youngster. She may nip or grab the scruff of the neck and give one or two vigorous, intimidating, but harmless, shakes. At this point the puppy usually "ki-yi's." Do not step in and discipline the dam if her swift punishment stops the moment

Puppy "attacks" on the dam normally follow a certain behavioral pattern. The dam remains tolerant up to a point, after which, the puppy is disciplined.
Alaskan Malamutes: Beth Harris, Vera Goldsmith and Leland Fong

it is given. If she becomes overzealous and continues her corrections, and the puppy's cries continue, admonish the matron.

Puppies become less dam- and sibling-oriented and increasingly people-oriented between six and nine weeks. When the puppies depend less on their dam and siblings, ignoring their presence and demand attention from you, they are ready to leave home. The environment into which puppies are placed must also maintain the positive reinforcement you have provided to this time. The interaction between environment and heredity is a delicate balance in well-socialized puppies' development.

THE PUPPIES' FIRST MEALS

Puppies are completely supported nutritionally by their dam unless tube or bottle feeding proves necessary. Small-litter puppies are generally not ready for an introduction to supplementary feeding for almost three weeks. Large-litter puppies develop slightly more rapidly than small-litter counterparts because of feeding competition. Some dams of any litter size are incapable of sustaining continuously increasing demands upon their abilities to produce milk. Puppies of these litters require early supplementary feedings while continuing full access to their dams.

An overly assertive puppy can develop into an aggressive adult. Although playing, a dam safely teaches her offspring the social interaction of submission.

Alaskan Malamutes: Robin Haggard

Puppies' interest in food is stimulated with a "mushy" diet that initially smells and tastes similar to the dam's milk. There are a variety of diets to start puppies, commercially prepared and homemade. These early feedings are essentially composed of a commercial bitch's milk replacement or orphan formula mixed with a commercially made weaning diet, commercially prepared canned puppy meat or homemade starting formula. Only diets that are highly palatable and digestible instinctively interest puppies. Commercial or homemade, one early balanced diet is not necessarily better than another.

It is easy to make your own puppy weaning formula. Boil and cool water to a warm temperature before mixing with the bitch's milk replacement or orphan formula (see Chapter 9, Orphan, Premature and Unthrifty Puppies). Beat an egg yolk, stopping before it froths, and stir well into the milk. Add a few drops of liquid vitamins formulated for puppies purchased from either your veterinarian or a well-stocked pet supplier. Mix with a powdered baby rice cereal or commercial weaning formula to a smooth gruel consistency. Stir only small portions in at a time to prevent lumps. Beating or vigorously whipping causes aeration, which in turn causes colicky distress. The mixture should neither be so thick that a

157

spoon "stands alone" nor should it be soupy. This formula is sufficient for the first few feedings as an introduction to semisolid foods.

Common sense must rule with first and subsequent diets you select. Gluten-based foods such as corn and wheat affect puppy and adult dog tolerances. Nor is a variety of dietary selections good. Stay with meat and high-quality protein feedings to avoid food allergies. The addition of any variety in a diet must be slow, mixing the new food in with the old, and only in small quantities for a taste "suggestion." The quantity of new food is slowly increased over a period of time as the puppies display a tolerance and avid interest. The tolerance to any new dietary addition is seen first in the puppies' stool. The stool should not be runny, foamy or discolored, indicating a dietary intolerance, but remain brown in color and of a soft, ropy consistency.

Some puppies are immediately ready to advance to the meat formula stage. The meat you select must be palatable and highly digestible to avoid gastric distress. Meats easily digested are boiled mashed chicken and strained lamb (human) baby food. You can also make your own puppy lamb formula. Boil a lean lamb roast adding *nothing* and refrigerate in its cooking liquid. Once cooled, the fat rises to the top and sets. Remove the fat by carefully inserting a fork or small spatula under it; the fat comes up in a "plate." Lamb is stringy meat and puppies need mush. Reheat the lamb and either puree it in a food processor or use a ricer. If the lamb is pureed, place it back in the refrigerator for 30 minutes before reheating and adding to the earlier milk formula. Pureeing adds minute amounts of air, the ingestion of which must be avoided. If the meat has been riced, it is ready for feeding.

Well-boiled chicken is usually soft enough to mash into the puppy formula. If it does not easily mash, follow the above steps for pureeing or ricing. Ground beef should not be used in the early feedings. Ground beef is lumpy and hard, and can cause a small puppy to choke. Boiled beef is initially hard to digest. Prepared canned puppy meats are often lumpy and should be riced or pureed. After one or two days the gruel is changed to a "paste." When meat is first added to the puppy formula, slowly decrease the cereal content. Use boiled water cooled to a warm temperature, not tap water, when fixing young puppy food. The paste should be thick enough to almost adhere to your fingers. If too thin, puppies suckle rather than rapidly learning to lap or bite the food. If the mixture is too thick, the puppies may get discouraged in their eating attempts, choke and be difficult feeding starters.

FINGER-FEEDING

Puppies' introduction to semisolid food during the first few feedings is always a bit of messy fun. If you have a sense of humor be absolutely certain to have your camera loaded, ready to make marvelously funny memories.

Finger-feeding: your fingers and the puppies' toes. Place the pan of puppy gruel in the whelping box where you can easily reach it. Some puppies immediately waddle over to the pan and waddle right through the middle of it. They smell the food and are excited, but they have not learned to lower their heads in order to eat. Face a puppy to the food pan and with a gentle but firm pressure, lower the puppy's head until the lower jaw and a small portion of the upper lip are in the food. Take care not to get food on the puppy's nose. Inhaled food can cause respiratory distress, even pneumonia. Many puppies quickly learn to eat with gentle pressure applied for only a few moments. Slower puppies require more attention. Sitting on the floor, dip a finger into the pan and gently put your gruel-covered finger into a puppy's mouth. Go on to the next puppy. Once the first four puppies are avidly sucking, biting or lapping food from your fingers, place a small amount of food between their forepaws. They will follow your fingers down to the floor to eat before eating from a pan. Then go on to the next three or four puppies and continue this pattern until all are eating. Generally the litter learns to eat well and independently from a pan (instead of the floor) within two or three days.

Not all puppies are created equal. There always seems to be a slower learner. Hold this puppy in your lap as you sit on the floor next to the whelping box. Dip your fingers into the gruel and place a small dab midway on the puppy's tongue. These puppies generally react negatively at first. Usually by the third time food is offered they eagerly accept being fed. A few puppies continue to refuse food, struggling against any introduction. They open their mouths widely and, wrinkling their lips, expel the gruel. Do not force these puppies. They will accept food as eagerly as other littermates in another day or two. If after two days these puppies do not accept food, consult the veterinarian.

It is okay to give the dam leftovers each time the puppies are fed. Always mix fresh food for each feeding no matter what the puppies' responses are. Once they are eating well, always prepare slightly more food than will be taken at one feeding. If puppies "polish" their dish and vie competitively for sufficient food, gluttony can result. Gluttonous eaters are more prone to gastric torsion (bloat). Gluttony can be controlled early by feeding these puppies separately with, instead of the entire litter, only one or two siblings sharing the dish. Serving portions must be sufficient to insure leftovers.

Orphaned puppies and those from large litters generally respond to feeding earlier (two-and-a-half to three weeks) than puppies fed by their dam. Most puppies respond to feeding at three-and-a-half to four weeks. Premature puppies' development for feeding initiation is usually counted *from the due date*, not the birth date. (See Chapter 9, Orphan, Premature and Unthrifty Puppies.) Food should be regularly offered from two-and-a-half weeks even if the puppies wade through and "wear" much of it.

INTRODUCING SEMISOLID AND NEW FOODS

The type of pan used for food introduction can have an effect on how quickly puppies learn to lower their heads to eat. "Flying saucer" puppy dishes can be purchased from a pet supplier or a catalog. When puppies have learned to eat without supervision, one of these low-sided metal dishes may be employed.

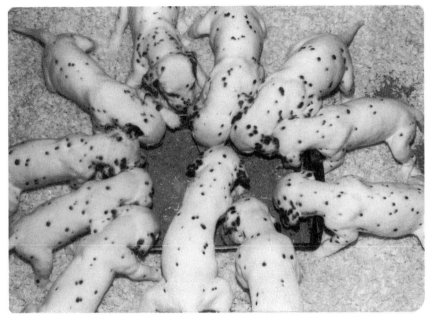

After one or two days, the puppies' milky gruel is thickened slowly to a paste-like consistency with the addition of small amounts of meat and well-soaked dry food or commercially-made weaning formula. Note the low-sided glass dish. *Dalmatians: Rambler Kennels*

Glass cake or pie pans also make serviceable puppy dishes. Initially puppies appear to "prefer" glass rather than metal dishes. Like babies, puppies take anything and everything into their mouths. Glass pans have no taste and are therefore not objectionable. Any metal other than stainless has a distinct taste from which many puppies initially recoil. A litter of small-breed puppies may never outgrow a pie-plate feeding dish during the time they are with the breeder. Large-breed puppies require additional pans to allow equal feeding opportunities. No puppy should be crowded and forced to vie aggressively for sufficient food.

Commercial dry foods that meet the special nutritional requirements of puppies are available. Some of them have the constitution and flavor of soggy cardboard. Care must be taken when selecting puppies' dry food to avoid puppies turning away, turning them into finicky eaters. The commercial dry puppy food can be added to the diet before puppy teeth grow through the gums. Add small amounts of the dry to the earlier formula while decreasing and finally deleting the cereal or commercial puppy weaning formula over a day's period. Allow the food to absorb all the moisture, softening, then add meat, (and by now) a small amount of warm tap water and stir before feeding.

After teeth penetrate the gums the puppies are ready for more texture in their food. By this time cereal is abandoned and the puppies no longer need milk mixed in their formula to excite eating. Continue to offer the bitch's milk replacement or the formula you have made in a separate bowl four or five times

160

daily. Continue to add a raw egg yolk each time. Discard old milk formula, giving it to the dam. Make fresh milk for each feeding. Always have fresh water in a clean bowl available to the puppies. Dry puppy food may also be left available for "demand feeding" by this time. Never leave food where it can attract flies.

There is no absolute rule about when puppies are ready to move from one stage of their feeding program to another. Each litter develops along general guidelines and every puppy is an individual character. As weaning approaches and the dam's support wanes, add a slightly increased amount of puppy vitamins and minerals to their meals. Be conservative; it is better to underdose than overdose. The brood matron should be continued on her supplementary therapy until weaning.

Initiate feeding between 18 and 21 days according to overall litter development. Once puppies eat with minimal assistance or voluntarily, offer food six times throughout the day at regular intervals. A schedule may look like the following: 7:00 A.M., 10:00 A.M., 1:00 P.M., 4:00 P.M., 7:00 P.M. and 10:00 P.M. It is important to offer food at three-hour intervals during the first one or two days of feeding. Puppies are not always ready to eat at the same time. A puppy ravenous for one meal may pick at the next. Brief intervals help puppies establish their feeding schedule, setting certain "Pavlovian" responses. After a few days the puppies can be moved to a somewhat more reasonable schedule, being fed five times daily.

Young puppies cannot ingest enough food at one time to hold them for long intervals between meals. Supplementary feeding helps to relieve puppies' increasing demands for milk production, setting matron and puppies up for weaning. Do not plan activities taking you away from the litter longer than a meal interval. Remember also to increase the amount of food offered to puppies as they grow. If they clean their pans, or begin growling and fighting in competition eating, the puppies are crowded and not being fed enough. There should always be at least a little food left over. Bacteria develop rapidly: discard old food and mix fresh for each feeding. The litter should stay on five daily meals until shortly before they leave your home. At this time they can be reduced to four meals a day and a "snack."

Very small portions of finely chopped raw liver added to the regular diet is good for older puppies and dogs. Early weanlings can be given a few drops of liver juice in their gruel. Too much liver in a diet causes diarrhea. If loose stools occur, immediately withdraw all liver for the next 24 hours. If the stools resume a normal shape and color, liver can be put back in smaller amounts. The initial feedings and those directly after a digestive upset must be bland to reestablish normalcy.

When the puppies begin social interaction and the meal interval is increased, you have more time to enjoy your litter. Further meal reduction is determined by the puppies, when they consistently ignore the same meal over a three-day period. While each puppy is an individual and will not always be hungry at the same time as littermates, in this instance the "democratic vote" with the majority ruling determines the ultimate numbers of meals offered. The quantity of food required by the litter varies from one litter to another. The time of year puppies are born and the exercise and stimuli available are all strongly influential factors upon the volume ingested. Puppy-formulated dry foods may be left available for "on-demand" feeding to supplement the hungriest puppies between regular meals. On-demand feeding also helps to prevent gluttony.

CHOOSING THE RIGHT DRY PUPPY FOOD

There are numerous dry puppy foods available on the market with wide price variations. The most expensive food is not necessarily the best for your breed. An inexpensive brand can prove costly in the long run by required volume for ingestion. Look for a good puppy food that can be safely fed either wet or dry. The food should be meat-based with high-quality protein. Meat alone is totally inadequate as diet and causes other problems. The list of ingredients is either on a side or back panel of the bag with the order of greatest volume first, the least amount last. If you are uncertain about which brand to select, ask the food dealer for samples or purchase test amounts. Use these following criteria to test the food selected. Does the puppy food swell markedly when mixed with water and allowed to stand for twenty minutes? If the food swells, so will puppy bellies. Gas forms as the result of a slowed gastric emptying time. If enough gas is formed, the puppies become colicky. Food swelling at the least can cause puppies to feel full and sluggish an inordinate amount of time after eating, limiting their necessary exercise. Puppies that do not vigorously challenge their developing muscles have a slower physical and emotional growth rate than counterparts on another feed. As a result, some of these sluggish puppies are never able to fully maximize their genetic potential. Ideally puppy food should disintegrate, becoming mush a few minutes after being mixed with warm water. If this mixture is allowed to dry in the pan it turns into "cement." Swelling, if any, should be negligible.

Look for puppy foods with a higher protein level than that offered adults by the same manufacturer. While certain breeds require higher or lower protein levels, puppy food should be of a high protein and caloric value. Also look for additives. Puppies need a food that is easily digested with a fast gastric emptying time, one which is palatable to them and not the owner. Nor do puppies need color added to their feed, making it attractive to the owner. Some dog food brands contain artificial food coloring that can stimulate tear duct inflammation. Once this type of response to artificial coloring occurs, it is usually always present. Tear duct inflammation is noted as a brownish tearing stain at the inner corner of each eye. The staining can also be an environmental allergic reaction or incubation of an illness. If there is a question about the cause for tear stains, or changing to a better food brand does not initiate some positive response within a few days, consult your veterinarian.

Never radically change any dog's food. Older dogs are more sophisticated and can handle a wider variety of foods and dietary indiscretions. Puppies cannot.

Sudden changes in food, water or a dietary indiscretion usually cause immediate fecal changes. Be particularly aware of diarrhetic conditions that cause precipitous and severe loss of body fluids, upsetting the electrolyte balance. Severe diarrhea can, if left unchecked, be fatal. Any change in puppies' feces must be noted and carefully observed. If these changes continue more than a few hours, call your veterinarian. Carefully observe the puppies' stools. If the stools become loose or poorly formed, the feed you selected might not be the right formula for them. Worms and other parasites can also cause loose stools. They will not be seen in a gross examination. The presence of undesirable "guests" can only be determined under microscopic examination by the veterinarian. (See Chapter 14, Parasites and Immunizations.)

Some dogs assimilate food more easily than others, utilizing almost everything they ingest. These are known as "easy keepers." The converse can also be found within a litter, with some puppies requiring ingestion of larger food quantities composed of higher fat and protein content. Constant observation coupled with weight checks at least twice weekly keeps the breeder well informed about each puppy's progress. The weight gain should be steady. A puppy that does not gain weight, or one that loses weight, is indicative of a puppy in dire trouble. The cause must be found without delay by taking the unthrifty puppy immediately to the veterinarian. (See chapter 9, Orphan, Premature and Unthrifty Puppies.)

Growth-chart guidelines have been developed for all breeds. Old-timers in your breed generally have rule-of-thumb guidelines also. While no puppy can grow beyond its genetic potential when everything is optimumly maximized, they can easily be irrevocably stunted by environment and dietary inadequacy. Puppies' most rapid growth occurs between birth and six months. This is the most crucial time of any dog's life. You only get what you pay for. The provision of a properly balanced diet during these weeks promotes maximizing a puppy's genetic potential. Puppies of certain breeds increase their weight 60 times during their first critical year. They require the best you have to offer.

Age (Months)	Adult Weight (%)
1	10
2	20
3	33
4	50
5	67
6	83
7	96
10	100

DENTAL DEVELOPMENT

With but the rarest of exceptions, puppies are toothless at birth. The outlines of the deciduous (first) teeth may be seen beneath the gums, if not at birth, within a few days. After another few days the presence of these "milk" teeth may be felt, as well as seen, as little bumps beneath the skin. Puppy teeth begin erupting through the gums about the time the puppies stand securely to eat. Generally by the time puppies are one month old, all the deciduous teeth have erupted. The teeth of medium- and large-breed puppies develop more rapidly than small-breed and Toy puppies. It is not unusual for Toy puppies to be a few weeks behind their large-breed counterparts.

While most puppies have no problems teething, there always can be the exceptional puppy. The first signs of teething problems may be noted by a change in stool and/or appetite depression. The gums may swell significantly and, on occasion, the sinuses become affected. These puppies can run a fever, become lethargic, eat little or not at all and appear generally unthrifty. Because of puppies' rapid development, the onset of these severe first teething reactions appear to occur suddenly. A puppy may be apparently fine during one portion of the day and distressed only a few hours later. Do not waste time. Any imbalance can be a major setback to a puppy's development.

Puppies begin shedding deciduous teeth between two and four months of age. During this period they may have a few days of apparent toothlessness as the incisors begin to appear: first the uppers and then the lowers. The last teeth to erupt through the gum line are the molars. By six months the puppy has shed all or almost all the deciduous teeth, and the permanent ones are in place. By eight months the average puppy's dentition is completed.

During the time of teething between deciduous and permanent teeth, puppies' mouths should be carefully checked at least once a week. Some puppies retain their puppy teeth even when the permanent ones have erupted. This is most often seen in the canines, the long "fang" teeth bracketing the front of a dog's mouth. Occasionally this "double" dentition is also seen with the incisors. The puppy's bite can be permanently disturbed with such an occurrence. In some cases, solidly set lower deciduous canines cause the permanent ones to penetrate the puppy's hard palate (roof of its mouth). This condition is painful, an invitation to infection and can often precipitate drastic personality changes in the puppy.

Make it a habit to "play" with puppies' mouths. Pull their lips back gently and rub your fingers along their gums. (Do not touch their sensitive noses.) Put your fingers in the puppies' mouths but do not allow them to chew. Praise them effusively while you make this examination. Then give the puppies a reward of a special treat, a tidbit of food. Within a few days the puppies readily and calmly accept oral examinations. Never correct a puppy harshly when examining the mouth, even if the puppy pulls away. This oral desensitization must always be performed in a positive manner to be successfully trained. Most puppies do not have problems teething although they gnaw on any object vigorously during this period. Provide the puppies with appropriate manufactured toys to play with, to exercise their jaws and irritated gums safely. Minor gum irritations can also be assuaged by providing the puppies with ice cubes for gnawing.

In addition to more vigorous and avid periods of gnawing, some puppies' gums become swollen, discolored (brightly pink) and sensitive or even painful to the touch. Canines and molars can cause more discomfort with (occasional) swelling and possible infection into sinus cavities. Undue gum swelling and discoloration and/or swelling of the jaw, lymphatic node area, muzzle and areas beneath the eyes during this period require *prompt* veterinary attention.

Teething commonly causes diarrhea in some puppies. Whether caused by teething, such stools should *always* be checked microscopically by the veterinarian for possible signs of parasitic infestation or microbiotic infection. Diarrhea is at this time also indicative of fever. Any puppy having diarrhea must be seen immediately by the veterinarian, along with a stool sample for appropriate treatment and to rule out possibility of other infection.

Periods of teething and rapid growth can also result in puppies' ears doing undesirable ''things'' for the breed. Prick-eared puppies whose ears have already become erect may have periods where the ears droop significantly. Rose-eared puppies' ears may become pendulous or pricked during this stage. Ear position is highly important to many breeds. Close attention must be paid to these puppies during their teething periods. Some puppies require having their ears' natural position reinforced during this time. Time is essential; if the ears of these puppies are left unattended and in the wrong position, the undesirable position often becomes permanent. Prick-eared puppies and those of large breeds particularly require a fortified puppy diet, including di-calcium phosphate supplements during their teething periods, optimizing their growth. The *only* di-calcium utilized should be formulated specifically for puppies. Either as a pill or carefully measured powder, this supplement given in a low dosage is added to their food once daily. Care must be taken *not to overdose* di-calcium phosphate, as growth may become compromised.

CANINE IMMUNIZATIONS

AGE:	5 Weeks	6 Weeks	9 Weeks	3 Months	4 Months	6 Months	1 Year
Measles	X						
Distemper		X	X	X	X	X	X
Hepatitis		X	X	X	X	X	X
Leptospirosis		X	X	X	X	X	X
Parvovirus		X	X	X	X	X	X
Parainfluenza		X	X	X	X	X	X
Coronavirus			X	X	X	X	X
Rabies					X		X
Heartworm Test*						X	X

(Between 6 and 12 months, depending upon the time of year.)
Suggested immunization schedule

14

Parasites and Immunizations

DOGS OF ALL AGES require protection against disease in order to remain healthy. Diseases can be contracted through airborne viruses, direct animal-to-animal transmission or by contact with infected feces, saliva or urine. Some diseases require an intermediate host such as a parasite or insect. Dogs not in regular contact with others lose immunities quicker than those exposed on a regular basis. When a dog is not inoculated annually, it becomes susceptible to disease.

Disease-producing organisms can be viral, protozoan, fungal, parasitic or bacterial. Infection occurs when a dog's body is invaded by one of these disease-producing organisms. An infectious disease, such as fungi, protozoa or bacteria, is parasitic and communicated by infection. A contagious disease is transmitted by contact: from one animal to another or animal to person. While not every infectious disease is contagious, contagious diseases are infectious.

Every dog's routine should include annual booster inoculations. Puppies are vaccinated through an early intensive course to build up their immunities. Once a prophylactic level has been initially reached, the animal must receive annual booster inoculations to help remain safe. This applies to all dogs, regardless of their environment and owner's life-style. No dog is exempt from ever coming in contact with a disease. Even the strictly backyard pet is prey to airborne viruses.

NATURAL IMMUNITY AND SUSCEPTIBILITY TO DISEASE

Shortly before birth and for a few days thereafter, dams secrete colostrum when lactating. Puppies' first immunities are found in their dam's antibodies through her colostrum. If the dam's inoculations against diseases are not current, her puppies receive no antibodies. Immunities acquired from the antibodies remain in effect through weaning and for approximately two weeks thereafter. Vaccination immediately subsequent to weaning is therefore critical to maintaining puppies' health.

It is every breeder's responsibility to initiate a prevention program through his or her veterinarian. Not all veterinarians follow the same program schedule. Some begin inoculating puppies shortly before or just at the time of weaning. Other veterinarians wait until the weaning process is completed. Vaccinations should be initiated prior to the time a breeder's home becomes an "entertainment center" for prospective puppy owners. Visitors may inadvertently carry disease on their clothing into a home. It is sad to lose a puppy from any cause, and a crime when loss is preventable.

Puppies of weaning age are highly susceptible. Unless you are prepared to keep your litter cocooned in a totally sterile environment, preventive care by immunization is requisite to rearing healthy puppies beyond weaning. A sterile environment does not mean merely placing the litter in the backyard and leaving it there. A sterile environment requires complete laboratory conditions, including special air filters and no personal contact. *This is not realistic.* As the breeder, it is your responsibility to insure your litter's initially healthy start.

Many veterinarians outline the following prophylactic immunizations. Interval periods may vary slightly from one practitioner to another. Some may suggest when necessary, initiating an early prophylactic program prior to weaning. Note: The measles vaccine is *not* inactivated by the dam's immunities. All inoculations should be given annually except for rabies, which is given every three years. If an area is in quarantine or the dog travels internationally, rabies vaccination may be required every two years. Puppies in urban or high-density suburban areas and puppies of owners who travel should also have the Bordetella (kennel cough) vaccine.

THE DHLPP, CORONA, BORDETELLA AND RABIES VACCINES

Canine distemper not too long ago was the most dreaded of all puppy diseases, occurring more frequently in young rather than adult dogs. This viral disease, highly contagious and universally present in all dog populations, is now totally avoidable when timely protection is given. Exposure normally occurs early in life, with transmission by object contamination or the aerosol-droplet route.

The incubation period is between six to nine days, with onset marked by

168

an elevated temperature lasting for one to three days before returning to normal, then rising again for approximately a week. Eyes appear reddened and matter collects at the inner corners, nasal discharge may be present and the puppy is sensitive to light. Depression, anorexia and diarrhea are also common indicators. Secondary pneumonia often develops and, if the dog recovers, it can succumb to other problems such as nervous system disorders including seizures and apparent disoriented wandering. Severity may be mild to severe: the course may last ten days to several months, during which time intermittent periods of apparent remission and activity occur.

Routine prophylactic inoculations make an occurrence of this disease unnecessary. When the virus is present, there is no direct treatment. Therapy is by support measures of intravenous fluids and antibiotics to avoid secondary infections. The prognosis depends on early discovery, therapy and severity.

Infectious canine hepatitis is a contagious viral disease often characterized by an elevated temperature, prolonged bleeding time, severe depression, mucous membrane congestion and marked leukopenia (reduction of the blood's leukocyte count). The incubation period is six to nine days, and dogs of all ages are susceptible. Infection usually occurs after ingestion of the virus. Direct transmission can also occur during acute stages of the illness, when the virus is present in all secretions and excretions. Eventually the virus localizes in the kidneys and is eliminated in the urine for several months afterward. Virus-containing urine from recovered dogs is believed to be the primary source of transmission.

Tests have exhibited that 80 percent of dogs over one year have been exposed to hepatitis. The disease's onset is abrupt and varies from slight fever to fatality. Indicators can mirror those of canine distemper. While rarely seen because of routine inoculations, young unimmunized puppies remain susceptible. Treatment of affected dogs is by support therapy and the prognosis among young puppies is poor.

Leptospirosis is a highly contagious bacterial disease affecting dogs of all ages. It can cause fever, oral ulcers, liver disease and renal (kidney) failure. It is transmitted from one dog to another and to humans. Infection occurs after oral and nasal mucosa are contaminated by infective urine. The incubation period is 5 to 15 days. The onset may be sudden and is characterized by an elevated temperature, appetite loss, vomiting, depression, weakness and possible jaundice. Treatment is by antibiotics and fluids. The prognosis is usually poor. The incidence among males is greater than females. Pets should be confined to their own yards if a local outbreak occurs. Fresh water must always be available to help avoid indiscriminate drinking, for example, from cesspools and ponds that can be contaminated by rat urine. Booster inoculations must be given on a regular basis.

Lyme disease is caused by a bacterial organism (*Borrelia burgdorferi*) and is transmitted primarily through insect contact, most notably by ticks. It may also be transmitted by flies and fleas. It affects dogs of all ages and humans. Clinical manifestations can be some or all of the following: lameness, swollen joints, loss of stamina and fever. Lameness may be mild to severe, one or more

Lyme disease cases continue to rise

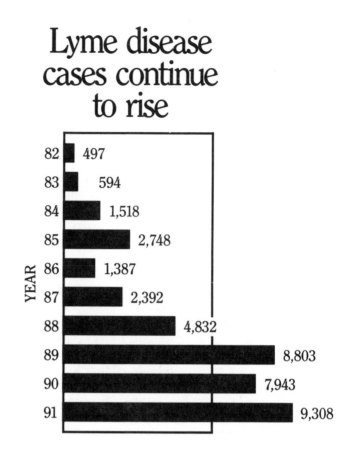

YEAR	Cases
82	497
83	594
84	1,518
85	2,748
86	1,387
87	2,392
88	4,832
89	8,803
90	7,943
91	9,308

U.S. Lyme disease incidence today.

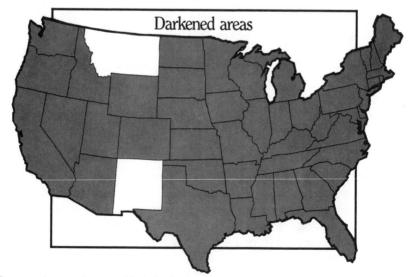

Darkened areas

Case numbers and geographical distribution of Lyme disease

Fort Dodge Laboratories

joints may be involved, usually the rear limbs. The bacteria migrate through the bloodstream to the joints, and in very severe cases, the bacteria colonize in the spinal cord joints, the effect of which may appear to be total paralyzation.

Definitive diagnosis is a blood test performed by a veterinarian and analyzed by a laboratory. Treatment and full recovery are normal. Reinfection can occur.

Canine parainfluenza is the most common viral isolate from dogs with upper respiratory disease. The disease is contagious and the virus replicates itself in the epithelial cells of the nasal mucosa, trachea, bronchi, bronchioli and peribronchial lymph nodes. Clinical signs of infection, including cough, are mild and of short duration, about six days.

Exposure and contamination is by aerosol-droplet and is usually found among high concentrations of animals such as may be found in shelters, boarding facilities and shows. The incubation period is approximately nine days. Treatment is by support therapy and antibiotics to help prevent secondary infection. Prophylaxis is by annual inoculation.

Canine parvovirus is highly contagious and infectious, and can affect dogs of any age. Transmission is primarily by contact with infected feces, or through clothing (including shoes) of people who have had contact with an infected animal. The incubation period is 3 to 12 days and onset sudden. Indications can be lack of appetite, fever, lethargy, bloody diarrhea, abdominal distress and vomiting.

Antibiotics help avoid secondary bacterial infections. Therapy includes withholding of food and water while supporting by intravenous fluids. The prognosis is guarded and affected by early determination and support therapy. Fatality can occur within two to four days of onset. Prophylaxis is by regular inoculations and environmental cleanliness. Use of chlorine bleach, such as Clorox, in kennel areas (and on shoe soles of visitors) and other areas where dogs habitually gather, helps to control transmission.

Canine coronavirus is a serious, highly contagious disease that causes severe gastroenteritis and affects dogs of all ages and breeds. It is particularly devastating to puppies. Secondary infection aggravates the disease's severity and complicates effective therapy. The onset is sudden with a 24-hour to two-week incubation period. Clinical manifestations include vomiting, followed shortly thereafter by hemorrhagic diarrhea and sudden death. The virus can remain active in feces for six to nine days, and in the soil and kennel areas for six months to several years. Transmission is contact and can be carried on shoes and equipment.

Initial symptoms include loss of appetite, shortly followed by (or simultaneous with) a soft or loose stool. Mucus and/or variable amounts of blood may be present in the feces. Stools, often "orangish," are characteristically fetid, having an unusually offensive, putrid odor. Vomiting of variable frequency may occur and can be tinged with blood. The diarrhea continues as a loose stool, or as an oozing of frothy yellow orange, semisolid material. Projectile diarrhea can occur either as a watery or bloody fluid. Relapses can occur within one to three weeks. Some animals have persistent diarrhea for three to four weeks even though they have received support therapy.

Affected young puppies may die suddenly before treatment can be effected. Stress, sudden temperature changes, fatigue or the presence of other infections significantly enhance the severity of coronaviral disease in dogs of any age. Treatment is by immediate veterinary care and includes support intravenous fluids. Warmth and absence of stress are conducive to recovery.

Kennel cough (tracheobronchitis) is highly contagious but self-limiting, involving the trachea and bronchi. Dogs of all ages are susceptible. It is rapidly spread among high-density dog populations, such as kennels (ergo the name), boarding facilities, veterinary hospitals and dog shows.

The exact cause is unknown but apparently airborne. It can be caused by a combination of the parainfluenza virus and Bordetella bacterium. Precipitating factors can be stress, drafts, high humidity and poorly ventilated areas. The incubation period is five to ten days.

Indicators are a harsh, dry cough followed by retching or gagging, in attempts to clear small amounts of mucus from the throat. Paroxysms can be aggravated by a tight collar, direct pressure applied to the throat and excitement. A slightly elevated temperature may occur if a secondary bacterial infection occurs. Stress can cause a relapse. Treatment is with antibiotics to avoid secondary infection and, if the dog is uncomfortable, a pediatric cough suppressant. Regular inoculations for parainfluenza (CPI) help to avoid contraction.

Rabies is an acute viral encephalomyelitis usually transmitted through saliva from an affected animal's bite. Contamination of existing fresh wounds can also occur but is rare. Transmission can occur prior to onset of clinical signs. Incubation is generally 15 to 50 days, but can go longer, up to several months. The prognosis for an affected animal is fatal.

Essentially there are three clinical stages: prodromal, excitative and paralytic. The first sign is a behavioral change, with affected animals usually not eating and drinking, and seeking solitude. Frequent urination may be noted. Also noted is erection in males and evidence of sexual desire stimulated by the genitourinary tract irritation. After the prodromal period of one to three days the animals either exhibit signs of viciousness or paralysis.

The paralytic form is characterized by inability to swallow, profuse salivation and dropping of the lower jaw. Paralysis rapidly progresses throughout the body and death occurs within a few hours.

A furious form is represented by the classical "mad dog" syndrome, whereby the dog becomes irrational and aggressively vicious. The facial expression is alert and anxious, with dilated pupils. Noise invites attack on any moving object, with loss of fear or caution of natural enemies. There is no evidence of paralysis during this excitatory stage. Dogs rarely live ten days beyond onset of signs.

Prevention is by regular booster inoculations every two or three years, depending upon the geographical area. The only positive diagnosis for rabies is by autopsy.

Continued research periodically offers improved vaccines. The above is intended as a guideline only. Intervals between prophylactic inoculations may vary slightly from one veterinary practitioner to another.

COMMON PARASITES

There are three basic forms of parasitism, that of internal organs, blood and skin. Most common are worms, fleas, ticks, mites and lice. Various geographical regions have problems peculiar to those areas. Becuase it is not possible to prevent a pet from ever coming in contact with one or more infestations, routine prevention proves less costly than treatment. An infested dog is often prone to secondary infections. Proper sanitation of the pet's quarters, including yard, is requisite for good health maintenance. Routine grooming, including therapeutic dips, sprays and collars help to insure a pet's health. No animal can feel good or be truly responsive when suffering an infestation.

The presence of fleas and ticks is easily determined by gross examination. Definitive diagnosis for the presence of most parasites is made, however, under microscopic examination with either a fecal or blood sample. Fresh uncontaminated samples are essential for a correct diagnosis of any parasitic condition. It is highly important to routinely submit a fecal sample and request a blood test when annual booster inoculations are given.

Worms are a common parasitic infestation and cause of diarrhea. The presence of diarrhea should not be consigned to a final determination by the owner as to whether the pet has worms. Definitive diagnosis is made by the veterinarian, under microscopic examination, of a fresh fecal or blood sample. *Only* the veterinarian who has made the determination of the *type* of parasitic infestation should prescribe, dose and monitor the drug therapy form used in eradication of parasites.

Chiggers (trombiculiasis) affecting man and dogs are prevalent in southern U.S. areas. Therapy is generally best effected by manual removal. Prevention is somewhat effective when limiting the dog to manicured grass.

Coccidiosis (*Isospora bigemina* or *Isospora rivolta*) are protozoans that cause an enteritis condition of young dogs (and cats). Severity may vary from mild to severe bloody diarrhea, lethargy and weakness from dehabilitation, anorexia and emaciation. Contraction is environmental or transmitted and onset indications rapid. Infestation is seldom fatal when treated by the veterinarian in a timely manner.

Fleas are the most common bane to dogs and their owners. Fleas constantly bite, producing toxic and allergenic salivary secretions. The sensitive dog scratches and chews, relieving the itch, only to produce a hotspot (or other dermatitis) condition, which often leads to secondary infection. Fleas also act as temporary hosts in tapeworms' life cycles. The dog acquires tapeworms as it chews, ingesting the fleas. Ridding a dog of tapeworm calls for repeated costly treatments.

The presence of fleas is determined by examining the dog's tail base and head near the eyes. A heavily infested dog can suffer pernicious anemia, which, if untreated, can produce irreversible damage. Treatment of the dog is effective only when the environment (house and yard) is included in therapies and prophylaxis. Flea control is comparatively easy through a wide selection of excellent products, including a choice of soaps, shampoos, sprays, powders and dips.

Because flea eggs are hatched every eight to ten days, an infested dog must be treated twice within this time period.

Flies can cause a condition commonly known as "fly struck," which can be fatal when conditions are sufficiently unsanitary. Generally flies attack dogs' ears and muzzles (on top near the nose). If untreated, fertilized eggs are deposited in the sites of bite wounds, and larvae develop to feed on the host dog and eventually perforate the skin.

Giardia is a protozoan infestation usually found around remote bodies of water. It occurs in dogs of any age and is transferable to and from humans. The noticeable onset is sudden, and indicators can be diarrhea, lethargy, lack of appetite and weight loss. Determination is made by fecal microscopic examination. Therapy is successful provided treatment is initiated early.

Heartworm (filariasis) infestation occurs in two forms throughout the lower forty-eight states. One is apparently harmless, the other if left untreated is lethal. When the dog is bitten by a female mosquito, microfilariae (larval heartworms) are discharged into the animal's bloodstream. It takes two to four months of migration for the larval worms to reach a dog's right ventricle, and an additional four months to reach maturity. Heartworm transmission between dogs is made indirectly by a mosquito biting the infected animal, serving as an intermediary host, then finally biting an uninfected dog. Diagnosis is made through a blood test. Unless the damage is in advanced stages, most dogs respond well to therapy. Regular safe prophylactic treatment is available and recommended.

Hookworms (*Ancylostoma*) are primarily found in the southern portions of the United States. Most infections are by ingestion but can also be caused by skin penetrations. Infection may also be transferred to puppies in utero. An infected dog may appear anemic, which in a young dog can include pneumonia and black tar-like stools. Diagnosis is made by microscopic fecal examination. Therapeutic treatment is successful. Prophylactic treatment is essentially that of clean, dry quarters.

Lice are wingless, live and reproduce on one host species. Dogs can be infested with either the biting (mallophaga) or suctorial (anoplura, blood-sucking). The lice and nits (eggs) may be observed without microscopic aid. The infected dog's coat is rough and dry, and may be matted. Sucking lice create small wounds subject to secondary infections. Lice constantly crawling, biting or piercing a dog's skin cause the animal to become very nervous and irritable. Infestation is usually by contact. Treatment is by therapeutic shampoo or dip and is successful.

Mange commonly occurs in one of two forms, being either *Demodex* or *Sarcoptes*, and is caused by microscopic mites that burrow into the skin. Positive identification can be made only by a veterinarian, under microscopic examination of skin samples taken from affected areas. These conditions are readily treated when diagnosis occurs early. **Demodectic** mange is commonly known as follicular or juvenile mange, and is caused by a mite affecting hair follicles, primarily among young dogs. It is also less well known as "red mange," because of discoloration of the skin and infected hair follicles that develop small pustules on the dog's skin. Afflicted dogs suffer reddened and thickened skin and allopecia (hair loss). The onset is marked by hair loss around the dog's eyes, muzzle or forepaws. Often certain family lines are prone to this condition. Fortunately, however, treatment has proven successful and response rapid. **Sarcoptic** mange, highly uncomfortable and highly contagious, causes severe itching. The affected animal often develops a secondary skin infection from lesions caused by vigorous and prolonged scratching. Indicators can be vigorous and prolonged scratching, allopecia resulting from scratching and thickened skin at infested sites. The skin may also exude an uncharacteristic, mouse-like odor. Positive identification is made through microscopic examination of a skin sampling taken with a sterile blade. Treatment to effect a cure is often prolonged.

   Mites are related to spiders. Multiple varieties cause dogs problems, including *Demodex canis* and *Sarcoptes scabiei canis* (see above), *Cheyletiella parasitivorax* and *Otodectes cyanotis*. **Cheyletiella** is found most often among puppies, appears as dandruff along the spine and is highly contagious to people. *Otodectes cyanotis* are the most commonly found mites. They cause ear infections (otorrhea), at times of such severity to nerve endings located at the ear canal base that "running fits" may be produced. The presence of these mites may be noted during routine grooming. The affected inner ears appear reddened. Tissue swelling may be present. As untreated infestation progresses, the ear produces an offensive odor and a dark reddish or blackish waxy exudate is noted at the ear canal's head. Definitive diagnosis is made of the exudate under microscopic examination. These mites appear as tiny white specks. Early treatment is effective and simple. Preventative care is managed by routine examination and cleaning of the pet's ears. Preventative care products are available through most pet suppliers.

   Roundworms (ascarids) are the most commonly found worm variety among dogs. They are particularly common among puppies that have been infected by their mothers while in utero. Their presence is usually not, however, a problem for adults. Roundworms can be transmitted to people through ingestion of the eggs, but will grow only to the larval stage. Larvae migrating into human tissue is a rare occurrence. Only dogs complete the life cycle of the roundworm. Infested puppies may appear unthrifty and have bloated bellies. Treatment and prophylactic management are easily effected.

   Tapeworms (cestodes) go through an intermediate host such as fleas to complete a life cycle. The flea ingests the tapeworm eggs and hosts them through the larval stage. Only when a dog bites (and ingests) the flea is the tapeworm able to complete its life cycle. Flea control is absolutely essential for effective eradication of tapeworms or the dog reinfests. Clinical signs and microscopic examinations may be negligible. Diarrhea may not be present. Occasionally tape segments or "rice grains" may be seen in the gross examination of a heavily infected dog's stool. This dog may drag its rectum along the ground. Whenever a dog is infested with more fleas, it probably has tapeworms.

   Ticks are common to most geographical areas and are usually found in the

Lone Star tick locations.

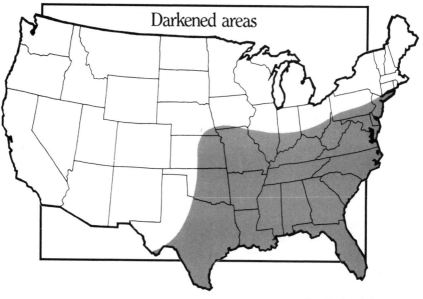

Darkened areas

Fort Dodge Laboratories

dog's ears, between the toes and on its neck. Redness or crusts may appear at the site of attachment after the tick drops off the dog. The female tick, when found on a dog, is engorged with blood. Therapeutic dips are effective in eradication and control. Care must be taken to remove the tick's head if the tick is manually removed with tweezers.

Whipworms (*Trichuris vulpis*) are contracted through ingestion of infective eggs. The life cycle is direct, continuing through larval development and maturity in the large intestine. Eggs contained in a moist environment are viable up to five years. Weight loss and diarrhea can be indicative of infestation. Diagnosis is made through microscopic fecal examination. Therapy is successful. Prophylaxis is by cleanliness and dryness of the dog's quarters.

Treatment of any parasitic infestation is at best toxic. Not every dog responds well or positively to treatment, some reacting negatively to therapeutic measures taken for parasitic control. Treatment should always be diagnosed and administered by the veterinarian. Should a negative reaction to drug therapy occur, countermeasures can be taken immediately by the veterinarian. Normally, adverse reactions do not occur. It is best to have all parasitic drug therapy administered and monitored at the veterinary hospital on at least the first occasion.

Once a puppy's tolerances are known, it may be possible for the owner to administer future therapies dispensed by the veterinarian. The veterinarian may allow a dog to be wormed at home if, for example, the infestation has been successfully treated before and no complications occurred. The owner should be able to, in this case, confine the dog to a suitable area that can be adequately disinfected.

Broad-spectrum over-the-counter parasitic drug therapies are usually not a wise choice. Few dogs host more than one parasitic infestation at a given time. Broad-spectrum treatments are unnecessary to these cases, and at times can be harmful or even lethal. Always remember that ridding a dog of any parasite is managed through safe levels of toxic therapies. Each parasitic infestation requires its own form of drug therapy. Through careful study, drug therapies are now manufactured that do not cause injury to dogs' delicate intestinal linings or organs. Advanced research has made drugs toxic only to the parasites, and negligibly toxic to the dogs.

Dogs can live with certain parasites although they are better off without them. Sometimes it is inadvisable to worm a dog, for instance, one that is very young or old, actively or recently ill. When to treat for parasitic infestation can be determined only through microscopic examination of the feces or a blood sample, by a qualified veterinary technician or doctor of veterinary medicine.

Unless you keep your dogs under optimum conditions, picking up their feces several times daily, regularly disinfecting their quarters and treating the area to discourage flies and mosquitoes, your animals will have to be repeatedly treated for parasitic infestations. Even when optimum conditions are met at home, parasite, airborne and contact diseases make regular checkups, inoculations and specific drug therapies necessary.

Puppy Performance. The most active puppy could be fast asleep and refuse to awaken, to put on a "performance." Warn visitors in advance that puppies, being baby dogs, have highly active and deeply quiet periods.

Artist: Jan Walker

15

Evaluating and Placing the Litter

T HERE has been, and always will be, controversy about methods used when grading litters and individual puppies. Each breed develops differently from any other, and individual lines mature at varying rates within a given breed. Some breeders "wet grade," selecting their best puppies from their moment of birth, while still wet from the sac. Other breeders believe that the puppies must be six weeks or older before the quality of an individual may be known.

You have been unconsciously grading your puppies also from birth, either labeling them as "cute," or basing your opinions on past experience. Formulating opinions as your litter matures is a natural reaction to their development. The perceptive breeder is able to see beyond color and markings, looking at bone, head shapes, angulation and other criteria. Many puppies change radically as they develop. As a result, most knowledgeable breeders make few comments about litter individuals other than early speculation. A few breeders have the natural ability to discern a puppy's balance. Others must work toward developing this ability, to see the animal's balance against the background of the breed Standard. Unfortunately, some people begin and end their dog experience in "kennel blindness," being incapable of reasonably assessing the merits, or lack thereof, in an animal.

Kennel blindness is usually found among those breeders who perceive that all puppies are "cute." Worse is the breeder who, infected with this "disease," infects others. The final and worst kennel blindness is found in "near" or "real" puppy mills, where one litter after another is bred. The reasoning behind these so-called "breeders" is, "This is what the public wants." The real root of this dread disease is found in these people's pocketbook.

A good breeder knows that opinions may change as the litter matures. Such opinion changes are not indicative necessarily of assessment inability, but may be proof of careful litter observations. Early breeder opinions are often more on an *idea* level. Final opinions about an individual's potential take time. An exception might be breeders who, completely familiar with their line's development, are often able to make an early determination between "pet-only" and show-prospect puppies. These people also encounter the "wait-and-see" puppies.

There is a strong misconception among the general populace that puppies left behind in a litter, after a few weeks have passed, are those that no one wants. Very often the reverse is true. Some final decisions may take extra weeks or even months between one or two very good quality puppies. The last decision in a well-bred litter is often the hardest for a breeder to make. It is not uncommon for a breeder with years of experience to call upon other knowledgeable people. A consensus, followed or not, can be helpful in final puppy selection. As a new breeder, it is wise to follow the procedure of requesting an opinion from those familiar with your breed, another breeder or handler of top dogs. When they help you grade your litter, ask them why exactly they feel one puppy is superior to another. It is easy to suffer kennel blindness, even if only to a small degree. It is easy also to lose perspective with adult dogs, and harder indeed to grasp perspective with adorable puppies.

Ask the professional handler, breeder or judge if he or she charges a fee when helping to grade a litter. Few breed professionals charge at all, while the fees of others normally cover only their expenses. If neither fees nor expenses are incurred, a gift of appreciation for their time and services is in order.

Because of indifferent quality, poorly bred and poorly cared-for litters are usually the easiest to grade. These litters are often spur-of-the moment breedings. A large well-bred litter is also easy to grade, normally having a range of puppies, from those showing promise to those that are pet quality. The small well-bred litter is the hardest to grade, with members exhibiting a high ratio of uniformity and promise.

Each breed Standard has its own criteria, setting that breed apart from all others. The only commonality may be said to be the fact that every dog has a head, four legs and a gait. Certain breed Standards call for specific gait types. While some call for a hackney or rolling action, by other Standards the mere presence of these gaits would be considered a major fault. Even if your Standard demands a very specific gait, the adult movement will be periodically exhibited by the puppies at about six weeks. A gait is the type movement exhibited when dogs trot, pace, canter or gallop. The desired gait for grading individuals is the trot, the very moment evaluated by bench show judges. In this gait a dog's four legs move alternately opposite: the right foreleg and left rear, then the left foreleg and right rear.

Grading puppies is never an easy task. A well bred puppy often exhibits its good breeding by standing correctly naturally, independently striking a "show pose."

Pug: Marshall Kelly

With the exception of a few breeds, a generalized gait exhibits good reach in the forequarters. The dog articulates (bends) the foreleg slightly, lifting to the stride's apex, just before "reaching" for the ground. An observer should be able to drop an imaginary plumb line from the dog's chin to the reaching forepaw as the animal gaits. When constructed correctly, the follow-through of the rear leg matches in a descriptive arc, the same extension of movement exhibited by the foreleg. Angulation, affecting gait types, varies from one breed to another. A dog of any breed should be able to travel, gaiting, in a straight line.

PUPPY PERSONALITIES

Be aware of the individual puppies as they play. Of course when they are first let out in the morning there is always the mad scramble and flying gallop. As the puppies settle down to their explorations, most will move in a gait. This is when the puppies should be carefully observed, grading them in their natural movement. Always be suspicious of a puppy that has difficulty in rising from a prone position. Suspect a puppy that never trots, moving its hindlegs independently, but instead consistently only gallops or "bunny-hops." Some of these puppies may even gait with the forelegs while hopping or galloping with the

Puppies should not be graded standing, on their looks alone. Their movement must also be graded according to the breed's Standard. *Alaskan Malamute: Barbara Curtis*

rear. Have a knowledgeable veterinarian examine these puppies carefully before a sale is made. Veterinary palpation might, in some cases, disclose dysplasia candidates.

The puppy that exhibits good breeding not only moves well, but also often stands correctly, striking a show pose. This pose is called a "stack." When adults, these puppies move from a gait into free stack without prompting, never requiring hours of training. The puppy that is put together correctly exhibits these moves, of gaiting and free stacking even if only momentarily, from about the time it is six weeks old. Often the puppies that strike the show pose, stacking voluntarily, prove to be better movers than others in the litter. These puppies are usually more naturally appealing to the eye when at rest and in motion.

Look at Me

If you are contemplating keeping a puppy or have a show home placement, choosing the right candidate from a well-bred litter does not always prove to be an easy task. Of course selection is biased toward the individual that appears to most closely meet the Standard's ideal criteria. Sometimes the choice between one or two puppies appears, at first, to be very close. This is not always the case,

182

Ring presence is a "Look at me!" attitude, no matter where the dog may be.

Shar Pei puppies: Carl Lindemaier, photographer: courtesy of M. Kelly

however, upon closer examination. When two puppies appear to be of identical merit, the automatic attraction gravitates toward the individual possessed of that elusive and hard-to-find quality, "ring presence." This is also a good prospect for a lively household.

Ring presence is the natural extra "oomph" a puppy has, coupled with a "Look at me!" attitude. No matter where this type of dog happens to be, in the Group ring or at the neighborhood barbecue, it possesses that truly undefinable aura that attracts people. For some dogs it is a regal manner, in others it is the extra sparkle that mesmerizes. This presence is quite real in the sense that it can definitely be felt and seen. When such an animal enters your view, the eye is automatically attracted, and lingers. Sometimes it is this intangible quality that makes the difference between a blue ribbon and that of another color. This "Look at me!" attitude in a puppy closely meeting the Standard's requirements should be a strong measurement of criteria when selecting a show prospect puppy.

A "deadhead" dog, no matter how conformationally perfect, can never be a show dog in the real sense of the term. At times these dogs can be cajoled into sparkling during periodic moments. Without expert guidance in handling, shows soon lose their interest, and the dogs soon once more revert to type. A show-prospect puppy, one which exhibits the criteria of closely meeting the breed Standard, must have a mien demanding attention. This attitude in a puppy must be cherished and fostered. If reared in a "No!" atmosphere, one where almost

If a puppy is to compete at all levels as an adult, it must exhibit certain character traits, including, open curiosity, friendliness, and lack of fear of loud noises and strange situations.
Alaskan Malamute: Monte and Debi Biss

every performance is berated, positive reinforcement is lacking and there are no appropriate toys to stimulate neural synapses, the puppy soon becomes discouraged and loses its sparkle, often permanently. This puppy will become a behavioral problem dog.

There are specific requirements for the people who want to train for work in the field, obedience and the bench show ring. Their puppy must have certain character traits beyond meeting the Standard if it is to compete at all levels. Their puppy must exhibit open curiosity and friendliness, and lack fear of loud noises and strange situations. The candidate should exhibit considerable sparkle and a lively interest in all that surrounds him. This puppy moves forward when greeting a new and strange encounter, without exhibition of fear or animosity. This special puppy should also exhibit earlier and more complete agility than siblings. The puppy exhibiting additional zest, agility and obvious sparkling intelligence is a good candidate for all work.

The puppy that is not lively, as well as slow to respond, aggressive, spooky, sulky, shy, clumsy or short of temper, is not a good candidate for trials or breeding, particularly when these problems are genetic rather than traumatized traits.

I'll Wait and See

The urban dweller of an apartment, duplex or home with a small yard is generally better suited to the quieter puppy. The older couple and those whose lives are of a more sedentary nature are also good candidates for a moderately quiet puppy. A family with older children might be best suited to the rambunctiously outward-going individual. The family who engages in a variety of outdoor activities and expects the dog to participate should be motivated toward the puppy that has a considerable amount of stamina. This puppy is the first one up to play and the last one to sleep.

The shy puppy needs a special home. Barring defects of hearing or sight, this puppy needs a quiet home that will faithfully take him to shopping centers, family outings and training classes: an environment where the puppy's psyche is consistently and gently positively reinforced. This puppy should not be placed with very young or rambunctious children. Such a placement could be disastrous, turning the puppy into a "fear biter."

GRADING PROSPECTIVE OWNERS

When parents visit, insist that they bring their children—all of them. How the children behave and interact with their parents in your home is indicative of the environment they offer a puppy. Certainly be very wary if the children are unruly, destructive or speak rudely to their parents. Such families often have a bad track record. Frequently this type of family has had many pets, losing or "getting rid" of their dogs because the animals also became unruly and troublesome. *When children are well mannered and polite through respect and not fear of their parents, their home offers a superior environment for the puppy that meets, by personality, their life-style.*

In addition to grading the litter, you will find yourself grading prospective purchasers also. This helps to insure the proper placement of every puppy into the correct environment for each personality type. There is no point in selling a puppy to the first viewers on a first-come, first-served and "how cute" basis. Each puppy has its own personality that is "right" only in certain homes. If the puppy is "mis-placed" it will either (hopefully) come back to you for replacement, end up unloved and unwanted in a backyard or shelter, be shuffled from one home to another or become so destructive that it is euthanized.

A puppy not of show quality should never be bred. If it is not a good enough breed representative to show, then it is not good enough for breeding, and will only produce more of its own kind. More "pet-onlies" are not necessary in an already overpopulated country of unwanted, "disposable" animals. Granted, there are pet-quality puppies in every litter. They are due the same consideration and time in rearing and placement as the finest show prospect. This fact of pets remains true no matter how many illustrious antecedents may be found in the pedigree. Irrevocable withdrawal from any breeding possibility must be made perfectly clear to prospective clients. If they insist that they want

185

to breed, either sell them the show-quality puppy at a show price or sell them no puppy at all.

Always detail the differences between the pet puppy your clients are looking at and a show-quality littermate, offering them the opportunity of making an informed decision predicated upon values and not price alone. Detail the American Kennel Club's breeding ineligibility policy. Explain that while their pet-only puppy issues from registered parents, and is itself eligible for registration, that offspring, should any occur, will *not* be eligible for registration. Specifically, show them where on the "blue slip" (the Application for Individual Registration) their puppy is shown as ineligible for a breeding program. Most people are aggreable to the idea of spaying or neutering when given the opportunity of acquiring a well-bred registered puppy at a price they can afford. Very often this will be a family's first registered animal. Often the pet-puppy interview takes a breeder's additional interest and time. It is time all breeders should wisely spend.

FINANCIAL CONCERNS

How do you establish and justify the price of your puppies? Did you objectively grade your litter alone or obtain expert outside opinion? Is your price commensurate with others of your breed, and in your area? Is your price based on objective assessment, or on emotional involvement, arbitrarily selecting a figure because it "sounds good"? It is not easy for the new breeder to equitably establish a purchase price for show prospect and pet puppies. When making objective litter assessments, a number of variables affecting price are due consideration. Is the litter champion-bred, rare or difficult to breed and whelp? Are there referrals from other breeders and the stud's owner?

The purchase price an established breeder charges is not necessarily the same for a new breeder, one who may lack effective networking. Established breeders of closely related dogs are often willing to help a sincere newcomer to the breed. The price selected must be made by objective assessment of each individual, and not an arbitrary price made by emotional involvement. The price norm is not what the market will bear, but instead the quality value of individual puppies. If your price is predicated on the dam's purchase and rearing, breeding and whelping investment, plus litter rearing and advertising fees, the sum when divided by the number of puppies present in the litter becomes astronomical. Certainly you do not want to price yourself out of the market, nor do you want to undersell, underestimating the value of your breeding.

*If you question how you are to "make money" from your litter, the answer is **never**.* Established breeders are satisfied when sales prices equal the amount spent when rearing a litter. Even if a slight loss is incurred, these breeders remain content with their performance and breeding program. Never predicate puppies' price by sex. Uninformed callers usually ask, "How much for your puppies?" After being told the difference between pet and show prospects, their next question is, "How much for your males?" and then, "Well, how much do you want for your females?'' Your first statement indicating prices are predicated only on quality is often misunderstood and ignored. Do not turn these people off by tuning them out. Invite them to visit the litter. You will have ample opportunity for education once they are in your home and captivated by the puppies' antics. Educating people why females are never less than males is very important. A response of this form helps to demonstrate the respect and value you place on all your puppies, predicated on quality alone.

Show puppies of most breeds are generally priced within a closely given range. The highest value is placed on those hardest to breed in accordance with their Standards' rigid idealized specifications. It is harder, for example, to breed an outstanding Bulldog or Brussels Griffon than many other breed types, even when the sires and dams are of comparable quality. Arriving at a just price for the pet-only quality puppy varies from one breeder to another. As a general guideline, pet puppies, regardless of sex, are normally offered at one half the price (or slightly less) than a show prospect from the same litter. Always, when speaking with prospective clients, make the price difference and reasons why perfectly clear from the very beginning.

ADVERTISING YOUR LITTER

New breeders are prone to make a mistake by not planning any puppy advertisements until after the litter has arrived. Some of these people panic as the puppies demand more food, personalized attention and costly veterinary care. Turning to their first available promotional source, they advertise in their local newspaper, in order to quickly ''get rid of'' the puppies. Quite often these are the people who bred with little or no forethought.

Both well-bred and puppies of indifferent quality are commonly available, and are more abundantly so during holiday seasons. Unless you are located in an exceptionally good area, waiting until the litter is seven weeks or older before advertising is inadvisable. Even if your litter becomes available for placement during a time when few puppies are advertised, they very rarely sell like hotcakes. Successful advertising, like successful breeding, takes very careful planning: *Where, when and how* are the key words.

Where: There are numerous marketplaces in which to advertise: local and out-of-town daily and weekly newspapers, local and national club publications, nationally distributed all-breed magazines and even when appropriate general sporting, hunting and fishing magazines. If your focus is strictly through your local newspaper, your advertisement can be telephoned within a day or two of its appearance. Realize, however, that newspaper advertisements are limited. Only a relatively small number of people scan the pet columns. Of these readers, some are strictly ''looky-lous.'' Realize that few sincerely interested people consider purchasing a show prospect through newspaper advertisements; the majority of these callers seek the pet-only companion.

All-breed dog magazines, which are sold at pet suppliers, shows and newsstands, are excellent advertising sources. Although expensive when initially compared with newspapers, dollar for dollar they reach the greatest number of sincerely interested consumers of both pet and show companions.

When: If your decision is to advertise in a limited or all-breed magazine, plan your campaign well in advance of the desired publication date. The majority of national publications have a two- or three-month lead time deadline. If your ad copy reaches the advertising editor the week your female is bred, your advertisement will not appear until the puppies are born or are even a month old. Some breeders submit advertising copy even before a breeding occurs. When copy is submitted for publication in advance of a breeding, be sure to include the month puppies are expected.

Advanced advertising allows readers the opportunity of contacting you in a timely manner and allows you to correspond without undue pressure for immediate puppy placements. This interim period also allows you time to politely investigate long-distance buyers. The investigation is bilateral: while you offer information about the sire and dam and send photographs, prospective clients share details about their life-styles, yards and commitment to a puppy.

Advance copy can be submitted to the editor, with a letter of instruction, even if you do not want to advertise before the litter's arrival. Succinctly indicate the starting month in which you want your advertisement to appear, always planning for publication by the puppies' due date. Remember the two- or three-month lead time. If the breeding or pregnancy does not occur, copy can be canceled. Be aware, however, that many magazines also have a policy of one month's lead time for cancellations.

There are two forms of magazine promotion, display and line advertisements. The latter advertisements generally appear alphabetically by breed, at the back of the magazine. Copy is limited to words only. Display advertising can include artwork or photographs in addition to informative copy. Displays cost more than other forms of advertisements, but are generally well worth the money spent.

How: Always plan your advertising campaign with the same carefully detailed attention you spent planning the breeding. If your copy does not specifically state what it is that you are offering for sale and in simple terms, you could lose the entire benefit of your dollars spent in advertising. You may wish to design your own display, or utilize the magazine's layout department. Commercial artists spend years of study to perfect this art. It is no disgrace, therefore, to require the abilities of design experts. When submitting copy to the advertising editor, include specific instructions and information for the insertion date and design department to use at their discretion.

Few people are motivated to respond to an advertisement that simply states, ''Puppies for sale.'' Your copy format will have a direct bearing on the responses you receive. When advertising before the puppies' birth, state their expected month of arrival. If your breed has different sizes, colors or coat types, specifically list them. If your breeding is closely based on a famous line, or the parents are titled, include these criteria also in your copy. Be prepared to wait several months for replies when advertising in a magazine. There appears to be an interim progression to magazine responses. If your copy first appears in the May issue, for example, you may not receive an inquiry that month, but should by June or July.

Or, if you employ your local newspaper, advertise well in advance of the puppies' readiness for their new homes. The best form of local advertising is short but explicit in content. Newspaper advertisement copy should include the following information: breed, color, size, Kennel Club, parents' titles and a telephone number. If you are available only during certain hours, include the times when callers may telephone.

While local advertisements seem to bring a disproportionate number of crank callers, do treat each caller with respect. Many of these people are poorly informed, lacking education in the realm of the better-bred, purebred pet. By treating these people with courtesy, painlessly and gently educating them, you may be able to bring new and sincere fanciers into your breed. Remember, these callers would not have initially telephoned unless interested.

Figure the spaces and lines when planning newspaper copy. Most newspapers have 33 spaces to a line; many have special four-day, weekly and monthly rates. Your advertisement should always cover Friday, Saturday and Sunday. Many people do not have time during the week to look at puppies. As a result, they may read only the weekend advertisements.

Alaskan Malamute puppies AKC reg.
Champion sire & dam. Large-boned.
Blk/wht m & fe. (202) 555-4444 5-9 pm

This advertisement covers a lot of information: you have large-boned, male and female, black-and-white, champion-bred Alaskan Malamute puppies that are registered with the American Kennel Club. You can be reached only during specific evening hours. If show and pet puppies are available, or you have placement preferences, state these in your advertisement also.

Whippet puppies AKC CH sire & dam.
Pet & show quality companions. 3 mos.
White & brindle. (407) 955-8185

or

Bull Terrier AKC white show/home.
Pref kids. CH sire. (818) 999-2705 5-9 pm

When price is stated in an advertisement, it is possible to lose an excellent placement. Proper placement of a puppy into the right environment for that individual and prospective family is more important than any monetary consideration. Always allow yourself opportunity to make an informed decision *after* having met prospective owners.

Local advertising often catches the attention of those aggressive callers who first ask about price. These people are not knowledgeable enough to ask about bloodlines, pedigrees, registration and inoculations. Their education becomes your responsibility when you engage them in conversation. Without mentioning price, politely respond to these callers by asking if they are interested in a pet or show-companion puppy. This opens an avenue of focus to the conversation, where the caller is able to request information about the differences between the two types of puppies (usually meaning the price difference).

Many callers have the misconception that show dogs are not pets, envisioning these dogs as pampered animals. Invite these people to your home to see the litter, in order to physically exhibit the difference between the two types of puppies. When the differences have been explained in person, why one puppy is strictly a pet and the other a show prospect, these people will be able to make an educated and focused informed decision. *Nevertheless, some callers absolutely insist on obtaining a price over the telephone. They are price shoppers only and often care little about quality.* In such cases, and although you may quote two prices of top show and pet-only puppies, invite these people into your home to physically see the differences, to be made aware of why there is a price difference.

The important item to remember when advertising is that your copy must attract people in order to generate a response. Think of your advertisement as advance public relations work. If you act gruffly when answering your telephone or a letter of inquiry, you will lose sales. You may, as the result of a lost sale, lose the opportunity of making a lifetime friendship, one which is so often initiated through a successful puppy placement.

PUPPY PRESENTATION

You have advertised, inquiries are being made and you are ready to set up visiting appointments. The manner in which the puppies are presented to strangers in your home will have a vast influence on your placements. Cottage or castle, how your home is kept is important, indicative to prospective clients of the pride you have in hearth and family. If junk is found lying about the yard, prospective buyers could assume this sloppiness extends to the care of your matron and puppies. There is a difference between the normal household clutter of a family and slovenliness. A neat appearance is important, indicative of caring.

Making sound puppy placements is time-consuming hard work. There is far more to making good placements than merely allowing prospective clients to view puppies randomly running around the yard. You may find that for many people this will be their first experience with a purebred registered dog. These people may not understand what "papers" are, or their value, but they do know that they want their dog to have them.

Prepare an orderly presentation of items to cover with your visitors. You need to devote adequate time to each visiting family, planning their visits at least two hours apart. Photographs of the sire and dam, including win pictures taken at shows, should be among your items. Have a list of necessary articles that a family needs to welcome a puppy into its home. This list should include complete feeding instructions, an inoculation record of shots already given, those due and when and a copy of the puppies' pedigree for each client to keep. It is imortant for visitors to have a copy of the litter's pedigree, illustrating illustrious ancestors for no less than three generations. Pedigree forms are available through pet suppliers and feed stores for a very nominal sum. Pedigrees can also be obtained through the American Kennel Club and through professional pedigree services. These services may be found advertised in the back portion of any national dog publication. Services need the registered names and numbers of the sire and dam, and the numbers in parentheses following their names, on their individual registration forms in order to make up a pedigree. The American Kennel Club will make a pedigree only once the dog is individually registered with the Club.

The numbers in parentheses following the sire's and dam's names are the dates on which these dogs first appear in the stud books. These records, while kept by the AKC, are also for sale through their offices. Every registered dog that has sired or whelped a litter is automatically entered in this historical record, providing the litter has been registered with the American Kennel Club. Pedigree services, subscribing to the periodically published stud books, are able to trace accurate pedigrees through the numbers in parentheses.

If the puppies are inside your home when visitors arrive, place a barrier such as an exercise pen between these people and the dam and her puppies. When stared at, dogs become nervous, feeling threatened. A new mother's protective instincts, although generally uncharacteristic of her temperament, as a result frequently rise in this situation. The dam will in most cases be relaxed and friendly with visitors when a "buffer zone" is established, one where strangers cannot move too closely to "threaten" her offspring's security.

Babies of any kind are irresistible. Never allow your puppies to be picked up or indiscriminately touched by visitors. Handling of this nature can make even the most relaxed dam nervous. More importantly, such handling is not healthy for the puppies. You never know what the visitors may bring into your home.

If your prospective clients have recently looked at other litters, you particularly do not want your puppies handled until the youngsters have been given either a measles complex vaccine or their first DHLPP vaccination. The intervening buffer zone allows you to safely pick up individuals to show prospective clients *only* those puppies in which they are the most interested (show quality or pet, male or female). No one, aside from the regular caretakers, should handle puppies until they are independently active and have had their first shots. Of course your buyers want to hold "their" puppy. Once selection is narrowed to a choice between two or three puppies, and shots have been given, clients may be allowed to hold their potential future companion.

Always teach your clients exactly how to pick up and hold a puppy: *never* by the scruff of the neck, ears, tail or legs! A puppy of any age must only be picked up (much as you would support a newborn baby) securely with either one hand under the stomach, through the hindlegs and forelegs (called the football carry), or one hand supporting the rear and the other holding the forequarters. Clients must be taught how to hold a puppy securely, yet never so tightly that it feels trapped and struggles for freedom. When a puppy is picked up in a manner so its legs are never against any surface, against which it can push, there is far less chance of dropping the youngster and causing injury.

You must be on a fact-finding mission when initially interviewing prospective visitors during the first telephone conversation. Inquire if the people have had a dog before, and if so, ask how long they had it. It is important to find out what kind of record they have had with previous pets: if they have had a succession of numerous animals through their home and what happened to them. There are families who have had numerous pets as a result of failure to inoculate in a timely manner, therefore losing them to diseases; failing to have adequately fenced yards and subsequently losing them to cars or wandering; failing to make proper pet selections and finding out months or even years later that the dog does not fit their life-styles, and so is brought to the local pound and dumped. *These are families with whom you want to avoid doing any business.* Certainly, also, if you receive a call from someone (bereft or not) whose pet died of a communicable disease, you do not want them to visit, exposing your puppies and contaminating your home.

Many families "puppy hunt" on weekends, much as one plans a recreational excursion to the beach or mountains. As one of their favorite pastimes, they visit puppies from different litters and various breeds. As a result, always preinterview visitors when they first telephone. By screening you are able to discern if they are just looking "for fun," or if they are serious buyers, and find out if they have or intend to view other litters before visiting your home. These families are often easily recognized by their children: generally two or more, aggressive in attitude and poorly behaved. Frequently these children can be heard yelling in the background or pestering their parents, who are on the telephone with you. Invite these people into your home, and you may invite disaster.

During a visit the parents distract you, usually with fairly good questions about your dogs, as they have developed some "looky-lou" expertise. By holding your attention, before you can become aware, the children may trample on your furniture (with their shoes on), run through your home and treat it as their playground. These free-for-all kids behave as they have been allowed to do in their own home. It is fine to desire placements into families because your breed is so good with children. It is best, however, to qualify this placement by seeking those families with well-mannered kids. No puppy likes to be picked up and squeezed or dropped. No dog likes to have its eyes poked, ears tugged, mouth and lips roughly explored by strange hands. There is no faster way to teach your puppies not to like children than to allow them to be subjected to such treatment for even one afternoon.

Always carefully supervise children who visit your home. When they want to hold a puppy, tell them no. Explain to the parents that the children might drop a wiggly puppy, and then watch their reactions. If they take their offspring aside to tell them why they may not hold the puppies, but that they may pet them on the ground, and the children listen respectfully and obey willingly, this home offers a more rational environment than almost any other. If the parents, however, slap their children or tell them no without explanation, be wary. These children, more often than not, will attempt to pick a puppy up as soon as adult backs are turned.

One does not normally think of those boisterous into-everything furry balls as being very delicate. They run, crashing into each other, rolling across the ground, falling up and down, and squeeze into corners, then whine anxiously about having to back out. *But puppies are delicate.* Their bones at six or ten weeks have not finished forming. They can be injured when lovingly squished in an affectionate embrace, just as much as by being dropped. Therefore, your puppies may be held at ground level after the visitor, adult or young, receives puppy-holding instruction.

An older dog that has been injured "understands" hurt, and instinctively knows how to manage so recuperation is not offset by undue stress. Puppies, having the attention span of a microsecond, are incapable of understanding an injury. They must be able to run, jump, wrestle and play hard and long with littermates. A dropped puppy is going to hurt quite badly. Such injuries, even if only incurring a temporary physical incapacity, can leave permanent scars on a puppy's personality. If the injury is serious enough, the puppy can defensively become a fear biter as someone approaches. Early negative conditioning by injury may stay with a puppy to some degree throughout its life.

If your visitors are older and cannot easily bend down, provide them with a chair. Once they are seated, place their potential puppy in their lap. Do not allow children or adult visitors to hold a puppy even from a chair unless you are close by and are prepared to catch the youngster should it leap. A squirming, leaping-to-freedom puppy can still be grievously injured even from the height of a lap.

You are better off losing a sale to the person who insists on holding a puppy against your expressed wishes than exposing it to such an unreasonable prospective owner. Those people who refuse to listen to the reason why you do things a certain way and respect you do not deserve to have one of your puppies: a life you are responsible for bringing into the world, the love and care for which you can never be adequately compensated. Satisfaction comes only through good puppy placements and contacts from owners over years of time, knowing that this dog is a beloved family member.

The puppies should be confined to a large, clean yard when they reach an active playful stage. They should not only be confined to this area when visitors arrive, but also be safely confined to this or another area during feedings, at night and when you are not at home. Puppies spread throughout a yard while you are trying to count dashing playful bodies do not always present a good image to prospective buyers. So Stuffy was asleep under the azaleas and could not be found! Those people had wanted a nice, easygoing puppy, not one of those boisterous youngsters that were so much in evidence. You lost the placement of this quiet, well-mannered puppy into possibly the best home for it.

Because you have lived with the puppies since their birth, you are able to know one from another, even if your breed has no easily discernible markings or colorings, just as a mother of twins can tell her youngsters apart. Realize that visitors usually cannot recognize one grown dog from another, let alone a "passel of puppies." If you have adequately preinterviewed your prospective buyers, you know what they desire and expect from their pet. If your visitors want a show companion or pet, one that is mischievous or sedate, there is no viable reason why they should need to inspect the entire litter, only to become confused by the number of puppies present. Perhaps there is your dream puppy, which you are not about to sell. Or the litter has several show prospects and your buyers adamantly want a pet. Do not confuse these people; show them only the available puppies in which they are most interested. Remember, it is up to the breeder to aid clients in puppy selection.

Try to schedule visiting times to those hours the puppies are habitually awake and most active. If clients desire a rambunctious youngster and the visit is not timed well, your most active puppy could be fast asleep and refuse to awaken, to put on a "performance." Warn visitors in advance that puppies, being baby dogs, have highly active and deeply quiet periods. Let them know that several visits could be necessary to find "their puppy" normally active. Do not allow prospective purchasers to randomly choose a puppy. If allowed to do so, very often the choice is an unwise one, a decision made after having viewed the puppies for only a brief time. As the breeder, you have had the opportunity of weeks of observation and know the puppies well.

All puppies are cute, but they do grow up. Newspaper classified advertisements display numerous adult dogs available to new homes. The breeders of these animals did not wisely aid their purchasers in the correct selection of a puppy for their life-styles. The dog, once grown and no longer little and cute, suddenly does not fit into their plans and can no longer be tolerated. Many of these purebred registered dogs end up in shelters and being euthanized. As the breeder, only you can insure your puppies' proper start in life by aiding in puppy selection, placing the puppy into the proper environment for each individual's requirements and family's life-style.

THEY COME WITH INSTRUCTIONS

Once the sale of a puppy has been agreed on by you and the buyer, you must insure the puppy's proper welcome into its new home. Provide the purchasers with full instructions of *what, when* and *how* frequently to feed. Also give them an alternative feeding schedule if no family member is available for middle-of-the-day feedings. Puppy instructions should include the inoculations the veterinarian gave and the pharmaceutical company's name. Advise the new owners if the puppy had any adverse reactions to a therapeutic drug, what future vaccinations are required and when. Include the date of the puppy's last fecal examination, the worming done and when the next fecal test is due.

Make sure the new owners have the feeding and health instruction sheets in their hands at least several days before they take their puppy home. The interim period gives the purchasers time for "buyers' remorse" (in case they change their minds), and allows them the opportunity of time to acquire the puppy's "layette," to purchase all items necessary.

Never allow a buyer to come, view, select and take a puppy home on the same day. If people insist on taking the puppy with them immediately, be very wary. Impulse buyers rarely offer a sound home and are most often those who grow tired of their dog once it starts to mature, growing out of the cuddly stage. These are the people who advertise "free to good home" in the newspapers or end up taking the dog to the pound. These are also the people who invest no time or effort in training their pets. The sincere, reasonable buyer appreciates the time and interest you have invested in your puppies, and is gratified that you are a conscientious breeder.

Toys are necessary to stimulate a puppy's mental capacity. A wide variety of toy types and colors can apparently help to increase a puppy's intelligence.

Linvicta Norwegian Elkhound: Ken and Judy Strakbein

16

New Owners' Puppy Care Instructions

INSTRUCT new owners to take the puppy directly home, not to visit relatives, friends and neighbors en route. Nor should they allow anyone outside those in the household to visit for several days. The puppy will be going through a traumatic experience, never before having been away from the dam and littermates. If the puppy becomes overly stressed and confused by too many people, it can become frightened, withdrawn or even ill. New owners must keep confusion and distraction to a minimum, offering their puppy the peace of quiet acceptance and much loving comfort in the new home. The first few days have a crucial influence on a puppy's emotional stability. How the puppy is initially managed can have strong bearing on the type of dog it becomes: nervous and afraid or openly curious without fear, yet not aggressive to new stimuli.

PICKING UP PUPPY

Instruct the owners to purchase a leash and collar in advance, bringing them to the airport. Walk the puppy as soon as it is released from the shipping crate. They should also offer the puppy a small amount of bottled water if it has been crated for more than three or four hours. Carefully instruct the owners where exactly at the airport they are to pick up their puppy. Some airlines ship only between air freight offices, others have a special counter-to-counter service.

197

When a puppy is picked up, either from the breeder or airline, instruct owners to bring three towels. Not every puppy is a good traveler and the puppy could mess in its crate, or could do so during the car ride home. One towel should be dampened and put in a plastic bag in case of an accident, one used for drying, and the third towel employed as a lap protector during the car ride. The puppy should be snuggled all the way home, being offered reassurance in consideration of the day's traumatic events. Make it clear to the owners that your puppy has been raised with a lot of love and gentle handling and positive reinforcement must be continued at every opportunity. Puppies grow incredibly fast, and if a medium or large breed, it will not be too long before the youngster cannot fit in a lap.

The airbill envelope on top of the crate should not only include the airbill but also the puppy's health certificate and duplicates of proof of veterinary examination: what shots have been given and when, and the type vaccine used. Some breeders also include the puppy's individual registration application rather than sending it under separate cover. The detailed puppy care instructions should be received by new owners no less than a week before their puppy arrives. The instructions should include the dates of vaccinations and type; what shots are due next and when; the dates of worming; when the next fecal exam is due and when to give the final booster and rabies shots (by five months of age, after the permanent teeth have started through the gums).

THE PUPPY'S DIET

List the type of kibble (dry food) and meat the puppy has been fed, and one or two brand-name choices. Indicate the amounts to be fed at each meal and when. If the food is mixed, write explicit directions. As the puppy matures and feedings are reduced numerically, write the directions of when, what and how much during each critical growth period.

Cottage cheese, an excellent meat substitute, is lean and high in protein and may also be fed frozen as a summertime treat. Vitamin/mineral supplements, either pill or powdered, help to insure optimum growth. It is more economical to purchase a year's supply. Dosage should be slightly less than indicated by directions on the label for a conservative approach. Di-calcium phosphate formulated for dogs also may be purchased either as pills or powder, and like the vitamins are generally quite palatable to the pet. Dosage should be very conservative, slightly less than indicated by the label's directions.

Feedings: Puppies under three months should be fed five times per day. It is best to offer more feedings of smaller amounts than fewer meals of a substantially larger size. The first morning feeding should be given as soon as the owner awakens, once the puppy has been allowed outside to relieve itself. Once fed, the puppy is put outside again. Remind owners that puppies generally must relieve themselves within five minutes of awakening and within five minutes of eating.

The *first meal* of meat and kibble is usually the heaviest. This is usually the best time of day to add supplements to the food—when the puppy is hungriest.

The *second meal*, fed midmorning, is a "snack" type and can be a slightly smaller repetition of breakfast or kibble alone. The *third feeding* at noon can be, for example, cottage cheese fed separately from the kibble. Because cottage cheese does not spoil easily, it is a safe food to leave out for a few hours. Once left down, however, anything uneaten should not be refrigerated again for use later, but thrown away. The *fourth* meal, offered about 4:00 P.M., may be cottage cheese or meat and kibble. The *fifth and last meal* is meat and kibble, fed at about 8:00 or 9:00 P.M. If a small amount of table scraps is to be included in a meal, mix them in at this time. As a word of caution, no puppy should be fed table scraps during the first few weeks in a new home. Not only must digestive upset be avoided, but puppies become spoiled rapidly, and will expect scraps on a regular basis. This sets the foundation for a finicky eater.

When the puppy is *three months* old, the meals may be reduced to four per day. Either the midmorning or midafternoon meal may be omitted. The puppy will indicate which meal to delete by refusing to eat that portion over two or three consecutive days. When *four months* old, drop the other midmorning or afternoon feeding, and move the dinner hour to a more reasonable time for the puppy. At this time the puppy should be fed three meals daily, spaced evenly apart. At *six or seven months* the puppy can be reduced to two meals per day, and may be fed two meals a day throughout adulthood.

Generally dogs do not require oil added to their diet if the feeding program is well balanced. Any evidence of dry flaky skin should be checked by a veterinarian before oil (formulated for dogs) is added.

A puppy should never be so fat that it carries a big gut. A large stomach can be indicative of digestive problems or parasitic infestation such as worms. A large stomach also places strain on the puppy's hips, and can in certain instances, along with slippery floors, lead to traumatically induced hip dysplasia. Have the puppy and a fecal sample checked by the veterinarian. Sometimes large guts occur because a puppy "inhales" food. Once again offer additional meals of smaller amounts. If the puppy has been on a demand feeding program with dry food always left out, remove it and keep the puppy on a regularly timed feeding schedule. If, however, the puppy has not had free access to additional dry food, small amounts may be put down for demand feeding on a carefully observed trial basis, hopefully, to eliminate gluttonous eating.

If a puppy is a poor eater and it has been thoroughly checked by the veterinarian to rule out possible medical problems, a small can of cat food on occasion can spark an appetite. Most dogs love fish-flavored food and northern breeds go wild over it. This is not recommended, however, as a regular diet because cats' dietary requirements are vastly different from dogs.

Not all dry foods are the same. Some swell significantly once wet. Any kibble that is fed dry, not presoaked, must be of the type that has little or no swelling whatsoever. Food that swells significantly and is fed dry will, once ingested, swell in the puppy's stomach. These foods have a slow gastric emptying time and can in certain instances be a precursor to the condition commonly known as "bloat."

Eggs are an excellent source of high protein. At least one raw egg yolk should be fed to the puppy weekly. Instruct new owners never to feed the raw white because it contains the enzyme avidin, which binds up normal body functions and inhibits growth development. Cooking an entire egg helps to destroy the avidin, allowing it to be an excellent high-protein food.

Have the owners feed a bitch's milk replacement at least once a day: large, rapidly growing puppies are in particular need of this supplement. Once the puppy has outgrown a need for the milk, it will be refused. One day's refusal is not enough for a complete withdrawal of this supplement. Withdraw it only after the puppy has refused to drink it over a two- or three-day period. Instruct the owners to mix the milk fresh each time offered or, if refused at any time, to refrigerate it immediately if it is to be offered again at a later time. Cow's milk must never be used because that can cause a dog severe gastric distress. If a bitch's milk replacement (such as Esbilac) is not available, write down the alternative orphan formula or goat's milk, which may be substituted safely.

Write a growth guideline for your puppies and include this on the instruction sheets. Indicate the general weight gain per month for dogs and bitches until the apex of the growth curve is reached. The weight should be calculated from the first and middle of the puppy's month, according to its birth date, and not evaluated by the calendar month. The growth guideline is very beneficial to new owners; if their puppy is far above or below the norm for the breed and line, the youngster could be having problems. By following the guidelines, owners can easily become aware if they need to contact you or their veterinarian should problems be suspected.

COMING HOME

New owners must have a place set aside inside their home where the puppy feels absolutely secure. Fresh water, food, toys and a bed are to be habitually kept in this location. *A crate with bedding makes an excellent den of security for a puppy.* The youngster can also be confined to the crate during the night. Allow the pup to freely explore once settled into its new area.

HOUSE-TRAINING

House-training is a very important subject to cover in your instructions. Owners must be aware that consistency in training is the key to success. A single simple command must be repetitively used in a monotone voice, training the puppy to "go on command." Every time the puppy is put outside, the command must be said over and over again, until the puppy goes. At those moments, the puppy must be praised in warm tones, but yet not so excitedly that it forgets what it is doing and stops. Teaching a puppy to relieve itself on command is very helpful and time-efficient when traveling, visiting or attending shows. Commercially manufactured house-training pads can be purchased from well-stocked pet suppliers everywhere. These help house-training by focusing the puppy through scent to one area alone, when relief inside the house is necessary. Tacking them to the ground in the backyard with a tent stake is helpful to teach the puppy to relieve itself in only one area.

Newspapers have long been de rigueur for house-training. A newspaper sheet on which the puppy has already urinated can be left down by the door to the backyard, or staked in the yard, being used in the same manner as the manufactured sheet. When able to scent where it has already gone, a puppy quickly learns to head directly back to the same spot. Temporary use of soiled newsprint or a commercial sheet eliminates the need to spread papers all over the floor during initial stages of house-training. When these papers are placed by the door through which the puppy customarily goes outside, soon enough control is developed to "ask" to be let out. It is not necessary to leave a soiled paper down too long, certainly not after the puppy has learned that there is one spot inside the house (on the paper) that is "all right," or when it has learned to go outside.

Puppies display a "dedicated attitude" directly prior to relieving themselves. They appear very busy, with a "nose-to-the-ground, fast-walking-sniffing" and "pacing-with-great-concentration" attitude. This behavior means the puppy is about to go. Immediately pick the puppy up, go outside and, speaking in a monotone, repetitiously command the word chosen for relief. The puppy must be enthusiastically praised once successful. Putting the puppy out directly after having awakened, immediately after having eaten and by careful observation in between times, when the puppy displays the about-to-go attitude in conjunction with the availability of paper, allows it to be essentially house-trained within a week of having arrived in the new home. Barring any physical or medical problems, how long house-training takes ultimately depends entirely on the owner's diligent observation of the puppy.

House-training Accidents

Never call a puppy to the scene of a "crime." *Always* pick up the puppy, and go to the "anointed" spot. Contrary to popular opinion, if there is only one puppy in a household, you do not have to catch the pup in the "act" of an error (although it is best to be able to do so). At this time the owner's vocal tones must change to one of "horror" for what the puppy has done. Simple yet strongly different tonal quality changes are more effective for training than yelling.

Just as no puppy should be called to an accident site, no puppy should be struck for having had an accident, because this can cause the pup to cower and may irredeemably change a puppy's personality. If a puppy must be physically reprimanded for an offense, *tapping* it on the side of the muzzle with one hand, while holding its head near the nape firmly with the other, coupled with strong vocal changes, is normally sufficient punishment. "No!" in a firm tone is a strong reprimand. If a puppy constantly hears its name in conjunction with "No!" it will think its name is "Puppy-No!"

Puppies need encouragement and praise in order to be well-rounded individuals. Owners need to be attentive to their puppies, praising them when they are well behaved, not just paying attention to them only when they are in error. This is called ''positive reinforcement.''

The first and one of the most important commands a puppy can learn is to come to the owner when called. A puppy that has been called to a crime scene, one in which the puppy has been corporally punished, will prove reluctant to respond in a positive manner when it has known only negativity from its owner. Puppies need to be called in a pleasant, somewhat excited tone of voice, first their name, then the command to come. At the exact same time, especially during early training, owners should lightly clap their hands or pat the ground invitingly. As soon as the puppy comes, you must give a good physical reward, lavish petting in addition to excited tonal qualities of verbal praise.

TEACHING PUPPY TO ''DROP IT''

Possibly the second most important command a puppy can learn is to release any object they may have in their mouth on command. The command ''No!'' by itself is inadequate. Always preface a command with the puppy's name. Whatever command is intended, the cue word must always be the same to elicit a response. Getting a puppy to release a treasured object is not an easily learned lesson. Social conditioning among littermates has taught a puppy otherwise: that what it has must be firmly kept between its jaws. Teaching this command is contrary to a dog's innate nature.

Teaching the puppy to ''Drop it'' or ''Give it'' on command should be started by the owner as playful training. Give the puppy a toy or other treat: do not release the object when the puppy takes it. As the puppy holds the toy, stroke the pup's head and nape, then give the command for release. Of course the untrained puppy will not respond. While still holding the toy or bone, repeatedly tap one side of the puppy's muzzle. Begin with light taps, then slightly increase pressure, until the puppy releases its treasure. Stroke and praise the puppy again, then carefully ''examine'' the toy while continuing to speak sweetly. After a few brief moments, return the toy, allowing the puppy to play for another few minutes. Then start the lesson again. Usually after two or three such lessons, when the puppy learns that the toy will be returned, it will immediately be released on command.

TOYS

There is a valid reason why indulgent owners often appear to have extraordinarily intelligent pets. As with children, toys are necessary to stimulate any puppy's mental capacity. The wider the variety of type and colors of the puppy's toys, the more responsively intelligent a puppy will be. Knotted ropes or a string of knotted socks are good for gentle tug-of-war games. Puppies also inventively

Some toys are inappropriate, or may even be dangerous to puppies.

Pug: Blanch McGee

play by themselves with these articles, tossing them around. Firmly knotted socks with a ball and bell knotted inside a toe can give a puppy hours of exercise.

Many breeds are able to manage sturdy rawhide bones, chewies or even raw knuckle bones. During teething and hot weather periods these can be frozen for especially soothing treats. A number of breeds should have neither rawhide nor real bones, but may have instead specially manufactured hard plastic-type substitutes. Any of these items can be tied to a long sturdy rope suspended from a tree limb or porch rafter. A puppy can dive, tug and chew on this toy for many contented hours by itself.

Very hard English rubber balls that cannot be chewed up or swallowed also give puppies hours of wonderful exercise. Pet suppliers everywhere sell them, some with bells inside. Great care must be taken to inspect these balls, insuring that the bells cannot fall out. Very large balls are also wonderful for inventive play. Puppies love squeaky toys. Care must also be taken when purchasing these that the squeaker cannot fall out. Many latex squeaky toys are manufactured with the squeaker portion incorporated into the design. These are safe for all ages and may be found not only at pet suppliers, but as well in the infant department of many supermarkets and stores.

PUPPIES AND STAIRS

Puppies should not be allowed to go up or down flights of stairs until their physical coordination has become very well developed. Consistent movement in either direction can place unnatural strain on certain portions of a puppy's body.

203

Puppy patellas (kneecaps) and carpal areas are delicate and particularly susceptible to injury.

CHANGE OF WATER

Owners of puppies being picked up by car should be advised to bring one or two empty gallon jugs, such as a Thermos or cleaned milk containers. The containers are filled with the water to which the puppies are accustomed at the breeder's home. This familiar water is put in the puppy's water dish once in the new home. The container is then immediately refilled from the owner's tap. By the end of one or two days, the puppy will have been gradually weaned onto the new owner's local tap water. The slow transition from one type of water to another usually avoids causing the puppy digestive upset.

DIGESTIVE UPSET

If the puppy develops a loose stool (and many do from the stress of change in environment), feed hard-boiled eggs, cooked white rice, very little meat and regular puppy dry food. If the diarrhea persists into the second day, the puppy should be immediately seen by the veterinarian. After examination ruling out other factors, the veterinarian will be able to prescribe pills or liquid to clear the condition up before it can become serious. A stool sample should be submitted for microscopic examination at the same time the puppy is examined.

It should be recommended that a puppy always be seen by the owner's veterinarian within the first 24 hours of being in the new home. Not only does this help to establish a relationship between the doctor, client and pet, but if there are any physical problems present, they will be discovered. In the event of a problem, an informed decision can then be made if the puppy is to be returned to the breeder before strong emotional attachments have been made.

17

Registration

LITTERS are registered by the American Kennel Club (or other registry) through the Litter Registration Application, a form that may be obtained by writing directly to the registry in question. The AKC application is free of charge and may be requested at any time. A litter is not registered until the application, correctly filled out and with the proper remittance, has been received and processed. Before any litter's application can be accepted, *both* the sire and dam must have already been individually recorded by the AKC: "The Sire and Dam must have been AKC registered and recorded in the ownership of the persons who were the actual owners on the dates of mating and whelping, before [the] application is submitted to the AKC. If registration or transfer applications for Sire or Dam accompany [the] application, all applications will be returned."

REGISTERING THE LITTER

In accordance with AKC policy, the application form is to be partially completed and signed by the sire's owner on the date of mating. Some breeders fail to comply with these regulations prior to the litter's birth. Many stud dog owners are reluctant to give carte blanche discretionary powers to a dam's owner when this person is not well known to them. A few stud owners insist on seeing the puppies in person, or their photographs, before signing an application. They want to verify the number and sex of puppies present and verify also, in some cases, that the litter is purebred.

Be very careful when you initially make a determination of each puppy's sex as it is born. Even breeders with years of experience have been known to make a mistake when overtired. Before completing the litter's application, once again check the sex of each puppy. The AKC records the number of viable puppies of each sex from your litter application. Include only those puppies that are alive at the time of your litter application.

Certainly the form's request should be made by the time a matron's pregnancy is known. The American Kennel Club's volume of mail is so great that a response may not be made until some weeks have passed. The Litter Registration Application is essentially self-explanatory. If, however, confusion reigns when reading the form, turn to the reverse side. There the form is fictitiously completed.

If your bitch's pregnancy resulted from insemination *other* than by a natural breeding (physical coupling of the sire and dam), one of the following forms must be requested. Each artificial insemination type of breeding requires a specific form for registration. When both the sire and dam are present for the A.I. (artificial insemination), the mating is called a "fresh semen" breeding and the Fresh Semen Form R94-3 must be requested in addition to the Litter Registration Application. Fresh extended (cooled) semen requires Form R207 in addition to the Litter Registration Application. Use of frozen semen requires Form R198-2 alone: no other form is needed. The fee stipulation of this form is slightly higher than that required by the other applications.

Many breeders do not complete the application until the litter is a week old. They want to be positive that all puppies born are thrifty and living at the time application is made. Once the form has been completed and signed by all parties involved, it is submitted with a check or money order (never cash) for the full amount to:

The American Kennel Club
5580 Centerview Drive
Raleigh, NC 27606

Write "Litter Registration Application" on the lower left-hand corner of the envelope to help facilitate delivery to the correct department. Do not expect an immediate response. Time is required to process the hundreds of letters and applications received daily. Normally it takes between three to eight weeks for a litter application to be processed, after which time the breeder receives a "Litter Kit." The Litter Kit contains several items, including a breeding record sheet and an appropriate number of partially completed individual registration application forms commonly known as "blue slips," attached in a series by perforated edges.

Correctly detailed record keeping is very important. The American Kennel Club booklet *Rules Applying to Registration and Dog Shows* state, Chapter 3, Section 2:

> Each person who breeds, keeps, transfers ownership or possession of, or deals in dogs which are registered or to be registered with The American Kennel Club, whether he acts as a principal or agent or sells on consignment, must make in

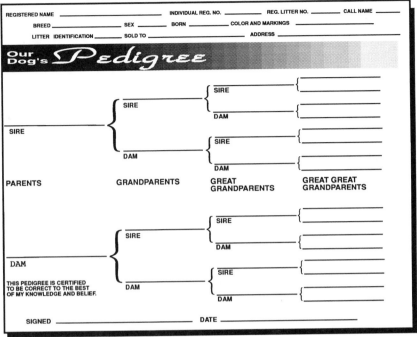

REGISTERED NAME _____ INDIVIDUAL REG. NO. _____ REG. LITTER NO. _____ CALL NAME _____

BREED _____ SEX _____ BORN _____ COLOR AND MARKINGS _____

LITTER IDENTIFICATION _____ SOLD TO _____ ADDRESS _____

Our Dog's *Pedigree*

SIRE

SIRE { SIRE

DAM

SIRE

DAM { SIRE

DAM

PARENTS   GRANDPARENTS   GREAT GRANDPARENTS   GREAT GREAT GRANDPARENTS

SIRE

SIRE { SIRE

DAM

DAM

THIS PEDIGREE IS CERTIFIED TO BE CORRECT TO THE BEST OF MY KNOWLEDGE AND BELIEF.   DAM { SIRE

DAM

SIGNED _____ DATE _____

Pedigree form

connection therewith and preserve for five years adequate and accurate records. The Board of Directors shall by regulation designate the specific information which must be included in such records.

Section 6. The American Kennel Club may refuse to register any dog or litter or to record the transfer of any dog, for the sole reason that the application is not supported by the records required by these rules and the regulations adopted under them.

The record sheet kept by the breeder has spaces marked for the following information: the breed, registered name and number of the sire and dam, the litter's owner, date of mating, date of whelping, sex and number of puppies whelped and space for the Litter Number (found on the blue slip). There are also sections where each puppy is listed individually: color, sex, date of sale (or death), names of new owners, name and number of puppy if registered by the breeder, when registration was applied for and bill of sale.

Registration applications should not be separated until the sale of a puppy has been made and payment in full has been received. *These are applications only and are not registrations of individual puppies in the litter.* No dog is individually recognized (registered) with the American Kennel Club until the application has been received and approved by the AKC. Each breeder is required to complete the front portion of every application, indicating the puppy's sex and color. The back portion is filled out when the breeder either decides to keep or sell an individual. The American Kennel Club must be immediately notified of a mistake if an error has been made when sexing the puppies. The number of males and females present in the litter is recorded by the AKC from the Litter Registration Application. Any changes in the number of a sex must be first cleared by their office.

The Litter Number is displayed on the right-hand portion of the individual Registration Application. This number should be transferred onto the breeder's record sheet and kept for future reference for no less than five years. Should any question ever arise about a dog's registration, or record keeping, an AKC field representative can demand to review these records.

There are a series of (pink) boxes at the top portion of each Registration Application. Here the dog's owner at the time of application fills in the desired name of their pet. The person who owns the dog at the time the application is submitted to the AKC has the privilege of naming the animal. All names are subject to AKC approval. Each box is limited to one letter only and one space is skipped between each word in the name. The AKC will then assign a permanent number belonging to each dog.

REGISTERING THE INDIVIDUAL PUPPY

A buyer is entitled to see the individual Registration Application when a deposit is made. People must be aware that their pet is neither already registered with nor individually recognized until the application has been received and recorded. They must clearly understand that they are responsible for their pet's registration, and should the application be lost, that replacement may not always be possible.

Some new owners are undecided about a name when they acquire their puppy's registration application. Many experienced breeders keep a list of names appropriate for their breed. Other breeders follow a litter format, where each puppy is named, for example, according to geographical locations or the alphabet. An "A" litter might carry names such as "Aaron" or "Amy," a B litter, "Bravo" and "Belle." A few breeders select names, registering the animals first, then later transferring ownership. Some breeders, however, are happy to allow owners the selection, when preceded by their kennel name. Prefacing a dog's name with a kennel name designates where the puppy was born and by whom it was bred. If the new owner also has a kennel name, it is placed afterward, signifying ownership. "Mac's Tartan of Terryworth" demonstrates that Tartan was bred by the Mac kennels and is owned by Terryworth kennels.

The American Kennel Club limits a name to 28 spaces. These spaces may be used by any reasonable combination of letters. Applications are given only one name choice. Often people have a favorite but common name that they wish to use. These people need to be told that "King" or "Queenie" have most likely already been used by numerous dog owners. If they insist on registering their pet with the common name, advise them that the AKC has the right to suffix the name with a number. For example, "Fido XXVI." An unusual spelling of a name is appropriate when clients insist upon commonly naming their dog. Suggest they apply for registration by spelling the name "Fydeau," which, when pronounced, is still their "Fido."

Permanently registering a dog's name with the AKC is a serious business. New owners must understand that the naming process must not be treated as a joke. The AKC will not tolerate applications of names that are irreverent or in bad taste. There are a number of dogs that have been registered with one name alone. When a single name is selected, it should be unique. One notable example is that of the Best in Show winning champion "Kougarok." The dog's entire registered name, short and simple, is not easily forgotten.

Once the application for individual registration has been completely and correctly filled out, and signed in the appropriate places, it should be immediately submitted with a check or money order made payable to the Kennel Club in the proper amount. Cash should never be sent through the mail, nor are stamps acceptable. Puppy buyers will receive their dog's permanent registered name and number from the Kennel Club usually within three to eight weeks. This will, in the case of the American Kennel Club, be a white slip with a royal purple border if the registration is not limited. If limited registration is designated by the breeder, the individual certificate will have an orange border. Offspring of dog's with limited registration may NOT be registered.

The information contained includes the dog's permanent registered name and number (which cannot be changed), the names and numbers of the sire and dam and the dates on which they first appeared in the American Kennel Club's Stud Books. Should the permanent registration of a dog ever become lost or destroyed, it can be easily replaced for a nominal sum by writing to the AKC and requesting a duplicate. If the Registration Application should become lost or destroyed, only the breeder (in almost every instance) is able to request and obtain a duplicate form. There is no guarantee that the AKC will approve a duplicate Registration Application. There have been times when this request has been denied, or when granted, a detailed explanation of why it is necessary has been asked for.

Quite often a puppy is already placed in a new home before the Litter Kit arrives at the breeder's. When a puppy is ready for placement, the breeder is wise to supply new owners with a bill of sale that identifies the sire and dam with their registered names and numbers. Time payment sales should also identify the litter's sire and dam in the same manner. The conscientious breeder also supplies each new owner with a pedigree of three or more generations and other forms of identification. An Individual Registration Application or an individual registration certificate should *not* be turned over to new owners until full payment and other obligations have been completed.

NEUTER/SPAY AGREEMENT

The following contractual agreement is between ___(breeder)___, hereafter referred to as "Seller," and _____, hereafter referred to as "Purchaser."

In consideration for the purchase price of $____, $____ is refundable to Purchaser by Seller upon Purchaser's supplying Seller with a veterinarian's letter as proof of a ___(Spay/Neuter)___ by ____ (age). At the time Seller receives proof of ___(Spay/Neuter)___ by a licensed veterinarian, Seller shall immediately refund to Purchaser the amount of ____ dollars.

It is understood by all parties that this dog of the _____ breed, ___(male/female)___ sex, from the registered litter (number) _____, is not of show/breeding quality.

_____   _____
Date & Time of Signature   Breeder/Seller

                                 _____
                                 Purchaser

_____   _____
Witness of the Agreement   Co-Purchaser

18

Spaying and Neutering

$\mathbf{G}$ENERALLY when people call about a puppy, their first question is, "How much?" Rather than reply directly, respond by asking, "Pet or show quality?" This allows a gracious lead-in opportunity of educating a layperson, helping to initiate a sound placement.

Usually the caller's response to the breeder's query is that they do not want a show-prospect puppy because they want a housepet. The majority of newcomers to the realm of the better-bred dog are under the misconception that a show dog cannot be a pet as well. They do not realize the two are entirely compatible: that the dog that loves to eat ice cream and beg for an occasional table scrap may also be a fine show dog. Explain the differences between a show prospect and pet-only puppy. Some breeders predicate the difference on size variation, coat color or structure, none of which make a puppy any less desirable as a pet. It must be made clear, without question, that any puppy sold as a pet is *not* to be bred.

Be a strong advocate of neutering pet puppies by spay (ovarian hysterectomy) or castration.

It is your responsibility to explain fully and in a positive manner that each form of withdrawal from a breeding program does not affect a dog's personality. Nor does neutering cause a dog (male or female) to become fat and sluggish, providing of course that the proper nutritional and exercise levels of the dog are met. (See also Chapter 1, Breeding Responsibly: Ask Questions—Give Information.)

Be assertively positive when explaining the whys of neutering. Explain in detail the lack of effect except for reproduction. Present a positive and sincere attitude when offering information about all the opportunities available within your breed and the never-ending excitement of obedience work. If you follow these basic guidelines of being a responsible breeder, and are placing puppies into responsible homes, offering a sound educational program and are thorough in your follow-up care, then you are indeed a "breeder" truly worthy of this honorable title.

NEUTER/SPAY AGREEMENT

Some people anthropomorphize their pets, giving them human characteristics. The people who do so most often strongly object to neutering or spaying, not realizing that dogs do not possess the libido of humans. Breeding is not recreational for dogs, nor is it demonstration of a deep abiding affection. For dogs, breeding is a strictly hormonal necessity dictated by respective hormonal changes incurring in both sexes.

An agreement to surgically irrevocably withdraw a dog from any breeding program can be structured from the Sales Agreement information. A paragraph can be added as an amendment to the Sales Agreement, stating the animal is not of show/breeding quality; that the sales agreement is predicated on the fact that the buyer agrees to alter (spay/neuter) the animal within a specified time period. An added incentive to irrevocably withdrawing a pet from a possible breeding can be the offer of a specific refund to help cover surgery costs.

Some breeders withhold the registration application or give limited registration until the neuter or spay has been performed. Temporary *withholding* of registration papers is not legal without a contract and specified time period. Nor is withholding the registration application in agreement with the American Kennel Club's rules and regulations. A safe alternative is to have the dog surgically withdrawn from any breeding program by your own veterinarian if the animal is old enough or to have specific requirements written into the contract. The AKC limited registration is another safeguard against breeding, but will not prevent future health problems as neutering will.

Thorough testing has shown that later-life problems are rarely encountered by pets neutered or spayed at a very young age. Spaying prevents a female from ever "coming in season" and being an "attractive" neighborhood nuisance. The side effect of such early alteration is that females often develop to be substantially larger, more "doggie" in appearance. These doggie characteristics occur because the females are incapable of producing the hormone estrogen once they are spayed. Often this characteristic is an added purchasing incentive for the pet buyer who wants a doggie animal. Tubal ligation allows a female to apparently have an estral cycle; she is, however, incapable of a complete season and conception.

Males may be neutered by castration or vasectomy once their testicles have descended into the scrotal sac. Castration usually lowers a male's inclination to attempt a breeding: it always removes his reproductive ability. Neutering by castration is recommended by veterinarians for males not of breeding quality. Intact males bred infrequently, or never, or a male with one or both testicles retained is often (but not inevitably) a candidate for testicular cancer.

While vasectomy prevents a male from siring a litter, it removes neither the ability nor inclination to the breeding act. Neutering by vasectomy allows a dog to fully develop as an intact male with all inherent hormonal growth changes including those of doggie appearance. Early castration of a male before hormonal changes occur may leave a male with a more refined, effeminate appearance. Consult a veterinarian regarding the details of specific neutering options and the age at which each is best performed.

RECEIPT & HOLDING AGREEMENT

The following agreement is between ____(breeder)____, hereafter known as "Seller," and _____, hereafter known as "Purchaser."

In consideration of a deposit of $_____, of which $_____ is Surety of Action, and $_____ is prepayment, Seller assigns Purchaser the option to acquire the dog described below, guaranteeing that the dog will not be sold to any party other than Purchaser for a period of _____ days. At the time Purchaser acquires physical possession of the dog, that portion of the deposit taken and known as Surety of Action shall be applied to the purchase price.

Breed: _____
Sire: _____ (AKC #_____)
Dam: _____ (AKC #_____)
Sex: __(m/fe)_____ Date of Birth: _____
Color & Markings: _____
AKC Litter #: _____
"Puppy Name": _____

Purchaser assumes all responsibilities for the dog as of the date and time of this agreement. Seller will not be held responsible for illness and/or injury to the dog except as that illness and/or injury would have been avoided by the exercise of reasonable and normal care.

The Surety of Action deposit received by Seller in the amount of $_____ is nonrefundable and $_____ over the Surety of Action amount is refundable.

We the undersigned have read, understood and agree with the terms of this contract.

_____   _____
Date & Time of Signature   Breeder/Seller

_____   _____
Witness to the Agreement   Purchaser

                                  _____
                                  Co-Purchaser

19

Contracts

EVERY PUREBRED PUPPY from parents with *un*limited registration is entitled to registration with the American Kennel Club, without regard to breeding quality. *This does not imply, however, that each purebred dog is eligible for a breeding program.* Only the breeder can make the stipulation of whether a dog may be eligible for a breeding program by virtue of being show quality. Selling a dog from registered parents without papers is a ''no-no'' according to the American Kennel Club. Box 1, Section A, of an Individual Registration Application form is specifically dedicated to dogs of purebred ancestry whose quality for whatever reason renders them irrevocably ineligible for a breeding program. This box refers to limited registration. Any progeny, accidental or intentional, from this animal, will *never* be eligible for registration.

Encourage new owners to irrevocably withdraw their pet-only dogs from even an accidental breeding. Females may be altered either by tubal ligation or spay (ovarian hysterectomy). Males can be neutered by vasectomy or castration. Responsible breeders feel very strongly about pet overpopulation, and may offer a bonus to new owners via a refund amount after receiving notification of neutering from a veterinarian. This contract can be drawn up in simple terms.

A contract must include the seller's and buyer's names; terms of the contract; a time frame within which these actions are to be performed; the location of the contract and action; the signatures of all parties involved; the time and date upon which the contract is entered into by all parties and, when possible, the signature of an impartial witness (one who is outside any involvement with the contract and action). Everything in the contract should be identified: the breed, sex of animal, parents' registered names and numbers. This same basic format may also be used for deposit receipts (Surety of Action), purchasing agreements and time payment contracts.

215

BUSINESS IS BUSINESS

No matter how well known a puppy purchaser may be, business is business. Keeping the legal transaction of a sale (transfer of ownership) business-like does not diminish the personal relationship between the seller and purchaser. This professionalism insures the protection of all parties: breeder/seller, purchaser and puppy. A clear and concise contract leaves no questions about performance obligations.

If the puppy buyers are unknown to you, request at least two references as well as driver's license number (and state), the home address and telephone (and how long the buyer has resided there) and the firm and length of employment. You need not be embarrassed by asking these questions. Your purchasers are not acquiring a used car. They are taking a cherished puppy in which you have invested a great amount of time, love, energy and expense. It is your responsibility to protect this puppy, insuring it the best new home possible.

The best home is not always indicated by a luxury car and fat bank account. It does mean a home that encompasses adequate financial resources to provide the puppy with good continued dietary support, veterinary follow-up care and, of equal importance, dedication of sane affection by the new owners. You perform no service to your puppy or breed if your placement is a home that cannot, or will not, provide all necessary measurements of support. Those purchasers who have their new puppy's best interests at heart will be pleased with your dedication.

Whether you use a contract or a handshake at the time a sale is made, identify the puppy being purchased and the new owner with a photograph. Take two instant snapshots, give one to the owner and keep one copy for yourself. While a snapshot is a gracious memento of the occasion for the new owners, it is also identification of their newest family member. Mistakes about a puppy's identity can rarely be made with a photograph at hand.

The contracts included may be used as a guideline. They are easily altered to fit individuals' requirements.

216

SALES AGREEMENT

The following agreement is between _____
(breeder), hereafter referred to as "Seller," and _____
_____ , hereafter referred to as "Purchaser."

In consideration of a purchase price of _____
dollars ($____.___), of which _____ dollars is
a nonrefundable deposit, the Seller transfers in fee simple all rights,
privileges and responsibilities associated with the ownership of the
___(male/female)___ dog of the _____
breed to Purchaser as of the date and time specified below.

Seller guarantees the dog specified above to be free of the following
conditions (genetic and disease): _____
_____
_____
_____

In the event of emergence of any above condition subsequent to the
sale of the dog, Seller binds himself/herself to:

A. Replace the dog with one of equivalent quality from the first litter
   bred by the Seller if:
   1) the genetic condition is sufficiently serious in the opinion of two
      qualified veterinarians, at least one of whom is selected by the
      Seller, to warrant euthanization of the dog.
   2) the original purchase price of the dog was greater than or equal
      to $_____.

B. Offer Purchaser a refund in the amount of $_____, less the
   nonrefundable Surety of Action deposit.

C. Allow a credit less the nonrefundable deposit toward the purchase
   of another animal from Seller if the original purchase price was less
   than $_____.

Purchaser has the right to return the dog to Seller during the first 24
hours from the date and time of signature of this agreement for credit
in the amount of the purchase price toward the acquisition of another
animal from Seller; or for a refund of the purchase price less the
nonrefundable Surety of Action deposit portion on all local sales. Local
sales are defined as being within _____ hours by car between Seller's
and Purchaser's residences.

Long-distance sales are defined as being beyond _____ hours by
car. In such cases Purchaser has the right to return the dog to Seller
within _____ days from the time and date of this agreement for credit
in the amount of the purchase price toward the acquisition of another
dog from Seller; or for a refund of the purchase price less the nonrefundable Surety of Action deposit.

We the undersigned have read, understood and agree with the terms of this contract.

_____ _____
Date & Time of Signature Seller

          _____
          Purchaser

_____ _____
Witness to the Agreement Co-Purchaser

TIME PAYMENT AGREEMENTS

Time Payment Agreements between _____
(breeder), hereafter known as "Seller," and _____
_____ , hereafter referred to as "Purchaser."

Seller does hereby agree to sell the _____(male/female)_____ dog of the
_____ breed,
Sired by: _____,
AKC Reg. #_____ out of Dam: _____,
AKC Reg. #_____, whelped on (date) _____, 19___,
and of AKC Litter or Individual Registration #: _____.

Consideration for this sale is $_____, to be paid in addition to
conditions to be performed by Purchaser which are set forth below.

Buyer agrees to pay Seller the first payment of $_____ as a Surety
of Action deposit and does hereby agree to pay $_____ as the
balance due Seller, in equal monthly payments of $_____, due on
or before the _____ day of each month commencing with
the month of _____, at which time the first installment is
due and payable. Payments will continue for _____
months, at which time the final payment having been made, Seller will
furnish Purchaser with the registration papers of the _____
Kennel Club, of the dog specified in this agreement. It is also understood that should Purchaser be more than _____ days late
in payment, a service fee of $_____ will be added to the amount of
each month late.

The death, loss, destruction or injury to the dog from any cause whatsoever before the final payment has been made and papers transferred
does not relieve Purchaser from the obligation of further and all payments due Seller.

Buyer agrees that until the full purchase price is met, the dog shall not
be sold, or removed from Purchaser's custody without written consent
of Seller. Purchaser also agrees that the dog shall not be removed
from the state of _____ except for such recreational
purposes of a nonpermanent length of time being not more than
_____ consecutive days.

Buyer agrees to take good and reasonable care, providing the dog
with a fenced yard or other roomy enclosure (if other, so specify)
_____; agrees to feed
and provide at own expense protective vaccinations as per the instructions sheet with which Seller provided Purchaser; agrees to control
the dog on lead when off the Purchaser's premises; protect the dog in
every reasonable and normal way possible against loss through theft,
injury, running or other.

The information set forth on this Agreement is declared to be true by all parties.

_____	_____
Date & Time of Signature	Seller

_____
Purchaser

_____   _____
Witness to the Agreement   Co-Purchaser

APPENDIX I

Emergency First Aid

SOME BASIC KNOWLEDGE of emergency first aid is essential for all dog owners. Such knowledge may prevent additional complications to an injury, alleviate some of the animal's pain and possibly save the dog's life. Dogs can get into as much trouble as any child or adult. Problems that may be encountered in the lives shared by dogs and owners can be shock, poisoning, broken bones, cuts (bleeding), heatstroke and porcupine and skunk encounters, to name a few. Smart dog owners have some degree of preparation in the event of an accident. All owners should know how to immobilize their pet, apply temporary splints and a tourniquet and have basic knowledge of CPR. Outlined here are initial steps only, which must *always* be *immediately* followed by *veterinary care*.

MUZZLES

A simple means of restraint is necessary to handle any injured dog. Even the most lovable pet can become frenzied or panic-stricken after being injured and while help is being given. A dog in great pain, or one that is panic-stricken, may bite, being incapable of recognizing the owner. A muzzle is the quickest and easiest way to prevent other injuries from occurring.

A muzzle can be simply made from a two-foot (approximately) piece of rope, belt, stocking or gauze strips. Practice tying a loose knot in the middle of the muzzle: leave a large loop, slip it over the dog's muzzle and pull the knot tight. Bring the loose ends down under the chin and tie another knot. Pull the ends around behind the ears to the back of the head, and tie yet one more knot. Muzzling a dog will not interfere with breathing, providing no head or jaw injury has been sustained.

STRETCHERS

A injured dog requires immediate transportation to a veterinarian, with the least amount of further trauma possible. The ideal canine stretcher is a large flat surface, such as a piece of plywood or for smaller dogs a drawer will do fine. Maneuver the dog carefully onto a blanket or a sheet, supporting as much of the animal as possible while doing so. With one person at each end, pull the sheet taut and lift the dog onto the board. (This method makes it easier to transfer the dog onto an examination table at the veterinary hospital.) If a board is not available, the blanket or sheet alone will suffice.

If the dog is injured and no blanket or plywood board is available, such as in a wilderness area, it can be transported by carrying the dog over your shoulders and around your neck, holding the legs in front of you. This latter, however, is a last resort method. It can be in certain instances critically important to keep pressure off the abdomen and chest to maximize breathing. A puppy can be transported with one hand under the head and neck, the other hand supporting the chest. A small (young) puppy can also be transported safely by picking it up by the loose scruff of the neck, allowing the puppy to hang straight down. This method also keeps the spine straight while allowing for maximum breathing capacity.

INTERNAL BLEEDING

Internal bleeding can initiate shock and can occur following injury, such as falling or being hit by a car. A dog that might have internal bleeding requires extremely gentle handling. Any moving should be performed on a stretcher or blanket. The blanket should be large enough to also cover the dog, helping to maintain body temperature, which aids in preventing shock. Internal bleeding is not always easily apparent. A suspect case must be transported to a veterinarian as soon as possible. Outward signs in extreme cases can be bleeding from the mouth or nose, and some amount of turgidness to the abdominal area. This is only for a veterinarian to determine and is never a layperson's decision.

EXTERNAL BLEEDING

Visible bleeding from cuts or contusions may be controlled before the dog is transported to the veterinarian. A pressure bandage can be applied to control all but the most severe bleeding. Bleeding may also be moderately slowed with a cool pack. Do not, however, apply ice or a cold pack directly to an open traumatized site. Nor should a cool pack be used if there is any possibility whatsoever that the dog is in danger of going into shock.

TOURNIQUETS

Severe bleeding from a leg wound can usually be controlled by increasing the tightness of a pressure bandage. Only when absolutely necessary should a tourniquet ever be applied to help stop major bleeding. If the veterinary service is farther away than 12 or 15 minutes, periodic releasing of the tourniquet must be made to prevent other trauma from occurring to the limb. Skin tissues are very delicate, and tissue death begins to occur after 20 minutes *or less*, which in turn allows the possible onset of life-threatening gangrene.

A tourniquet can be simply made with a piece of rope, belt, stocking or gauze strips. Traditionally a loop is made around the limb a few inches above the laceration site. Place a stick, board or even a pen or a pencil over the loop and then make a second loop. Twist the stick until the fabric of the tourniquet is pulled moderately tight: tight enough to help ease the flow of blood. *Never* attempt to stop the flow of blood altogether. It is very important to time the period a tourniquet is tightened. Prolonged periods of tightness not only staunch the flow of blood to a limb, but with time will cut off all circulation. The tourniquet should remain tightened for periods of 12 to 15 minutes, followed by 3 or 4 minutes when the tourniquet is moderately loosened before tightening it again.

SHOCK

A dog suffering shock becomes completely prostrate; its breathing may be shallow and rapid. The eyes may dilate (the pupils wide open), the pupillary reaction may be slow and the eyes may have a rather glassy look to them. Mucous membranes, such as the gums, are often pale.

Unless the weather is hot, cover the dog with a blanket to keep it warm. If the weather is warm, cover the dog lightly with a lightweight blanket or sheet. If the dog is injured during cold months, an emergency hot-water bottle can be made by filling a plastic bleach or detergent bottle with very warm (not hot) water, and placing it next to the dog. A large dog needs multiple warm-water bottles to help prevent shock. A dog suffering shock requires *immediate* transportation to the veterinary hospital. If low blood pressure (shock) persists too long, and remains unsupported by therapy, irreversible changes can occur.

DISLOCATIONS, FRACTURES AND SPLINTS

Fractures or dislocations are usually quite evident, with most dogs forgoing use of the injured limb. The sooner a fracture or dislocation is set by a veterinarian, the less serious any aftereffects of the injury will be.

If a leg bone is severely out of line, a temporary splint or support can be helpful to prevent further trauma to the injured leg. A simple splint can be made by wrapping two short boards or sticks in fabric such as cloth or gauze strips. Place these carefully on either side of the injury site, then gently wrap the limb with additional gauze or cloth strips. Stockings or pantyhose can be used in lieu of cloth or gauze. The injured dog requires immediate transportation to the veterinarian's, in a manner that prevents any further trauma to the injury site. Do not spend time worrying about a splint, however, if the dog is in shock. Use the blanket-carrying method discussed under Stretchers and immediately transport the animal.

POISON

Puppies and some adult dogs may be indiscriminate in what they ingest. Any dog with the propensity to eat anything and everything in sight could easily become poisoned. Treatment of poisoning presents special medical problems. It can be critically important to know exactly what poison the animal has ingested.

When the poison is known, the veterinarian can immediately initiate the proper antidote. Unfortunately many poisons have no specific antidote and may only be partially controlled. If the exact poison is not known, the owner must become a "sleuth," helping the veterinarian to determine what possibilities could have affected the dog. Possible sources of poisoning are poisoned bait such as that used for foxes and coyotes or mice and rats, paint, plant sprays and weed killers, insect sprays and chocolate. Certain plants are also poisonous to animals. Lists of these plants may be obtained through your veterinary hospital, a local university, animal control, a poison center or a state agency.

Chocolate toxicosis affects many pets around the holidays. Milk chocolate is less toxic than darker varieties. Baking chocolate is approximately nine times stronger in its effect—one-half an ounce can prove fatal. Chocolate contains caffeine and theobromine, which are toxic to animals. Clinical signs may include vomiting, hyperactivity, increased heart and respiration rates, diarrhea, muscle tremors, staggering, increased urination, vomiting, seizures, coma and death. A pet that exhibits any of these symptoms must be seen by the veterinarian immediately.

Warfarin is a common poison used on rodent populations. Any dog that has ingested this substance requires *immediate* medical attention. Strychnine, often used for varmint control, results in a dog's having rigid extensions of the legs and neck. A dog that has been poisoned by ingestion of a corrosive chemical should *never* be forced to vomit, as this procedure can be extremely dangerous.

If the pet has actually been observed ingesting a poisonous substance other than strychnine, causing the animal to vomit can be beneficial. Several teaspoons of salt placed at the back of the tongue may be enough to induce vomiting. A mustard and water solution, or a strong saltwater solution (six teaspoons of salt mixed with a glass of water), can also produce the desired effect. Directly after the dog has been caused to vomit it should be given milk. The dog must then be immediately seen by the veterinarian.

HEATSTROKE

Heatstroke may be one of the greatest causes of death in dogs. The most frequent case occurs when a dog is confined to an automobile on a warm day, or even when the car is exposed to direct sunlight on a mild day. The auto's metal body acts exactly like an oven. Temperatures rise within *brief minutes* from double-digit to triple-digit figures. The signs of heatstroke are difficulty breathing accompanied by very rapid and shallow panting. If a dog has reached this point, it is in a state of collapse and death can be imminent.

The dog's temperature must be reduced immediately. Do *not* wait to get the dog to a veterinarian before initiating treatment. Time and quick reactions by the owner are the most critical factors initially to saving the dog's life. The dog's temperature can be reduced quickly by immersing it in a tub of cool-to-cold water, NOT ICE. The pet can be hosed off thoroughly, or it can be placed in a shower stall with cold water sprayed on it. A cool-water enema can also be administered. En route to the veterinarian, loosely wrap the dog in towels drenched with cold water. Ice can also be applied to the groin area, around the ears and between the forelegs (''armpits''). Elevate the dog's head and chest slightly during the ride to the hospital to facilitate easier breathing.

Once a dog has heatstroke, it becomes incapable of regulating its body temperature. It is *critical* that the dog be placed under veterinary care as quickly as possible. An animal is prone to recurrence of heatstroke once suffering this condition. Each year one hears about dogs (and small children) that die of heatstroke from having been left unattended in a closed or poorly ventilated car.

PORCUPINE QUILLS

Few dogs are canny enough to win against a porcupine. Quills can easily become embedded anywhere in a dog's anatomy: legs, chest, neck, throat or head. Any dog suffering multiple punctures from a porcupine immediately distresses. If the quills embed around the mouth, face or neck, the situation becomes life-threatening.

Quill removal is painful. Application of vinegar to the quills softens them. A good measure of success is experienced in quill removal by cutting them at the point farthest away from the dog's body. Once severed, the quills partially collapse, aiding in their withdrawal. The quills may then be removed, as carefully and gently as possible, with either a pair of hemostats or pliers, either of which give a good grip. Quills have small barb-like projections that perform similar to a fish hook, and which make removal painful and difficult. Small quills can quickly become totally embedded, to be felt beneath the dog's skin: *these must be surgically removed as quickly as possible*. Complete quill removal usually requires veterinary attention because the withdrawal process is so painful, and the animal already in pain often panics. The dog should always see a veterinarian after this type of injury. Treatment with anti-inflammatory drugs and antibiotic drugs is commonly necessary.

SKUNKS

Undeniably, skunks are the most "popular" bane of dogs and their owners. Few dogs have the canniness and ability to be victorious over a skunk. Skunks are infamous for carrying diseases such as leptospirosis and rabies. Few things distress either an owner or dog more than the dog that has been "hit" by a skunk.

The odor of a skunk needs to be neutralized as quickly as possible. The dog should be bathed repeatedly with tomato puree, then rinsed each time with water. After several repeated applications of the tomato puree and rinsing, the dog should then be bathed with soap and water. Diluted tomato paste, tomato juice, catsup or even tomato soup can be used as alternatives to tomato puree. There are also a number of good commercial products available that aid in skunk odor removal, some of which are applied to dogs, and others to carpeting, clothing and furniture. These products are excellent for first and final applications.

FOREIGN OBJECTS

Puppies teethe by chewing; there is little that they will not try at least once. Adults often relieve boredom or find recreation in chewing. Smart owners always have safe, suitable chewing objects readily available to their pets.

Many dogs are known to swallow much if not all of what they chew. They have been known to swallow bones, golf balls, hard rubber balls, squeakers from toys, bells from balls, entire pantyhose and bath mats! A dog that has ingested a foreign object may attempt to vomit persistently, strain to defecate, suffer loss of appetite, display a generalized lackluster air and exhibit signs of abdominal distress. First aid for this *life-threatening* condition is immediately taking the dog to the veterinary hospital. Occasionally emergency surgery is required to clear an obstructed intestinal tract.

The jaw power of a large dog can be awesome. Some have been known to shear large pieces of bone, sticks or other objects with their molars. On a rare occasion, an item can become lodged in the roof of a dog's mouth, between its teeth or jaws, or caught in the back of the throat. When an object is caught, the dog attempts dislodgement by pawing its mouth, usually while holding its head slightly to one side. If the object can be seen it can normally be removed with the aid of a pair of pliers. Dog's saliva makes an object quite slippery. Using fingers alone can at times cause an object to slip dangerously toward the throat, to potentially block the trachea (airway). *Never* attempt to remove an object by fingers alone. Even the most tractable dog can panic when an object is caught in its mouth and may inadvertently bite. Sometimes an object is so firmly embedded that only a veterinarian can remove it after having given the dog a mild, general anesthetic.

BURNS

Burns, while uncommon, are not rare to dogs. They can occur from hot grease or water, or from simply touching a hot object (such as a radiator, iron or stovetop). A burn site should initially be flushed with cool-to-cold water. A syringe without a needle or a spray bottle can be ideal for flushing. *Once the burn site has cooled,* generally after an hour or so, sterile ointment can be applied to protect the damaged area. In lieu of a sterile burn ointment, Vaseline, shortening or even sweet butter (butter without salt) may be used. Also, products such as Solarcaine or an aloe vera compound help to control localized pain.

A large burned area requires immediate veterinary attention. A dressing can be applied to give added protection against infection. The dog also requires antibiotics. A severely burned dog may require additional medical support, such as stabilizing intravenous or subcutaneous fluids.

Dogs burned by acids must have their wounds *thoroughly flushed* with baking soda and cool water. Alkaline burns can be thoroughly rinsed with lemon juice and water. Once flushed, the injury site can then be treated as other burns, with the application of a sterile burn ointment. A dog always requires veterinary care following any immediate emergency treatment.

The eyes must be flushed with water continuously for at least fifteen minutes if they are the site of a caustic solution type of burn. Following this initial emergency first-aid treatment, the dog requires immediate veterinary follow-up care in order to save its sight.

Products such as turpentine or kerosene, when used as paint removers on a dog's coat, also produce a very painful burn. These products should never be used for removal of tar, grease or paint from dogs. The best treatment for these burns is by irrigation of the sites, followed by an application of a vegetable oil, then washing the area with a mild soap and again applying vegetable oil. (Vegetable oil can be soothing in addition to healing.) Following emergency first-aid applications, the dog must be seen by its veterinarian. Veterinarians often have a list of products that can be used safely on a dog for the removal of paints, greases and tar. If the affected area is small enough, the hair can simply be allowed to wear off, or it can be scissored without "damaging" the dog's appearance.

Burns can remain painful for long periods of time. They are prone to

227

infection and are slow to heal. Any dog that has suffered anything more than a minor burn must be seen by a veterinarian. *If a large area is burned, or the burn is deep enough, the dog can go into shock.* A dog's electrolyte balance is also easily upset by burning. In such cases the dog requires immediate supportive electrolyte therapy.

ELECTROCUTION AND CARDIOPULMONARY RESUSCITATION

Some puppies and adults may attempt chewing on an electric cord. Normally such an action results in giving the dog a severe, painful jolt. A burn caused by the electricity can also occur. Worse, the animal can receive a bad electrical shock, and suddenly stiffen and fall over in a rigid posture. *The dog may be incapable of releasing the cord, and the shock may, therefore, be continuous!* No matter how much you love your pet, *never* touch the dog first! Your first response must be to pull the plug from the wall! If rubber gloves are handy, don them as an added safety precaution *before* pulling the plug, and *before* touching the dog.

A dog that has suffered electric shock may have arrested heartbeat and breathing. Place the dog fully prone on its right side. Pull the left foreleg back toward the rib cage; the point of the elbow will be close to the site of the heart. Feel for the heartbeat there. Watch the rib cage for a brief moment, noting if there is involuntary breathing. If there is neither respiration nor apparent heartbeat, *CPR must be started immediately!* If someone is nearby, have them call the veterinarian for additional instructions and notification that you will be transporting a case of cardiopulmonary arrest.

CPR

Cardiopulmonary resuscitation is best performed by two people. Although it can be effectively performed by one person, it is harder and riskier to the animal. First check the dog's mouth, making sure that the tongue is not blocking the airway: pull the tongue forward to clear the trachea. With the dog prone on its right side, and on a firm flat surface, alternately depress and release the animal's chest, pressing firmly on the rib cage just posterior to the fifth to sixth rib. Count a rhythm as the dog's chest is depressed and released. It is a three-part cadence: one for depression; two for release; three for a brief pause before starting over.

The chest should be depressed and released alternately five times before "breathing" for the dog. While ideally a second person breathes for the pet, this can be performed by a single person. Extend the dog's head and neck, place both hands around and cup the dog's muzzle (preventing air from escaping through the lips), then envelope the pet's mouth *and* nose with your mouth. Blow air from your mouth (not from your lungs) firmly, with a moderately sustained pressure. Observe the rib cage for evidence of elevation, response to the blowing.

Then again, depress and release the chest five times before "breathing" for the dog once more. Repeat the procedure as necessary until the dog is breathing on its own.

If the dog's heart has stopped beating, give a quick thump over the organ after having cleared the trachea (pulling the tongue) and before depressing and releasing the chest. This procedure, too, must be repeated until the heart begins beating, or all hope has elapsed.

Resuscitation by these methods may take as long as twenty minutes, or even an hour, before the animal responds well enough to have a steady heartbeat and breathe on its own.

In the ideal situation two people work on the dog while a third person drives everyone to the veterinary hospital. Even if an apparently normal heartbeat and respiration have been restored, the animal must still be immediately seen by the veterinarian. In cases where the heart has continued to beat and there has been no apparent respiratory arrest, but the dog was unconscious, aromatic stimulants prove beneficial. In lieu of anything else, a small amount of ammonia can be used as a stimulant.

CONVULSIONS

Convulsions are an uncommon occurrence in dogs. An episode is more upsetting and dismaying to the owner than the pet. An episode can be caused by a viral infection that has reached the brain, such as distemper, for example. Ear infections, epilepsy, certain parasitic infestations, in addition to other causal factors, can also initiate an episode of convulsions.

If a pet convulses, make sure that it is out of harm's way, and cannot become entangled in furniture or other objects, and it is not up against a wall. When a dog is out of danger, *leave it alone*. If, however, the animal is in a dangerous site, do not attempt to handle or move it. Cover the dog with a blanket to restrain it from injury. Be certain to keep your fingers and hands (and other portions of your anatomy) away from the dog's head: dogs often bite actively as they convulse. A convulsing dog is totally oblivious to its surroundings. While the dog will not intentionally attack anyone, or otherwise be vicious, it can easily inflict injury upon those who come too close to its head during an episode.

Any dog that has convulsed requires veterinary attention to determine the cause. Dogs that have convulsed should *never* be wormed by the owner; under certain conditions, this may cause another episode. Owner-given treatments such as worming or other over-the-counter remedies can, in certain instances, even cause death to the dog that has previously convulsed.

FISH HOOKS

Fish hooks are barbed and usually require veterinary attention to be withdrawn safely and painlessly. Because the barbed portion normally must be pushed forward, removal causes the dog much distress. The fish hook's eye usually must be severed before the barbed portion can be pushed through the skin. It is wise to seek veterinary care even for something as simple as a fish hook removal. Veterinarians are equipped to remove these with little or no pain, with the application of a topical or general anesthetic. Often a veterinarian will also want the dog to have antibiotics.

SNAKE BITES

Only a few varieties of snakes in North America are poisonous to dogs. The rattlesnake, copperhead, water moccasin (the cottonmouth), mangrove, coral and California lyre are the most commonly found poisonous reptiles. Of these, the rattlesnake's bite accounts for approximately 80 percent of all fatalities.

Snake bites demand immediate first-aid treatment by the owner and intensive veterinary treatment as quickly as possible. The venom's progress can be restricted by use of a tourniquet when the bite is on a leg or tail. Place the tourniquet snugly *above* the wound site (as tightly as when, for example, a nurse draws blood). The tourniquet may be fashioned from hosiery, rope, a rubber band, a bungee cord or even a shirt sleeve. The tourniquet's pressure is necessary to impede the venom's progress toward vital organs, the heart, brain and spinal cord.

Next, make a single-line incision through the cutaneous layer, slightly into the muscle fascia at the bite site. Express the venom by squeezing the wound. If a bulb syringe is available, use it. *Never* suck the venom from a wound with your mouth! Doing so could prove fatal! Allow the wound site to slowly ooze blood. If ice is available, pack it around the area but not directly over the wound. Ice also helps to slow the venom's progress.

Immobilize the dog: do not allow it to walk. Carry the dog to your vehicle for quick, direct transportation to the nearest veterinary clinic. Any movement of the dog will increase heart, metabolic and respiration rates and, at the same time, the spread of the venom.

If ever confronted by an emergency, the owner of the animal must respond quickly in order to prevent further possible irreversible damage or to save the dog's life. The dog's heartbeat and breathing require the first attention. Bleeding sites should be checked next. Check the extent of any other injuries last in emergency first aid. Emergency first aid is just what is implied, the *first aid only*. Dogs that have encountered any one of these conditions (in addition to others) should always be seen by a veterinarian as quickly as possible. *First aid never replaces the requirement for qualified veterinary attention.*

230

APPENDIX II

By Air

THERE IS ALWAYS an element of risk in travel and commercial carriers can be no better than the staff. Use major airlines which are best equipped and more adept at handling live cargo due to their flight volume. Small, commuter airlines may present hazardous conditions if their cargo holds are not pressurized.

Weather embargos also occur. You should schedule the pup's departure and arrival time between 85° and 45°F because airport ground temperatures can change precipitously from 130°F to -0°F and adversely affect a waiting dog.

Flight types are: direct, through, change of planes with the same carrier, and change of planes between one or more companies. Direct shipment is best because the dog flies nonstop to its destination. Through flights have stops: plane and carrier changes may require a layover of several hours. Some airlines allow one or two dogs, small enough to fit under a seat in a flight-approved crate, to travel in the cabin when accompanied by an owner who is ticketed first class. Reservations must be booked a week in advance when flying with a pet booked as carry-on or excess baggage.

Reserved Air Freight (priority shipping) should be booked no less than four days before flight time. Baggage and cargo limit compartment space and displace available oxygen. Pet travel during holidays or weekends is not always possible nor in an animal's best interests. Also, without adequate notice of a live shipment, dry ice (which rapidly depletes oxygen) could be routed in the same compartment, causing suffocation.

CRATE REQUIREMENTS

The FAA has specific crate requirements which say that a dog must be able to stand, sit, and lie down comfortably; it must be sturdy; have spacer bars to prevent direct baggage contact; and enough holes for maximum ventilation. Crate sizes, designated by numbers 100 through 700, indicate cubic inch and air displacement. The 600 and 700 crates (for giant breeds) are restricted to certain flights because they do not conform to all aircraft designs. Many airlines also have weight limitations their employees may handle. Reserve the purchase of a crate when booking a flight if you do not already have a crate for the pup.

HEALTH REQUIREMENTS

A health certificate, proof of veterinary examination, is required for shipping. The dog's inoculation status, shipper's and consignee's names, addresses, and telephone numbers are included. Give booster vaccinations no less than a week before a flight. The health certificate is dated according to the veterinary examination (not flight date), and remains in effect for ten days. If a breeding is completed within that period, a bitch may return utilizing the same document.

Some areas have a rabies quarantine. Additional requirements must be checked before a shipment into or out of these areas is attempted.

THE CARE PACKAGE

Assemble a ''care package'' for any lengthy trip, by air or car: include shavings, soft toys, and freeze a very large ice cube, perhaps in a margarine tub. Ice placed in a crate door's removable bowl will not spill during travel. Fill the bowl with water a fraction from the top before freezing. These bowls, of a similar size for all crates, are inadequate for large breeds.

Coarse pine and cedar shavings combined can be purchased from a pet supplier. If a dog relieves itself in the crate during travel, it may still emerge sweet smelling and moderately clean. Fine shavings can be inhaled, causing trauma. The scent of cedar alone can be overwhelming in a crate's confines.

Include the dog's name and a brief personality description on the ''Live Animal'' notice attached to the crate's top. Airline employees, like most people, are fond of dogs and will often comply with legibly written, simple care instructions. Consignee care instructions can be attached to the crate in a second see-through airbill envelope. Although mailed, duplicate instructions help to insure a brood bitch's safety and comfort at the stud's home, or welcome a puppy's arrival.

232

DEPARTURE

Call the airline on flight day because problems causing changes can occur. Check the advance time required to conclude airbill paperwork and when the dog must be there, one or more hours prior to the flight. While dogs flying as excess baggage are not insured through the airlines, their value (up to five hundred dollars) can be declared, or insurance purchased for a nominal fee.

Brood bitch owners pay for the crate, shipping, kenneling, and stud fee. Puppy purchasers also pay for a crate and air shipment, prepaid or by collection.

As a courtesy, the consignee should always call the breeder when the dog arrives. A progress report made within the first few days is also reassuring.

Glossary of Terms

Acetabulum: The cup-shaped socket in the hip-bone into which the head of the femur fits.

AKC: American Kennel Club.

AKC Litter Registration Application: The application form submitted to the American Kennel Club for a litter registration "kit." This form is also signed by the owner of the stud dog at the time of service. It is filled out in its entirety by the owner or lessee of the dam at the time of whelping.

AKC Litter Registration Kit: A series of forms for the breeder and prospective owners of puppies consisting of individual AKC Registration Application forms.

AKC papers: Those papers given by the American Kennel Club that certify the dog's registration with an individual number, the dog's registered name, the breeder's name, the owner's name and address, the name of the sire and dam, along with their respective registration numbers, and, in parentheses, the stud book date in which the sire's and dam's names first appear.

AKC Registration Application: The application form that must, by AKC rules and regulations, accompany each puppy eligible to be registered as an individual with the American Kennel Club.

Alpha personality: Designates the first position, chief or highest-ranking animal of dominance in a social hierarchy such as a canid pack.

American Kennel Club (AKC): A registering and governing body that oversees, regulates and forms the rules and regulations relating to dog registrations, dog shows, field, obedience and tracking trials and dog-show–giving clubs. This governing body performs as the registering body for all breeds of dogs recognized as being purebred by the American Kennel Club; also those breeds whose pending recognition has placed them in the Miscellaneous Class.

Amnion: The thin, transparent, silvery and tough membrane lining (known as placenta) that produces, at the very earliest period of fetation, the amniotic fluid.

Amniotic fluid: The fluid that surrounds the fetus.

Anconeal: Pertaining to the elbow.

Anconeal dysplasia: Known in lay terms as "elbow dysplasia," it is an ununited anconeal process, and involves three small bones of the elbow joint that unite as the dogs grow. It is a developmental abnormality of the elbow that can cause the animal much pain.

Angulation: 1. The formation of an angle. 2. The angles formed by a meeting of the bones; mainly the shoulder, upper arm, stifle and hock.

Aunty: Any canid, male or female, not necessarily related to whelps, that fulfills the capacity as "puppy-sitter."

Autoradiograph: A radiograph of an object or tissue made by its own radioactivity, especially after the purposeful introduction into it of radioactive material.

Autosomal: Pertains to an *autosome*, which is any ordinary paired chromosome as distinguished from a sex chromosome.

Barrel: Rounded rib section.

Bench(ed) show: 1. A dog show at which the dogs competing for prizes are required to remain in a designated place for a specific time. 2. Also, a conformation show.

Best Brace in Show (BBIS): Two dogs of the same breed and identical ownership compete at the Breed and Group levels, winning in each category, then compete against the Brace winners from the other six Groups, one to be ultimately selected as the Best Brace in Show, all-breeds, for that show.

Best in Show (BIS): In all-breed shows, one dog that through the process of elimination has been selected as the Best in Show dog at that show.

Best of Breed, Best of Variety: The award given to that breed or variety representative judged to be the breed's best at a given show.

Best of Opposite Sex: The award given to that breed representative as being the best of the opposite sex to the Best of Breed winner at a given show.

Best Team in Show (BTIS): Similar to Brace competition, except that four animals make up the unit.

Bitch: Any female canid (*familiaris* or *lupus*).

Bite: The relative position of the upper and lower teeth when the mouth is closed. (See **Level bite, Scissors bite, Undershot, Overshot.**)

Bloat: 1. A condition that can fatally affect dogs and other animals. It is caused either by the distention of the stomach, or the stomach turning over (volvulus), thereby blocking the entrance and exit to the stomach. 2. A common term for gastric dilatation-volvulus requiring immediate veterinary care to save the animal's life. 3. To make turgid, or cause to swell, as with air or liquid. 4. A flatulent distention of the abdomen that can arise from eating too rapidly.

Breeder: Any person who owns a pregnant bitch.

Brisket: The forepart of the body below the chest, between the forelegs, closest to the ribs.

Brood bitch: A female used for breeding. The dam of any litter in utero or postnatal. The same as brood matron.

Canadian Kennel Club (CKC): The governing and registering body of Canada, overseeing and regulating the rules and regulations pertaining to dog shows, field, obedience and tracking trials and show-giving clubs in Canada. It performs as the registering body for all breeds of dogs recognized as being purebred by the Canadian Kennel Club. Individuals as well as clubs may join the membership of the Canadian Kennel Club.

Canines: The two upper and two lower sharp-pointed teeth next to the incisors.

Canis familiaris: Any domesticated breed of dog.

Canis lupus: Wolf; there are over 300 subspecies.

Central progressive retinal atrophy (CPRA): A condition in which a central atrophy of the retina occurs.

Champion (Ch.): A prefix used with the name of a dog that has been recorded a Champion by AKC as a result of defeating a specified number of dogs in specified competition at a series of AKC licensed or member dog shows.

Character: Expression, individuality, and general appearance and personality considered as typical of a breed.

Choke collar: A leather, nylon or chain slip collar fitted to the dog's neck in such a manner that the degree of tension tightens or loosens it.

Chondrodysplasia (ChD): Known commonly as *Dwarfism*. It is a hereditary condition found in Alaskan Malamutes and other breeds. A simple recessive gene produces the condition. Both parents must be carriers for the condition to occur in offspring. Carriers should not be used in a breeding program.

Close-coupled: Comparatively short from withers to hip bones.

Coat: The dog's hairy covering.

Collar: A leather, nylon or chain for restraining or leading the dog when the leash is attached.

Companion Dog (CD): A suffix title used with the name of a dog that has been recorded by AKC as a result of having won minimum scores in Novice Classes at three AKC licensed or member Obedience Trials.

Companion Dog Excellent (CDX): A suffix title used with the name of a dog that has been recorded by AKC as a result of having won certain minimum scores in Open (Obedience) Classes at three AKC licensed or member Obedience Trials.

Condition: Health as shown by the coat, state of flesh, general appearance and deportment.

Conformation: The form and structure, make and shape; arrangement of the parts in conformity with breed Standard demands.

Coupling: The part of the body between the ribs and pelvis; the loin.

Cow-hocked: When the hocks turn toward each other.

Crest: The upper, arched portion of the neck.

Crossbred: A dog whose sire and dam are of two different breeds.

Croup: The back part of the back, above the hindlegs.

Crown: The highest part of the head; the topskull.

Cryptorchid: The adult whose testicles are abnormally retained in the abdominal cavity. Bilateral cryptorchidism involves both sides; that is, neither testicle has descended into the scrotum. Unilateral cryptorchidism involves one side only; that is, one testicle is retained or hidden and one is descended.

Culotte: The longer hair on the back of the thighs.

Cur: A mongrel dog; one of mixed ancestry.

Dam: Any female that has whelped a litter.

Dewclaw: An extra claw or functionless digit on the inside of the leg; a rudimentary fifth toe.

Dewlap: Loose, pendulous skin under the throat.

Disqualification: A decision made by a judge or by a Bench show committee following a determination that a dog has a condition that makes it ineligible for any further competition under the dog show rules or under the Standard for its breed.

Dog: A term in general usage referring to all *Canis familiaris* (male and female), or, more technically, referring to the male gender of the species.

Dog show: A competitive exhibition for dogs at which the dogs are judged in accordance with an established Standard of perfection for each breed.

Domed: Evenly rounded in topskull; convex instead of flat. Domy.

Double coat: An outer coat resistant to weather and protective against brush and brambles, together with an undercoat of softer hair for warmth and waterproofing.

Down in pastern: Weak or faulty pastern (metacarpus) set at a pronounced angle from the vertical.

Dudley nose: Flesh-colored.

Dwarfism: See **Chondrodysplasia**.

Dysplasia: Abnormality of development.

Dyspnea: Difficult or labored breathing.

Elbow: The joint between the upper arm and the forearm.

Elbows out: Turning out or off from the body; not held close (or in line).

Emesis: Vomiting; an act of vomiting.

Epilepsy: A functional disorder of the brain characterized by signs related to the nervous system (which is structurally unaltered). Epilepsy as found in canines is not completely comparable to that found in humans. Evidence of epilepsy may be convulsions, hysteria and unusual behavior patterns.

Estrus: The recurrent, restricted period of sexual receptivity in female mammals. Also, the cycle of changes in the genital tract that are produced as a result of ovarian hormonal activity.

Euthanasia: The act or practice of painlessly putting to death those animals

238

suffering from an incurable and distressing disease or from totally debilitating old age.

Expression: The general appearance of all features of the head as viewed from the front and as typical of the breed.

Eyeteeth: The upper canines.

Faking: To change the appearance of a dog by artificial means with the objective of deceiving the onlooker as to its real merit.

Fangs: See **Canines.**

Feathering: Longer fringe of hair on ears, legs, tail or body.

Feet east and west: The toes turned out.

Femur: The proximal bone of the hindlimb; the thighbone.

Feral: 1. A domesticated dog gone wild. 2. May also be a domestic (type) dog gone wild that can be reintroduced to domestication (e.g., the Australian Dingo). 3. Untamed, undomesticated, wild, savage.

Fetus: The unborn offspring of any viviparous animal; the developing young in the uterus.

Fiddle front: Forelegs out at elbows, pasterns close and feet turned out. French front.

Flank: The side of the body between the last rib and the hip.

Flat-sided: Ribs insufficiently rounded as they approach the sternum or breastbone.

Flews: Upper lips pendulous, particularly at their inner corners.

Forearm: The bone of the foreleg between the elbow and the pastern.

Foreface: The front part of the head before the eyes. Muzzle.

Foster mother: 1. A wet nurse. 2. A lactating female, human or animal, used to nurse offspring not her own.

Front: The forepart of the body as viewed head-on; i.e., forelegs, chest, brisket and shoulder line.

Futurity Stakes: Competition at selected dog shows for which young dogs have been nominated either at or before birth—with fees. Also, Field Trials.

Gait: The manner in whch a dog walks, trots or runs.

Gastric torsion: Pertains to torsion (twisting) of the stomach. (See **Torsion.**)

Genetics: The study of heredity.

Get: The product of a sire and dam.

Groom: To brush, comb, trim or otherwise make a dog's coat neat.

Groups: The breeds as grouped by "type" into seven divisions to facilitate judging in the United States: I Sporting; II Hound; III Working; IV Terrier; V Toy; VI Non-Sporting; VII Herding.

Guard hairs: The longer, smoother, stiffer hairs that grow through the undercoat and normally conceal it. Outer coat.

Hackles: Hair on neck and back raised involuntarily in fright or anger.

Ham: Muscular development of the hindleg just above the stifle.

Handler: A person who handles a dog in the show ring or at a Field Trial.

Haw: A third eyelid or membrane in the inside corner of the eye.

Heat: Seasonal period of the female.

Heel: 1. See **Hock**. 2. A command given to the dog to keep it close beside its handler.

Height: Vertical measurement of the dog from the withers to the ground. (See **Withers**.)

Hemeralopia: Known in lay terms as "day blindness," is a condition of defective vision in bright or normal daylight. The condition is an inherited one and may be discovered in puppies as young as seven weeks of age.

Hemophilia: Commonly termed the "bleeder's disease," it is characterized by unusual and prolific bleeding following even minor trauma and with a markedly significant coagulation time. Caused by a lack of coagulation factor in the blood, it is sex-linked and is transmitted by females to male offspring.

Hemostasis: 1. The arrest of an escape of blood. 2. The checking of the flow of blood through any part or vessel: i.e., effective hemostasis requires a normal vessel wall, normal levels of blood coagulation factors and adequate numbers of functional blood platelets. (Platelets must adhere to the vessel wall at sites of disruption (injury), then stick to each other to form a hemostatic plug.)

Hemostatic disorders: 1. May be acquired or genetic or, as in some cases, are defects in the hemostatic system. 2. A condition whereby an agent that arrests the flow of blood is lacking.

Hierarchy: A rank or order; a series classified in ranks, such as in natural science or logic.

High in Trial (HIT): The dog that scores the highest number of points in an Obedience Trial.

Hip dysplasia: A malformation of the acetabulum and/or head of the femur; may include a thickening of the neck of the femur. A condition that can be caused virally, congenitally or by trauma. Early arthritic changes can occur in the joint as a result of hip dysplasia. Mild cases may go unnoticed except by radiographic evaluation. The most severe cases are pronounced and require surgical intervention for the animal to live a near normal life.

Hock: The tarsus or collection of bones of the hindleg forming the joint between the second thigh and the metatarsus; the dog's true heel.

Hypothyroidism: A condition manifested by a low metabolic rate (among other clinical signs). It is a condition that is determined by a veterinarian. Treatment is ongoing and effective when detected early, before irreversible changes occur in the animal.

Hysterectomy: The operation of removing the uterus.

Inbreeding: The mating of two *closely* related dogs of the same breed, e.g., father/daughter, brother/sister, etc.

Incisors: The upper and lower front teeth between the canines.

In utero: Being within the uterus.

Jowls: Flesh of lips and jaws.

Judge: The arbiter in the dog show ring, Obedience Trial or Field Trial.

Kennel: Building or enclosure where dogs are kept.

Knuckling over: Faulty structure of carpus (wrist) joint allowing it to double forward under the weight of the standing dog; double-jointed wrist, often with slight swelling of the bones.

Laparotomy: Surgical incision through the flank; less correctly, but more generally, abdominal section at any point.

Layback: The angle of the shoulder blade.

Lead: A narrow length of leather, canvas or nylon used as a training or walking (leading) device to move an animal from one area to another.

Leather: The flap of the ear.

Level bite: When the front teeth (incisors) of the upper and lower jaws meet exactly edge to edge. Pincer bite.

Linebreeding: The mating of dogs within the line or family to a common ancestor, for example, a dog to his granddam or a bitch to her grandsire.

Litter: By AKC definition, a litter is comprised of two or more puppies, whelped at a single date by a dam.

Littermate: Is either a male or female sibling (brother or sister) in the same litter.

Loaded shoulders: When the shoulder blades are shoved out from the body by overdevelopment of the muscles.

Loin: Region of the body on either side of the vertebral column between the last ribs and the hindquarters.

Lower thigh: See **Second thigh**.

Lumbering: An awkward gait.

Mad dog: A rabid dog. Rabies can be definitely determined only by autopsy.

Mane: Long and profuse hair on top and sides of the neck.

Mask: Dark shading on the foreface.

Match Show: Usually an informal dog show at which no championship points are awarded.

Mate: To breed a dog and bitch.

Miscellaneous Class: A competitive class at dog shows for dogs of certain specified breeds for which no regular dog show classification is provided.

Mismarks: In some breeds, self colors with any area of white on back between withers and tail and on sides between elbows and hindquarters, dark colors on forelegs between the elbows and toes and on rear legs between the hock and toes.

Molera: Incomplete, imperfect or abnormal ossification of the skull.

Mongrel: A dog whose parents are of mixed-breed origin.

Monorchidism: The condition of having only one testis in the scrotum.

Muzzle: 1. The head in front of the eyes—nasal bone, nostrils and jaws. Foreface. 2. A strap or wire cage attached to the foreface to prevent the dog from biting or from picking up food.

Night-dogs: See **Hemeralopia**.

Nose: 1. Organ of smell. 2. The ability to detect by means of scent.

Obedience Trial (Licensed): An event held under AKC rules at which a "leg" toward Obedience degrees can be earned.

Obedience Trial Champion (OTCH): This is a title that has been awarded to UD dogs for class wins and placements in Obedience Trials.

Occiput: Upper, back point of the skull.

Offspring: The get (puppies or adults) of a breeding from a given sire and dam.

Open Class: A class at dog shows in which all dogs of a breed, champions and imported dogs included, may compete.

Orthopedic Foundation for Animals, Inc. (OFA): A body of specialist veterinarians who evaluate hips and elbows and perform radiographic consultations.

Out at elbows: Elbows turning out from the body as opposed to being held close.

Out at shoulder: With shoulder blades loosely attached to the body, leaving the shoulders jutting out in relief and increasing the breadth of the front.

Outcrossing: The mating of unrelated individuals of the same breed.

Ovariohysterectomy: Surgical removal of the uterus and ovaries.

Overshot: The front teeth (incisors) of the upper jaw overlap and do not touch the front teeth of the lower jaw when the mouth is closed.

Pace: A gait that tends to promote a rolling motion of the body. The left foreleg and left hindleg advance in unison, then the right foreleg and right hindleg.

Pack: A social group of canids that have established a social hierarchy.

Paddling: Moving with forefeet wide.

Pads: Tough, shock-absorbing projections on the underside of the feet. Soles.

Parent club: National club for the breed. Listing with name and address of secretary can be obtained from American Kennel Club, 51 Madison Avenue, New York, NY 10010.

Parturition: The act or process of giving birth.

Pastern: Commonly recognized as the region of the foreleg between the carpus or wrist and the digits.

Pedigree: 1. A table presenting a line of ancestors, a genealogical tree. 2. An ancestral line, lineage. 3. Ancestry, recorded known descent. 4. The genealogy of a given dog, prepared by a kennel club, a pedigree service or the breeder, consisting of three or more generations.

Pig jaw: See **Overshot**.

Pincer bite: See **Level bite**.

Placenta: The cake-like organ within the uterus that establishes communication between the mother and offspring by means of the umbilical cord. The chorion, superficial or fetal portion is surfaced by a smooth, shining membrane with the sheath of the cord (amnion).

Points: 1. Color on face, ears, legs and tail when correlated—usually white, black or tan. 2. A dog or bitch having won their respective Winners class (Winners Dog or Winners Bitch) is awarded points toward a championship. The number of points awarded is a scale based upon the actual number of dogs or bitches defeated in that breed (or variety).

Prick ear: Carried erect and usually pointed at the tip.

Professional handler: A person who shows dogs for a fee.

Progeny: The offspring of a stud dog or brood bitch.

Progressive retinal atrophy (PRA): A hereditary condition involving a progressively diminishing pupillary response to light. Cataracts may or may not be present with this condition. Transmission is by an autosomal recessive factor. Dogs with this condition should not be bred.

Puppy: A dog under twelve months of age.

Purebred: A dog whose sire and dam are the same breed.

Put down: 1. To prepare a dog for the show ring. 2. To denote a dog unplaced in competition. 3. To euthanize a dog.

Racy: Tall, of comparatively slight build.

Radiograph: A film or other record produced by the action of actinic rays on a sensitized surface, such as an autoradiogram or a roentgenogram.

Register: To record with an official registry a dog's breeding particulars.

Register of Merit (ROM): A suffix that is awarded to those dogs whose offspring have met the criteria as established by the breed's Parent Club.

Regurgitation reflex: Puppies effect the regurgitation reflex through stimulation by the licking of the salivary glands located along the lips toward the back of the mouth of an adult canid (such as dam or "aunty"). This reflex and initiation thereof is found in domestic puppies and feral whelps (domestic dogs of a "feral" type and feral canids). The effect of this reflex causes partially digested food (which has been partially broken down for digestibility through the enzymes found in salivation and gastric juices) to be brought up reflexively for young puppies (and whelps) to ingest.

Ring tail: Carried up and around almost in a circle.

Roach back: A convex curvature of the back toward the loin. Carp back.

Rudder: The tail.

Ruff: Thick, longer hair growth around the neck.

Saber tail: Carried in a semicircle.

Sable: A lacing of black hairs over a lighter ground color.

Saddle: A black marking over the back, like a saddle.

Scent: The odor left by an animal on the trail (ground scent) or wafting through the air (airborne scent).

Scissors bite: A bite in which the outer side of the lower incisors touches the inner side of the upper incisors.

Season: That period of time during which a female canid is in estrus. (See **Estrus.**)

Second thigh: That part of the hindquarter from the stifle to the hock corresponding to the human shin and calf. Lower leg.

Self-color: One color of whole color except for lighter shadings.

Seeing Eye dog: A dog trained by the institution The Seeing Eye, as a guide for the blind. (May also be known as a Guide Dog.)

Semislip collar: A collar easy to put on and remove, usually made from one-inch-wide webbing, and provided with two to three inches of slip (play) sufficient to allow the collar to slide over the dog's head as well as preventing it from coming off when the collar is pulled tight, but being unable to choke the dog.

Septum: The line extending vertically between the nostrils.

Shelly: A shallow, narrow body, lacking the correct amount of bone.

Shock: A condition of acute peripheral circulatory failure caused by derangement of circulatory control or loss of circulating fluid and brought about by injury. It is marked by pallor of the mucous membranes, decreased blood pressure, feeble rapid pulse, decreased respiration, restlessness, anxiety and sometimes unconsciousness.

Shoulder height: Height of a dog's body as measured from the withers to the ground. (See **Withers.**)

Sibling: Another offspring of the same parents, but not necessarily of the same birth date. Brothers and sisters but not necessarily littermates.

Sickle tail: Carried out and up in a semicircle.

Sighthound: A hound that hunts by sight: e.g., Saluki, Whippet, Greyhound.

Sire: The male parent.

Sloping shoulder: The shoulder blade set obliquely or "laid back." (See **Layback.**)

Smooth coat: Short hair, close-lying.

Snap tail: A tail that, when carried over the back, will have the major portion lying on the back, and the tail may extend to cover a portion of the loin or flank. Dogs with a snap tail will have a short, level or almost-level croup.

Snipy: A pointed, weak muzzle.

Social hierarchy: The order of dominance in a dog team or dog or wolf pack: in effect, the pecking order.

Sound: A descriptive term applied to a dog that appears to closely meet the breed Standard requirements.

Soundness: The state of mental and physical health when all organs and faculties are complete and functioning normally, each in its rightful relation to the other.

Spay: 1. To remove the ovaries of a female animal. To perform a surgical operation on the bitch's reproductive organs to prevent conception. (See **Ovariohysterectomy.**)

Spring of ribs: Curvature of ribs for heart and lung capacity.

Stance: Manner of standing.

Standard: A description of the ideal dog of each recognized breed, to serve as a word pattern by which dogs are judged at shows.

Standoff coat: A long or heavy coat that stands off from the body.

Station: Comparative height from the ground, as high-stationed, low-stationed.

Sternum: Breastbone.

Stifle: The joint of the hindleg between the thigh and the second thigh. The dog's knee joint.

Stilted: The choppy, up-and-down gait of the straight-hocked dog.

Stop: The step up from muzzle to skull; indentation between the eyes where the nasal bone and skull meet.

Straight-hocked: Lacking appreciable angulation at the hock joints. Straight behind.

Straight shoulders: The shoulder blades rather straight up and down, as opposed to "well laid back."

Stud book: 1. A record of the breeding particulars of dogs of recognized breeds. 2. A Kennel Club's stud books will contain the registered name and number of the sire and dam of a given litter. On a registration form or application the date of publication of the stud book in which the names first appear is shown in parentheses following the name of the sire or dam.

Stud dog: A male dog used for breeding purposes.

Subluxated hock: A hock that moves forward; double-jointed.

Substance: Bone.

Swayback: Concave curvature of the backline between the withers and the hip bones.

Tachycardia: Excessive rapidity of the heartbeat.

Teat: The nipple of the mammary gland.

Test-breeding: is the breeding of two animals together, one a known carrier of a condition, the other animal a suspect carrier of the condition. The progeny are evaluated by a veterinarian, and if the condition is found to be present in the offspring, the suspect animal is then known as a carrier. If the condition is not found to be present in the offspring, the suspect dog is then cleared.

Testes: (Sing. testis) The male gonad; an egg-shaped gland normally situated in the scrotum, which produces spermatozoa.

Thigh: The hindquarter from hip to stifle.

Thorax: That portion of the body (of man and other mammals) found between the neck and abdomen, in which the heart, lungs, esophagus, etc., are situated.

Thrifty dog: A dog that requires proportionately little food in ratio to the work performed (e.g., a dog that can haul a heavy load, over a long distance, on comparatively little nourishment).

Torsion: The act of twisting, the condition of being twisted. (See **Bloat.**)

Track: The course by which a dog moves.

Tracking Dog (TD): A suffix title used with the name of a dog that has been recorded a Tracking Dog as a result of having passed an AKC licensed or member club Tracking test. The title may be combined with the UD title and shown as a UDT.

Tracking Dog Excellent (TDX): A suffix title used with the name of a dog that has been recorded a Tracking Dog Excellent as a result of having passed an AKC licensed or member club Tracking Dog Excellent test. The title may be combined with the UD title and shown as a UDTX.

Tracking test: A trial in whch a dog covers a specified course in a specified manner. A dog must be certified by a qualified person before it can be entered in a Tracking test. Any dog of a recognized breed that successfully completes a test is awarded the suffix of Tracking Dog (TD) to its name.

Trail: 1. To hunt by following ground scent. 2. A track worn by passage through a wilderness or wild region.

Triangular eye: The eye set in surrounding tissue of triangular shape.

Trim: 1. To groom the coat by plucking or clipping. 2. Neat, tidy. 3. Without excess weight.

Tubal ligation: Male—tying off the vas deferens. Female—tying off the fallopian tubes.

Tuck-up: Characterized by markedly shallower body depth at the loin. Small-waisted.

Type: The characteristic qualities distinguishing a breed; the embodiment of a Standard's essentials.

Umbilical cord: The cord or stalk arising from the navel that connects the fetus with the placenta.

Undershot: The front teeth (incisors) of the lower jaw overlapping or projecting beyond the front teeth of the upper jaw when the mouth is closed.

Unilateral cryptorchid: See **Cryptorchid**.

Upper arm: The humerus or bone of the foreleg, between the shoulder blade and the forearm.

Uterus: The hollow muscular organ in female animals that is the abode and the place of nourishment of the embryo and fetus.

Utility Dog (UD): A suffix title used with the name of a dog that has been recorded a Utility Dog by AKC as a result of having won certain minimum scores in Utility classes at three AKC licensed or member Obedience Trials. The title may be combined with the TD or TDX title and the dog shown as a UDT or UDTX.

Vasectomy: Surgical removal of the ductus (vas) deferens, or of a portion of it.

Volvulus: Intestinal obstruction caused by a knotting and twisting of the bowel.

Weedy: An insufficient amount of bone; light-boned.

Wheel back: The backline arched markedly over the loin. Roached.

Whelp: 1. Unweaned puppy. 2. The young offspring of a dog or feral canid. 3. To give birth.

Whelping: The act of giving birth.

Whelping box: A box specifically designed to contain the bitch comfortably while whelping and later, with her puppies. Some whelping boxes are constructed with a guard rail which helps prevent puppies from being crushed against the side of the box by the dam's weight.

Withers: The highest point of shoulders, immediately behind the neck.

Wry mouth: Lower jaw does not line up with upper jaw.

Index

Children
    playing with bitches during pregnancy,
        62, 64
    of purchasers, supervision of, 192
Chinese Shar Peis, *183*
Chocolate toxicosis, 224
Chondrodysplasia, *112*, 115
Chondrodystrophy, 115
Clamber areas for mobile puppies,
    139–40
Cleft lip, 115–16
Cleft palate, 91, 116
Close line breeding, 11
Coat defects, 116
Coccidiosis, 173
Colic, 108, 116, 131
Colitis, 116
Collar, removal prior to whelping, 136
Colostrum, 89, 131, 168
"Come" command, 202
Commands, learning of, 202
Commercial dog food, 45–47
Conception, *14*, 15
    rates, 34
Confinement barriers, 69
Constipation, 116
Contracts for sale and payment, 214–20
Convulsions, 54, 117, 229
Coprophagy, 35, 40, 116
Coronavirus, 171–72
Corporal punishment, 40
CPR, 228–29
Crates for shipping, 232

Dalmatians, 44, *76*, 89, 117, *139*, *154*,
    160
Dams. *See* Bitches
Day blindness, 119
Deafness, 116–17
Demodectic mange. *See* Mange
Denning, *38*, 78–79
Dental development, 163–65
Depression, 57
Dewclaw removal, 134–35
Diabetes, 117
Diarrhea
    colitis and, 116
    coronavirus and, 171
    liver intake and, 50
    in puppies, 163, 165, 204
    remedy for, 133
    worms and, 173
Di-calcium phosphate, 53–55, 165
Diet. *See* Nutrition

Digestive system
    functioning of, 43–44
    medical problems of, 118–19, 121,
        124
Diseases, 167
    listing of, 168–72
Dislocations, 224
Distemper, 168–69
Dog shows, xiv, *xvi*
"Drop it" command, 202
Dry delivery, 93–95
Dry puppy food, 160, 162–63
Dwarfism, *112*, 115

Ears
    medical problems of, 116–17
    position of, 165
Eclampsia, 54–55
Eggs as food, 105, 199–200
Ejaculation, 25, 26
Elbows
    examination of, 7–8
    medical problems of, 114
Electrical shock, 228
Elimination of body wastes, 104–5, 133
Embryo transplantation, 28
Emergency first aid, 221–30
Environment, temperament and, 17, 59
Epilepsy, 117
Epithelial cells, 21
Esophagus, medical problems of,
    121–22, 123
Estral cycle, 20–22
Estrogen, 32
Euthanasia, 91, 92, 97
Evaluation of puppies, 179
    assistance for, 180
    criteria for, 180–81
    kennel blindness and, 179–80
    techniques for, 181–85
Exercise program for pregnancy, 61–64
Eyes
    development of, 136–39, *137*
    examination of, 8
    medical problems of, 45, 115, 119,
        122, 123

Fading puppy syndrome, 114
Failure-to-thrive syndrome, 98–99, 100,
    103–4
False pregnancy, 39–41
Feet, inspection of, 62
Finger feeding, 158–59
First aid procedures, 221–30

Meats
  fresh or canned, 46–47
  for puppies, 158
Medical problems
  first aid procedures, 221–30
  listing of, 113–27
  See also Diseases; Parasitic infestations
Megaesophagus, 121–22
Milk production by bitches, 53, 110,
    125, 131–32, 152
Milk replacement formula, 72, 105–7,
    106
Mineral supplements. *See* Vitamin/
    mineral supplements
Mites, 175
Mothers. *See* Bitches
Mounting, 24–25
Mouth inspections, 164
Muscles, medical problems of, 122–23
Mushy foods (weaning formula), 156–58
Muzzling
  breeding and, 24
  of injured dog, 221–22

Nails, 62
Naming, registration and, 208–9
Natural breedings, 23
Neglectful mothers, 49
Nervous system disorders, 122
Neutering, 3, 210–11
  agreement form for, 210, 212–13
Newspapers
  for house-training, 201
  for whelping, 70
Number of puppies in litter, 15
Nursing, 89–91, *90, 91*
Nursing reflex, 99
Nutrition, 43
  caloric intake, 44–45, 46, 51–53, *52,*
    107
  cheeses, 47, 133
  commercial diets, 45–47
  di-calcium phosphate, 53–55, 165
  dietary support therapies, 49–55
  digestive processes, 43–44
  estral cycle and, 22
  individualistic requirements, 43, 48
  meats, fresh or canned, 46–47
  multiple smaller feedings, 43, 44
  pregnancy and, 47–55
  for puppies, 72, 105–7, *106,* 165,
    198–200
  vitamin/mineral supplements, 50–51,
    53, 161

well-balanced diet, 47
  See also Weaning
Nutritional anemia, 122
Nymphomania, 31–32

Obedience training, 4
Objectivity for breeding program, 9–10,
    16
Obligations of breeders, 1–5
Ophthalmis neonatorum, 122
Opisthotonos, 54
Oral desensitization, 164
Orphaned puppies, 103–10
Orthopedic Foundation for Animals, Inc.
    (OFA), 7–8
Osteochondritis, 122
Osteochondritis dessecans, 122
Outcrossing, 11–12, 13, 17
Outside tie, 25
Ovarian cysts, 41
Overweight conditions, 43, 51, 199
Ovulation. *See* Estral cycle
Oxytocin, 77, 78, 85, 130

Palate, 91, 116
Palpation test, 36–37
Pans for puppy food, 159–60, *160*
Parainfluenza, 171
Parasitic infestations, 173
  examination for, 8–9
  listing of, 173–76
  therapies for, 176–77
Parvovirus, 171
Patellar luxation, 122–23
Patent ductus arteriosus, 123
Payment agreement, 219–20
Pedigree documents, 190–91, *207*
Pedigrees, breeding decision and, 10–14
Penis, 19, 25, 27
Persistent right aortic arch, 123
Pet-quality puppies
  sale of, 2–3
  show-quality puppies, comparison
    with, 3–4
  spaying or neutering of, 3, 210–13
Pheromones, 21
Photographing puppies, 139
Picking up and holding a puppy, 60, 144,
    145, 146, 148, 149, 191, 193
Pituitary oxytocin, 77, 78, 85, 130
Placenta, 51, 82–85, *85*
Placing of puppies
  assessment of prospective purchasers,
    185–86, 192, 193, 194–95, 215

Vaccination. *See* Immunization
Vaginal discharge, postpartum, 133
Vaginal smear, 21
Vaginal structure, 22
Vaginitis, 32
Veterinarians
  breeding decision, role in, 7
  consultations with, 9
  postpartum examinations, 130
  puppies in new homes and, 204
  whelping and, 76
Vitamin/mineral supplements
  for adult dogs, 50–51, 53
  for puppies, 161
Vizslas, *146*
Volvulus, 44
Vomiting, 171
  poisoning and, 224–25
Von Willebrand's disease, 125, 126–27
  breeds known to have exhibited
    (chart), 126–27

Walks, 61
"Walrus puppy" condition, 125
Water for puppies, 141, 204
Water retention, 125
Weaning, 151
  amount of food offered, 161, 162
  binding technique, 153
  bitch's diet and, 152–53
  camphorated oil used for, 153
  dry food, choice of, 160, 162–63
  finger-feeding, 158–59
  mushy foods (weaning formula),
    156–58
  pans for, 159–60, *160*
  regurgitated food from bitch, 151
  schedule for feeding, 161–62
  semisolids, introduction of, 160–62,
    160
  timing of, 152
  vitamins and minerals, 161
Weather conditions
  breeding and, 22, 31
  exercise and, 61–62
Weight gain by puppies, 163
Wet delivery, 95–96
Whelping
  airway and lungs of puppy, clearing
    of, 85, *86*, 87–88, *87*
  behavior of bitch, 78–79

birth defects, 91–92
breech delivery, *94*, 95–96
calendar for, *36*
cesarean section, 51, 77
difficult deliveries, 92–96, *93*, *94*
dry delivery, 93–95
hot and cold dipping of puppies, 96
inertia, 51, 77
labor, 77–80
locations for, 69
look-alikes, identification of, 89
manual extraction of puppy, 93–96,
    93, *94*
normal deliveries, 82–89, *83*, *84*, *85*
nursing, 89–91, *90*, *91*
owner's role, 59–60
paper-changing, 70
physical changes in bitch prior to
    whelping, 75–77, *76*
placentas and, 51, 82–85, *85*
record-keeping for, 73, 75, 84
resuscitation of lifeless puppies,
    88–89, 92–93
smothering of puppies, prevention of,
    67–68
"trial run" by owner, 72
umbilical cord, 80–82, *81*, 83
unattended whelping, dangers of,
    69–70
veterinarian, communication with,
    76
wet delivery, 95–96
Whelping box, 65–69, *66*, *67*, *68*
Whelping equipment, 65
  confinement barriers, 69
  heating pad, 71
  heat lamp, 74
  hemostats, 80–81
  incubator, 99–100
  milk replacement, 72
  miscellaneous items, 72
  newspapers, 70
  puppy box, 70–71
  scale for weighing, 72–73
  towels, 72
  whelping box, 65–69, *66*, *67*, *68*
Whipworms, 176
Wobbler syndrome, 126
Worms, 173, 174, 175, 176

X-rays, 7–8